Jerusalem

Vanessa Betts

Credits

Footprint credits
Editor: Alan Murphy
Production and layout: Angus Dawson,
Emma Bryers
Maps: Kevin Feeney

Managing Director: Andy Riddle
Commercial Director: Patrick Dawson
Publisher: Alan Murphy
Publishing Managers: Felicity Laughton,
Nicola Gibbs.
Digital Editors: Jo Williams,
Tom Mellors
Marketing and PR: Liz Harper
Sales: Diane McEntee
Advertising: Renu Sibal
Finance and Administration:
Elizabeth Taylor

Photography credits
Front cover: Rostislav Glinsky/Shutterstock
Back cover: Roman Sigaev/Shutterstock

Printed in Great Britain by CPI Antony Rowe,
Chippenham, Wiltshire

FSC
www.fsc.org
MIX
Paper from
responsible sources
FSC® C013604

Publishing information
Footprint *Focus Jerusalem*
1st edition
© Footprint Handbooks Ltd
September 2011

ISBN: 978 1 908206 31 2
CIP DATA: A catalogue record for this book is
available from the British Library

® Footprint Handbooks and the Footprint
mark are a registered trademark of Footprint
Handbooks Ltd

Published by Footprint
6 Riverside Court
Lower Bristol Road
Bath BA2 3DZ, UK
T +44 (0)1225 469141
F +44 (0)1225 469461
footprinttravelguides.com

Distributed in the USA by Globe Pequot
Press, Guilford, Connecticut

The content of Footprint *Focus Jerusalem* has
been taken directly from Footprint's *Israel
Handbook*, which was written and researched
by Vanessa Betts and Dave Winter.

Contents

It would not be much of an over-statement to say that Jerusalem is the most famous city in the world. In many minds it is also the most important. Here is a city that is of fundamental spiritual importance to one third of humanity, sacred to Jews, Christians and Muslims alike. Three faiths based on a common creed that now present mutually exclusive claims to the same city.

A visit to Jerusalem can be an intense experience, yet it is one that should not be missed. In fact, almost all foreign tourists visiting Israel come to Jerusalem at some stage during their trip, on average spending around half of their time in the city. And there is plenty to justify a prolonged stay, with even the most ardent of non-believers becoming enthralled by its unique atmosphere. Not only is the first sight of the Dome of the Rock far better in reality than in the imagination, but the chaotic, crowded streets of the Old City retain a timeless exoticism despite the passage of many centuries of pilgrims and tourists. Layered beneath the city are remains of civilizations stretching back 3000 years, which can be explored via tunnels under the Old City itself or at countless other archaeological and architectural sites. Should the pervasive air of history and religion get too intense, there are excellent museums and nightly cultural activities – as well as a fine bar and dining scene in both East and West Jerusalem.

Jerusalem is a fairly easy city in which to orientate yourself, though it is a little more complex than just an 'Old' and a 'New' city. The places of interest in this book have been grouped according to location, though most of the attractions are in or close to the walled Old City. In fact, it's not difficult to see all the key attractions in just three to four days.

Planning your trip

When to go

There are two key factors to bear in mind when timetabling a visit to Israel: climate and religious holidays/festivals.

Climate
The climatic seasons in Israel are the same as those in Europe (and the northern hemisphere). Thus spring is roughly March-May, summer is June-August, autumn (fall) is September-October and winter is November-February. As a very general guide, winter tends to be rather wet and overcast, becoming colder and wetter the further north or the higher up you go. Many visitors are unprepared for just how cold it gets in Jerusalem and Bethlehem in the winter. Nevertheless, the Dead Sea Region and the Negev are particularly appealing at this time of year, with very comfortable day-time temperatures. Since Israel is so small, it does not take much travelling to escape from a cold and wet Jerusalem to a dry and sunny Eilat. Indeed, winter is an ideal time to take a beach holiday in Eilat.

Climatic conditions in spring are ideal across most of the country, notably in the Negev and Dead Sea Region, where day-time temperatures have not climbed too high. Temperatures are beginning to pick up on the Mediterranean coast and Jerusalem area, though there will be some rainy days. Galilee (notably Upper Galilee and Golan) may still be cloudy and wet.

Early summer is the best time to visit Galilee and the northern areas, with the cooling influence of the sea making the Mediterranean coast an appealing option. At the height of summer, however, the Dead Sea Region and Negev can get far too hot to be comfortable.

As summer turns to autumn around September, the entire country becomes an attractive proposition, with comfortable temperatures and little rainfall. As autumn draws to an end, however, the northern areas such as Galilee and Golan become cloudier and wetter.

Holidays
Unless you are coming to Israel specifically to celebrate a religious holiday (whether Jewish or Christian), the main holiday periods are best avoided. Flights to and from Israel just before or after religious holidays tend to be heavily booked, and you will almost certainly end up paying more for your ticket. Likewise, accommodation prices rocket (sometimes double), and in some places it can be difficult to find a room without an advance reservation.

The key Christian festivals are of course Easter and Christmas, though the accommodation shortfalls and problems of over-crowding at major sites only really affect visitors to Jerusalem and Bethlehem. Note, however, that different branches of the Church celebrate these events at different times, and hence the Christmas and Easter rush can become quite an extended period. Nevertheless, there is a special atmosphere in Jerusalem and Bethlehem at these times (even if you are non-observant).

Jewish holidays and festivals are numerous, though the key ones are Rosh Hashanah, Yom Kippur, Sukkot and Pesach. Though the holidays are generally brief (usually one day), you should bear in mind that the holiday affects all aspects of life in Israel. Not only do accommodation prices sky-rocket, but almost everything else closes down (including places to eat, sights, banks, post offices and transport). When several holidays come along together it can have a major impact on your visit. Dates of Jewish holidays follow the lunar calendar and thus change each year, though the approximate time of year remains the same. Thus, September/October may be a time to avoid since Rosh Hashanah, Yom Kippur and Sukkot all come along together. Likewise, April/May tends to feature Pesach, Independence Day and Holocaust Memorial Day. For full details of holidays and festivals see the section starting on page 13.

Getting there

Air
The majority of visitors to Israel arrive by air. Most arrivals are at **Ben-Gurion Airport** (at Lod, some 22 km southeast of Tel Aviv), though some charter flights land at **'Uvda Airport** (60 km north of Eilat). Ben-Gurion Airport can get very crowded during holidays when it can take almost an hour to clear immigration on arrival. For further details on Ben-Gurion Airport, including getting there and away, see below.

At peak periods not only do air-fares rise dramatically, but it can also be difficult getting a flight in or out of Israel. Such peak periods include the time around Jewish and Christian holidays, plus the peak periods associated with school holidays in the country of the flight's origin. You are advised to book tickets for these periods well in advance.

Ben-Gurion Airport
General Ben-Gurion Airport is located at Lod, some 22 km southeast of Tel Aviv. For general 24-hour airport information call T03-9755555 or *6663, or see www.iaa.gov.il. Recorded information for departures/arrivals/transportation, T03-9723332, in English, 24 hours. All international flights arrive at Terminal 3, and the vast majority also depart from there, save for a couple of low-cost airlines which check in at Terminal 1. Domestic flights also depart/arrive from the old Terminal 1.

To/from the airport Trains go from Tel Aviv's four terminals to the airport, and are the only form of public transport to/from the city (buses leave from outside the airport grounds, a long impractical walk away). The train service operates 24 hours. From Hagana train station in Tel Aviv it is a short walk to the Central Bus Station, from where buses/sheruts 4 and 5 pass most of the hostels.

Sheruts (24 hours) are the only means of public transport to/from Jerusalem, leaving from outside the arrivals hall (Nesher, T03-9759555, 1 hour). For Haifa/the north there are 24-hr sheruts (Amal, T04-8662324, 1½ hours), or the train service through Tel Aviv carries on to northern destinations. Taxis are also available 24 hours, departing from the ground floor next to Gate 2.

Arrival formalities You have to fill out a landing card on arrival. Immigration will stamp this card and not your passport, but only if you ask in advance. The card is then taken from you after passport control, leaving you with no record of your entry date. This generally only poses a problem when you cross borders (to the West Bank, Egypt, Jordan) when Israeli security officials might ask where your stamp is. A phone call to an authority figure follows, and then you will be allowed to pass. Do not mention any travel plans to the West Bank if questioned on arrival at Ben-Gurion, as this will only arouse suspicion.

Departure formalities Ensure that you arrive no less than three hours before your flight departs. Be prepared for thorough questioning by the security staff before you check in

Packing for Israel

Most travellers tend to take too much, particularly when you bear in mind that practically everything that you need is available in Israel. However, with few exceptions, most things bought in Israel will be more expensive than back home. There are a few things that you might like to bear in mind before packing your bag.

Taking appropriate clothing is essential. When selecting what to take, you should remember cultural and religious factors as well as climatic considerations. When passing through either Arab or religious Jewish areas, conservative dress is a must. This means no shorts or bare shoulders on either men or women, closed necklines, and loose unrevealing clothes. In Jewish religious areas women are requested to wear long skirts as opposed to trousers. At Jewish religious sites both men and women are requested to cover their heads; yarmulkes and scarfs are often provided, though it is as well to bring some sort of head-covering or hat of your own. You will be denied entry into churches, mosques and synagogues alike if you are inappropriately dressed. In summer light loose-fitting cottons are best, though desert and upland areas can get remarkably cold at night. With the exception of day-time in Eilat, the Negev and the Dead Sea Region, winter in Israel can get very cold and wet so bring appropriate warm clothing.

Toiletries, including tampons, sanitary towels and condoms, are readily available, though they tend to be more expensive than at home. Those staying in hostels should definitely bring their own cotton sleep-sheet and ear-plugs, and consider bringing an eye-mask.

(which can be lengthy). Bear in mind that this is done for your own safety. On exiting passport control, if you avoided an Israeli stamp when you arrived you can avoid getting one now, but only if you ask.

Airport facilities There are limitless opportunities for frenzied duty-free shopping upon arrival or departure. There is free Wi-Fi throughout Terminal 3. All the major car-hire firms have offices at the airport, most of which are open 24 hours. A number of companies offer cellular phone hire. Banks here do not offer the best deals: change just enough to tide you over until you can go to more competitive places in Tel Aviv or Jerusalem. VAT refunds are processed at the **Bank Leumi** in the Departures lounge. There's a post office and the **Buy & Bye** shopping area (including **Steimatzky** bookshop, cafés, restaurants) before exiting through passport control. Baggage storage facilities, T03-9754436, are found at the short-term car park, ground level, Sunday-Thursday 0800-1945, Fri 0800-1430, 20NIS per 24 hours.

Flights from the UK

A one-year open return can cost between £190 and £230 depending upon the season. Shorter stay tickets can be even cheaper. **British Airways** (BA; T03-606 1555; www.british airways. com), **Jet2** (from Manchester) and **EasyJet** (London Luton) offer cheap charter seats to Israel.

Flights from Europe

Discount flights to Israel can be picked up from most major cities in mainland Europe, though they tend to be slightly more expensive than flights from the UK. Airlines include

Air France, www.airfrance.com; **Alitalia**, www.alitalia.it; **Austrian Airlines**, www.aua.com; **Iberia**, www.iberia.com; **KLM**, www.klm.com; **Lufthansa**, www.lufthansa.com. The cheapest deals tend to be with Eastern European airlines.

Flights from the USA and Canada

It is possible to fly to Israel from Atlanta, Chicago, Los Angeles, Miami and Toronto, though the best deals and widest choice of flights are from New York. There are several daily direct flights from New York's JFK to Israel with **El Al**, www.elal.co.il. There are also flights with **American Airlines**, www.aa.com; **United**, www.united.com; and **Air Canada**, www.aircanada.com. Look out for special deals, though don't expect much change from $800.

Flights from Australasia

Flying from Australia/New Zealand will require either stop-overs or plane changes. The cheapest deals are with the national carriers operating via Cairo, Athens or Rome, though expect to pay between A$1,700 and A$2,500 during the low season. A better deal may be to include Israel as part of a round-the-world ticket.

Flights from Egypt

There are flights between Tel Aviv and Cairo, operated by **Air Sinai**. There are also flights on **El Al** linking Ben-Gurion airport to Cairo (US$100 one way).

Flights from Jordan

Flights between Tel Aviv and Amman on **Royal Jordanian**, www.rj.com) go daily (around US$130 one-way). El Al offer a similar service.

Airline security

For obvious reasons, airline security on planes flying in and out of Israel is probably the tightest in the world. Whether you are flying in or out of Israel, you should check-in at least three hours prior to departure. **El Al** also use their own airline security staff abroad.

Prior to checking-in at Ben-Gurion or 'Uvda Airport to board a flight out of Israel, you will be questioned thoroughly by the airline security service. How long this cross-examination lasts depends upon a number of factors: your name and ethnic background, the stamps in your passport, your appearance, and where in Israel you admit to having been. Dave Winter's personal record is one hour and 55 minutes!

Getting around

Though many of Jerusalem's sights are within walking distance of each other (notably in and around the Old City), you will almost certainly have to use the city bus service at some stage; few enjoy the walk from the Central Bus Station to the Old City carrying a backpack. Fares are currently 5.9NIS whether you go one stop or all the way across town. Buses from outside the Central Bus Station to the Old City leave from the opposite side of Jaffa (Yafo) Road from the bus station. To get to Jaffa Gate take 20; to Damascus Gate take 6 or 1 (the latter of which carries on to Dung Gate for the Western Wall).

Known as the '**Jerusalem City tour**' ① *Line 99, T1-700-70-75-75, www.egged.co.il, 2 hrs, 5 tours per day Sun-Thu, 3 tours on Fri, buy tickets on board*, links many of Jerusalem's main sights on one continuous loop, with the one-day (80/68 NIS) or two-day (130/110 NIS) ticket allowing you to hop on and off at any designated stop. Audio guides are available in eight languages.

When it is completed (supposedly 2011) the Light Rail tramway will be a handy, if controversial, connection between Mt Herzl in the west and the northern suburbs, going along the length of Jaffa Road passing the Central Bus Station and Damascus Gate.

Sleeping

Hotels
Israel has a very broad range of hotels and, as a general rule, the **$$$$** category hotels live up to their price tag, with facilities and service to match their 'luxury' pricing. Things can be a little more variable in the lower categories, with many of the hotels here holding themselves in too high esteem. If you are looking to stay in the 'top end' accommodation, it may be worth noting that the suites in some hotels offer very good value. For a guide to the classifications used, see box on next page or inside the front cover.

There are a number of considerations to bear in mind when booking/checking in to a hotel in Israel. Firstly, there is a huge variation in room charges according to the season. 'High' season generally coincides with Jewish and Christian religious festivals, and can see prices increase by between 25-50%! Note that the weekend (Friday-Saturday) is usually considered 'high' season.

Despite this blatant rip-off, in some places (notably Eilat, Tiberias and Jerusalem) it can be hard to find a bed during the 'high' season. Most of the rest of the year is designated 'regular' season, with a couple of weeks of 'low' season when tourist bookings are slack. The classifications in this Handbook are for the 'regular' season. Note that the prices used here are spot/rack rates: if you book as a group or through a travel agency, you may be getting a significant discount. With all hotel classifications, look out for hidden taxes. An Israeli breakfast is included within the price at many hotels.

Remember that by paying in a foreign hard currency you avoid paying the 17% VAT. High-end hotel prices are almost always quoted in US dollars, and this is the preferred means of payment. Many hotels have specific characteristics that reflect the Jewish nature of Israel, such as in-house synagogues, Shabbat elevators (that stop at every floor and don't require buttons to be pressed) and kosher restaurants.

NB All accommodation in Israel (from five-star hotels down to backpacker hostels) Is required by law to provide a free safe for depositing valuables.

Kibbutz guesthouses
Kibbutz guesthouses represent a relatively recent diversification by the beleaguered kibbutz movement. Almost all are located in rural environments, and on the plus side tend to be peaceful and quiet, well run, and with full access to kibbutz facilities such as swimming pools and private beaches, children's entertainment and restaurant/dining hall. The down side is that few are served by regular public transport.

Hospices
Christian hospices often provide excellent value. They are run by various denominations of the church and tend to be located close to major Christian pilgrimage sites. Advance reservations are recommended, and essential during major Christian holidays. They tend to be impeccably clean, though most have early curfews, early check-out times, and non-married couples might not be able to share a room. Half- and full-board deals can be good value.

Sleeping and eating price codes

Sleeping

$$$$ over US$150 $$$ US$66-150 $$ US$30-65
$ under US$30

Prices include taxes and service charge, but not meals. They are based on a double room, except in the $ range, where prices are almost always per person.

Eating

$$$ over US$30 $$ US$15-30 $ under US$15

Prices refer to the cost of a two-course meal for one person, excluding drinks or service charge.

Hostels

Jerusalem's hostels provide the cheapest accommodation in Israel (at $10-15), though generally you should expect to pay around $18-20 for dormitories in the other large cities. There is a big jump in price for double rooms, with the cheapest generally $45-$50. Some hostels in Israel allow you to sleep on the roof for less or give discounts for longer stays. Standards are highly variable. Dorm sizes vary between three and 46 beds, with some being single-sex and others mixed. Some hostels pride themselves on their 'party atmosphere', the idea being that they act as a meeting place for backpackers who want to go out and get drunk together.

A more than welcome addition to the hostelling scene is the **ILH organization**. This independent group of hostels/guesthouses has enrolled members whose beds are guaranteed to be clean, with a mix of dorm and private rooms, who nearly always provide kitchen facilities, have prices that are very fair and are in locations that are always interesting – and so might be the accommodation (in wood cabins, country kibbutzim or camel ranches). ILH hostels accommodate a range of budgets, are suitable for all ages, and are a good place to meet like-minded travellers, see www.hostels-israel.com. They are a real blessing for backpackers (and all independent travellers) in Israel.

You don't need to be a 'youth' to stay at any of Israel's Hostelling International (HI) hostels; in fact most have a number of family rooms. In some of the more remote places of interest, **IYHA** hostels provide the cheapest (or only) accommodation at about $30 per night. Without exception, they are spotlessly clean, offering a choice of spacious air-conditioned dormitories (usually single-sex); family rooms, sleeping four-eight, a/c; and private rooms; all with en suite shower. Sheets and blankets are provided. Breakfast is almost always included, and evening meals tend to be generous and reasonable value (but only available if enough people are staying). Bookings are recommended during holidays and weekends, though these hostels can get very noisy with kids at these times. For further details see www.iyha.org.il.

The **Society for the Protection of Nature in Israel** (SPNI) operates Field Schools throughout Israel, many of which have accommodation similar to IYHA hostels, though they are usually more basic, see www.aspni.org.

Camping

There are a number of fully equipped campsites in Israel, though they are only really for those who are dedicated to sleeping under canvas. Camping in a hostel grounds is cheaper than sleeping in a dorm and may be a good compromise. You can generally camp for free on beaches, though theft and security remain major risks. When trekking for a few days, 'wild' camping is an acceptable option (though of course you have to carry all your gear and camping equipment).

Private homes
Accommodation in private homes is available in a number of towns, notably Netanya, Nahariya, Safed, Eilat and Jerusalem. You can respond to advertisements in the paper, notes on the wall in hostels, or signs hung outside homes for rent, though it is recommended that you make enquiries through the local tourist office (who should have a list of licensed places). Daily rates vary from $40 to $60 per person, though weekly and monthly deals can be struck. Make sure that you see the place before handing over any money, and be sure that the deal is clear (eg heating, blankets, breakfast, etc).

Eating and drinking

Despite a common bond (Judaism) Israelis have a diverse cultural and ethnic background. Not surprisingly, therefore, the dining experience in Israel reflects this diversity. Dining out in Israel can, however, be an expensive business. The cheapest eating options are provided by the ubiquitous falafel and *shwarma* stands, though eating at these three times a day is neither good for your health nor morale. Expect to spend $20-$25 a day for one decent meal plus two 'street meals' (less – if you don't eat meat, and stick to falafel and pizza). Hostels with their own kitchens can reduce your food bill.

Israel is (for those with a bit of money) a gastronomic paradise. Everyone you meet will recommend the best place in town to eat, and they usually know what they are talking about. Yes, it costs money, but the size of portion and the quality of the meal is way above what many visitors are used to. Diners in Israel can choose from a global menu, with Argentinean, Mexican, Italian, French, Chinese, Southeast Asian and Indian restaurants in the main cities. In many cases, the owners/chefs have strong links to the country that their restaurant claims to represent.

The staple of many Arab restaurants is barbecued meat on skewers (*shashlik*), *shwarma* (known elsewhere as doner kebab) and grilled chicken. Accompaniments include salad, falafel, hummus, bread, and possibly chips (fries), though put together these side dishes can provide a filling meal. One of the most delicious (and cheap) meals served in Israel is *fuul*: a plate of mashed fava beans served in garlic-flavoured oil with hummus and bread. More specialist dishes include *mansaaf*, usually a whole leg of lamb served on a bed of rice with nuts and lemon juice. A diet-busting Arab sweet dish, often served in Jerusalem's Old City for breakfast, is *kanafeh*, a mild cheese mixed with pistachios and baked in a honey syrup shell.

Budget eating
It is possible to eat on a budget in Israel, though it is very easy to fall into a predictable diet of nutritionally poor food. The backpacker staple, considered to be Israel's national dish, is the falafel. This comprises ground-up chickpeas blended with herbs and spices, rolled into balls and then deep fried. They are usually served stuffed into a pitta bread with *tahini* (a thin paste made from sesame seeds) and salad. Such a sandwich costs 6NIS for a half and about 10NIS for a full sandwich, or even 15NIS (depending upon where you buy it). At many such streetside stalls you do the salad-stuffing yourself. A variation of this is the *shwarma*, where the falafel balls are substituted by a form of processed lamb or turkey cut from a revolving spit. Blokes who go down the pub in England know

Kosher

The eating habits of observant Jews are governed by the *kashrut* dietary laws laid down by God to Moses (*kosher* being the noun of *kashrut*). Given the standards of hygiene likely to have been practised at this time, many of them make good sense, particularly in the area of prevention of cross-contamination. Many people are familiar with the *kosher* prohibitions against eating pork and serving meat and dairy products at the same meal, though there is far more to the *kashrut* laws than just this.

Beasts that are clovenfooted and chew the cud can be eaten (*Leviticus 11:1-47; Deuteronomy 14:6-7*). Hence you can eat a cow, which fulfils this criteria, but not a camel (since it chews the cud but is not cleft-hooved). Conversely pigs, despite being clovenfooted, do not chew the cud and so are forbidden. Only birds that do not eat carrion can be considered 'clean', whilst fish must have fins and scales; thus shellfish are forbidden (*Deuteronomy 14:8-19*). However, to be considered *kosher*, animals have to be killed instantly and according to methods supervised by the religious authorities. Animals that have died of disease, or in pain, are not considered *kosher*.

A *kosher* kitchen, whether in a restaurant or private home, will keep separate plates and dishes for cooking and serving meat and dairy products and will not serve the two together (*Exodus 23:19; Deuteronomy 14:14-21*). Such have been the culinary habits developed by Israelis over the years, however, you will not simply be given a black coffee to finish off your meal – a milk substitute will be provided. It is permitted for *kosher* restaurants serving dairy products also to serve fish.

Visitors should note that many restaurants (especially in Jerusalem) are closed on Shabbat, though - bar a few extreme cases - finding somewhere to eat should not be a problem. Note that a restaurant that offers a *kosher* menu will not be given a *kashrut* certificate if it prepares or serves food on Shabbat.

Despite the strict regulations regarding *kashrut* dietary laws, few visitors to Israel will be inconvenienced by them, whilst the dining experience of vegetarians will be positively enhanced.

such a dish as a doner kebab. It's funny how a dish that in some cultures would only be eaten after consuming 10 pints of lager can become a staple in others.

Traditional Jewish

Some dishes associated with the Ashkenazi, or Eastern European, Jewish immigrants include good old fashioned Hungarian goulash, Viennese schnitzel, chicken livers and gefilte fish. Perhaps more appealing are the Sephardi/Mizrachi, or 'Oriental', restaurants that are becoming more and more popular. Food here reflects the Sephardi roots in the Middle East, with many dishes such as the grilled meats and chicken being very similar to those found in Arab restaurants. Goose livers, baked sinia and stuffed vegetables are all specialities. Falafel (see 'budget eating' above) and hummus (a thick paste made from ground chickpeas, garlic, seasoning and tahini) are also served as side dishes.

Vegetarian

Vegetarians, though not necessarily vegans, are pretty well catered for in Israel, usually as a by-product of the kashrut dietary laws. In addition to the chain of 'dairy' restaurants that can be found across Israel, Jerusalem and Tel Aviv have a number of notable restaurants that are preparing imaginative vegetarian dishes. In less cosmopolitan areas vegetarians may have to fall back on the tried and tested falafel and hummus formula, though many hotels prepare good-value eat-all-you-want breakfast salads.

Drink

You pay around $5-7 for a beer in a regular bar, though these prices can be almost halved if you look out for happy hours and backpacker-oriented bars.

It is still said that Israelis are not big drinkers, though the recent massive influx of Eastern Europeans into the country appears to have replaced one stereotype with another. The most popular locally produced beers are Goldstar (4.7%) and Maccabee (4.9%), the latter of which is considered marginally better. Locally brewed-under-licence Carlsberg, Tuborg and Heineken are readily available at similar prices. A half-litre glass in a regular bar will cost 18-22NIS, or 10-12NIS if you drink in one of the bars catering to the backpacker crowd. The German-style Ramallah-brewed Taybeh beer (see page 252) wins a lot of friends, though is not widely available outside of the West Bank.

A number of very good wines are produced in Israel, with notable labels coming from the Golan Heights Winery of Katzrin (see 'Lower Golan' on page 680), the Carmel Wine Cellars in Zichron Ya'akov (see 'North of Tel Aviv' on page 6) and the Carmel Winery in Rishon LeTzion (see 'South and southeast of Tel Aviv' on page 442). Imported wines tend to be expensive. A variety of spirits and fortified wines are also produced locally, with Israeli vodka renowned for its, er, cheapness.

Drinking coffee is a popular Israeli habit, with a wealth of cafés to choose from. Coffee served in Arab cafés tends to be the thick, bitter Turkish-style drink, complete with half a cup of sludge. It is usually served with a palate-cleansing glass of water. The tea served in Arab teahouses is particularly refreshing; it is served black, in a glass, often with a sprig of mint and plenty of sugar. Carbonated drinks are readily available. Expect to pay 6NIS for a can of Coke, while bottled water costs 4-5NIS for a litre (less in a big supermarket).

Festivals and events

Holidays and religious festivals in Israel and the Palestinian Authority areas present a very confusing picture. Not only are there 'secular', Jewish, Christian and Islamic holidays, but the dates that they fall on are variously governed by the Hebrew lunar calendar, the solar Gregorian calendar, plus sightings of the new moon at Mecca! It should also be noted that the various branches of the Christian Church celebrate key events on different days.

Jewish holidays

Israel works on the lunar Hebrew calendar (as opposed to the solar Gregorian calendar), and thus all Jewish religious and secular holidays fall on different dates of the Gregorian calendar each year. However, they always remain at roughly the same time of year. Most of the main Jewish holidays fall within the autumn season ('fall'). Unless you are coming to Israel specifically to celebrate one of these holidays, this is a good time to avoid visiting. Transport, banks, offices, shops and restaurants are all affected, whilst accommodation can be difficult to find in spite of the sky-rocketing prices. If you are here for one of the major holidays (Rosh Hashanah, Yom Kippur, Sukkot, Pesach), plan ahead. For details of the Jewish Sabbath (Shabbat) see under 'Business hours' above. Dates are given here for 2010 (where appropriate), 2011 and 2012. The holidays below are listed in the order in which they occur during the Hebrew calendar year, and not in order of importance.

Rosh Hashanah Rosh Hashanah celebrates the beginning of the Hebrew calendar year, though it is also a time of introspection as religious Jews examine their conduct over the previous 12 months. Because it is the only holiday in Israel that lasts for 2 consecutive days, it is considered to be the main vacation period. It is celebrated on the 1st and 2nd of Tishri. 2010: Sep 9-Sep 10; 2011: Sep 29-Sep 30; 2012: Sep 17-18.

Yom Kippur This is the holiest day of the year and the most important date in the Hebrew calendar. It marks the end of 10 days of penitence and moral introspection that began with Rosh Hashanah, and finishes with God's judgement and forgiveness: the Day of Atonement. Yom Kippur is characterized by a sunset to sunset fast that is usually observed by even the most 'secular' Israelis. Virtually everything in Israel closes down for Yom Kippur and the roads are totally empty. Since 1973 it has also acted as an unofficial memorial day, commemorating those who died in the surprise war that the Egyptians and Syrians launched on that date. It takes place on the 10th of Tishri. 2010: Sep 18; 2011: 8 Oct; 2012: 26 Sep.

Sukkot Sukkot commemorates the 40 years spent wandering in the wilderness after the Moses-led Exodus out of bondage in Egypt. Many Jews recreate the succah, or moveable shelter, in which the Israelites lived during their wanderings, taking all their meals there for a period of 7 days. Small plywood structures with a roof of loose thatch and branches are built in courtyards, on balconies, in gardens, on roof-tops, and in corners of rooms, all across the country. Many hotels also build a symbolic succah in reception. An oft-told story, said to derive from a case in the United States, tells how a Jew who had built a succah on his balcony was taken to court by a bigoted neighbour, who claimed it was an eye-sore. The judge (who was himself Jewish) found in the plaintiff's favour, ordering the Jew to remove the structure within 7 days! Sukkot is often referred to as the Feast of Tabernacles. Zionist tradition associates Sukkot with the celebration of the Harvest Festival. It takes place on the 15th to 21st of Tishri. 2010: 23-29 Sep; 2011: 13-19 Oct; 2012: 1-7 Oct.

Simchat Torah This is probably the only Jewish religious holiday in Israel that has no accompanying Zionist tradition. It celebrates the giving of the Torah (first five books of the Bible: *Genesis, Exodus, Leviticus, Numbers, Deuteronomy*); literally the Rejoicing of the Law. It falls 1 week after Sukkot, at the end of Tishri. 2010: 1 Oct; 2011: 21 Oct; 2012: 9 Oct.

Hanukkah Not an official public holiday, since it does not mark an event mentioned in the Torah, Hanukkah celebrates the Maccabean Revolt that began in the 2nd century BCE when the Jews rose up against the pagan reforms of the dominant Hellenistic culture. The revolt culminated in a return to Jewish self-rule under the Hasmonean dynasty (c.152-37 BCE). Hanukkah is celebrated by the nightly ceremonial lighting of the menorah, or 7-branched candelabra, and is thus often known as the Feast or Festival of Lights. British readers who used to watch Blue Peter at Christmas will understand. It falls during Kislev. 2010: 2-9 Dec; 2011: 21-28 Dec; 2012: 9-16 Dec.

Tu B'Shevat This is not a public holiday, though in recent years it has been used as an occasion for tree-planting. Its origins are in the Mishnah, when the 'New Year for Trees' was celebrated by eating fruit and nuts. 2011: 20 Jan; 2012: 8 Feb.

Purim Purim is probably the most bizarre holiday in the Hebrew calendar. It celebrates events in ancient Persia when the Jews were sentenced to death for refusing to bow to the secular

Months of the Hebrew calendar

Tishrey (Sep/Oct); **Cheshvan** (Oct/Nov); **Kislev** (Nov/Dec); **Tevet** (Dec/Jan); **Shvat** (Jan/Feb); **Adar** (Feb/Mar, Adar bet in a leap year); **Nisan** (Mar/Apr); **Iyar** (Apr/May); **Sivan** (May/Jun); **Tamuz** (Jun/Jul); **Av** (Jul/Aug); **Elul** (Aug/Sep).

authority. Their main persecutor was a man named Haman, though eventually it was Haman whom the authorities executed, whilst the Jews were left unmolested. For some reason Purim, or the Feast of Lots, has been turned into a sort of Jewish Halloween, with children dressing up and adults encouraged to get uncharacteristically drunk. 2011: 20 Mar; 2012: 8 Mar.

Pesach Pesach, or Passover, celebrates the Exodus out of Egypt. The festival lasts for a whole week and, even though only the first and last days are official public holidays, many shops (including food stores) close for the entire 7 days. Be prepared. During the Israelites' escape from Egypt, the Bible recalls how there wasn't even time for them to wait for their bread to be baked. As a symbolic gesture, no products containing yeast or other leavening agents are eaten. Anyone spending Pesach in Israel will have to content themselves with a special unleavened bread called *matzah*, a rather tasteless substitute in most people's minds. Even McDonald's produces a special bun! The Passover meal also has a symbolic significance in the Christian tradition. Pesach is celebrated from the 15th to 21st of *Nisan*. 2011: 19-25 Apr; 2012: 7-13 Apr.

Mimouna This takes places on the 22nd of *Nisan*, the day after the last day of Pesach. It is only really celebrated by Sephardi Jews, noticeably those from North Africa, and, though its exact origin is unclear, it is a good excuse for a party – usually in the form of a big barbecue. 2011: 26 Apr; 2012: 14 Apr.

Lag B'Omer Lag B'Omer is really a multiple celebration. Taking place on the 18th of *Iyar*, it marks the end of a 33-day period of mourning and represents a sort of rite of spring when a plague was lifted from the Jewish nation. There's really only one place to celebrate this event, and that's at the Tomb of Rabbi Shimon bar Yochai at Meiron, near Safed (see 'Galilee' section for full details). His teachings in the 2nd century CE were compiled into printed form some 1100 years after his death, with Lag B'Omer also used as a celebration of the giving of this *Zohar*, or central text of kabbalah. 2011: 22 May; 2012: 10 May.

Shavuot In its original form, Shavuot commemorated the 7 weeks that it took the Israelites to reach Mt Sinai, and is thus something of a celebration of the receiving of the Torah. In Hebrew shavuot means 'weeks', though many readers will know this festival as the Jewish Pentecost. Under the Zionist influence of the early kibbutzniks, however, Shavuot has come to represent something of a celebration of the productive capability of the land, and is often referred to as the 'kibbutz holiday'. It takes place on the 6th of *Sivan*. 2011: 8-9 Jun; 2012: 27-28 May.

Tisha B'av This is a solemn occasion commemorated mainly at the Western Wall in Jerusalem. It remembers the occasions upon which the First and Second Temples were destroyed. It falls on the 9th of *Av*. 2011: 9 Aug; 2012: 29 Jul. Some observant Jews also fast on the 17th of *Tamuz*, the date upon which the Romans destroyed Jerusalem's city walls.

Israeli 'secular' holidays

Yom HaSho'ah (Holocaust Memorial) Since 1951, the 27th of *Nisan* has been set aside as a day to remember both the victims of the Holocaust and the heroes of the Jewish resistance. Its official title is in fact Memorial to the Holocaust and the Heroism. At 11 o'clock sharp a siren is heard throughout the country, signalling all traffic (human and vehicular) to stop whilst 2 minutes of silence is observed. It really is a very unusual (and moving) sight, particularly if you are on a normally busy street at the time. Israeli television broadcasts a special service from Yad VaShem. Note that most businesses and places of entertainment close the evening before. 2011: 27 Jan; 2012: 27 Jan.

Yom Ha'Atzmaut (Independence Day) David Ben-Gurion declared Israel's independence on 14 May 1948. Or rather he declared it on the 5th day of the month of *Iyar*. Every 19 years the event can be celebrated on the same day, though otherwise the Hebrew calendar is used. Note that most businesses and places of entertainment close the evening before. 2011: 9 May; 2012: 26 Apr.

May Day May Day reflects the socialist leanings of the early Zionists, though International Labour Day is now only celebrated on some kibbutzim (1 May).

Christian holidays

All the major Christian festivals are celebrated in Israel, though none are official public holidays; Israeli life proceeds as normal. The key festivals are celebrated on different dates by the 'Eastern' Orthodox, 'Oriental' Orthodox and 'Western' Churches ('Latin' ie Roman Catholic, and Protestant).

Christmas Christmas Day is celebrated on 25 Dec by the 'Western' Church, with the highlight being the midnight mass held at the Church of the Nativity in Bethlehem on the night of Christmas Eve (24th). For full details see the 'Bethlehem' section. The Orthodox ('Eastern') Church celebrates Christmas on 7 Jan (except Greek Orthodox which also uses 24-25 Dec) whilst the Armenian Christmas falls on 19 Jan. These dates remain consistent.

Easter Easter is celebrated on different dates by the 'Western' Church, 'Oriental' and 'Eastern' Orthodox Churches, with the date also changing from year to year. 'Good Friday' commemorates the Crucifixion, with impressive crowds walking the Via Dolorosa. 'Easter Sunday' (two days later) celebrates the Resurrection. Note that the Orthodox 'Holy Saturday' is the day when the 'Miracle of the Holy Fire' is celebrated (arguably Jerusalem's most intense Christian celebration). 2011: 'Western' Good Friday, 22 Apr; 'Eastern' Orthodox Good Friday, 22 Apr (note that they both fall on the same day, which will be intense); 2012: 'Western' Good Friday, 6 Apr; 'Eastern' Orthodox Good Friday, 13 Apr.

Feast of the Annunciation This festival celebrates the revelation by the archangel Gabriel to the Virgin Mary that she was pregnant with Jesus. The most spectacular celebration is held at the Basilica of the Annunciation in Nazareth (25 Mar).

Other For details of various Christian festivals and holidays contact Christian Information Centre (Catholic), PO Box 14308, opposite Citadel, Jaffa Gate, Jerusalem, T02-6272692, www.cicts.org, and Franciscan Pilgrim Office (same location), T02-6272697.

Muslim holidays

The Islamic calendar The Islamic calendar begins on 16 July 622 AD, the date of the *Hijra* ('flight' or 'migration') of the Prophet Mohammad from Mecca to Medina in modern Saudi Arabia, which is denoted 1 AH (Anno Hegirae or year of the Hegira). The Islamic or Hijri calendar is lunar rather than solar, each year having 354 or 355 days, meaning that annual festivals do not occur on the same day each year according to the Gregorian calendar.

The 12 lunar months of the Islamic calendar, alternating between 29 and 30 days, are; *Muharram, Safar, Rabi-ul-Awwal, Rabi-ul-Sani, Jumada-ul-Awwal, Jumada-ul-Sani, Rajab, Shaban, Ramadan, Shawwal, Ziquad* and *Zilhaj*. To convert a date in the Hijra calendar to the Christian date, express the former in years and decimals of a year, multiply by 0.970225, add 621.54 and the total will correspond exactly with the Christian year!

Ras as-Sana/Al-Hijra (Islamic New Year) 1st *Muharram*. The first 10 days of the year are regarded as holy, especially the 10th. 2010: 5 Apr; 2011: 26 Nov; 2012: 15 Nov.

Moulid an-Nabi Birth of the Prophet Mohammad: 12th *Rabi-ul-Awwal*. 2011: 15 Feb; 2012: 4 Feb.

Leilat al-Meiraj Ascension of Mohammad from the Haram al-Sharif in Jerusalem: 27th *Rajab*. 2011: 28 Jun; 2012: 16 Jun.

Ramadan The holiest Islamic month, when Muslims observe a complete fast during daylight hours. Businesses and Muslim sites operate on reduced hours during Ramadan. 21st *Ramadan is the Shab-e-Qadr* or 'Night of Prayer'. 2010: 11 Aug-10 Sep; 2011: 1-30 Aug; 2012: 20 Jul-19 Aug.

Eid el-Fitr Literally 'the small feast'. 3 days of celebrations, beginning 1st *Shawwal*, to mark the end of Ramadan. 2010: 10 Sep; 2011: 30 Aug; 2012: 19 Aug.

Eid el-Adha Literally 'the great feast' or 'feast of the sacrifice'. 4 days beginning on 10th *Zilhaj*. The principal Islamic festival, commemorating Abraham's sacrifice of his son Ismail, and coinciding with the pilgrimage to Mecca. Marked by the sacrifice of a sheep, by feasting and by donations to the poor. 2010: 17 Nov; 2011: 6 Nov; 2012: 26 Oct.

Palestinian 'secular' holidays

There are a number of dates that are celebrated as 'secular' holidays in Palestinian areas, some of which have been designated public holidays by the PA (marked with an asterisk). **Fatah Day** 1 Jan*; **Jerusalem Day** 22 Feb; **Palestinian Land Day** 30 Mar; **Deir Yassin Day** 19 Apr; **Black September Day** 18 Sep; **Balfour Day** 2 Nov; **Independence Day** 15 Nov; **UN Palestine Day** 29 Nov.

Responsible travel

Bargaining

Israel provides almost unlimited shopping potential, particularly in the field of 'souvenirs' for pilgrims/tourists looking for some memento of their visit to the Holy Land. Much of the stuff is garbage, and much is concentrated in Jerusalem's Old City, where nothing has a price tag and you are expected to haggle a deal. There is great potential for the tourist to be heavily ripped off. Most dealers recognize the gullibility of travellers and start their offers at an exorbitant price. The dealer then appears to drop his price by a fair margin but remains at a final level well above the local price of the goods.

To protect yourself in this situation be relaxed in your approach. Talk at length to the dealer and take as much time as you can afford inspecting the goods and feeling out the last price the seller will accept. Do not belittle or mock the dealer; take the matter seriously but do not show commitment to any particular item you are bargaining for by being prepared to walk away empty handed. Also, it is better to try several shops if you are buying an expensive item such as a carpet or jewellery. This will give a sense of the price range. Walking away from the dealer normally brings the price down rapidly.

Clothing

Israelis tend to dress informally, particularly in Tel Aviv, Eilat and the coastal resorts. A highly visible exception to this rule are the ultra-orthodox Jews, who dress as per the Eastern European Jewish community of the 18th century. As mentioned elsewhere, visitors to Israel (both men and women) should be prepared to dress conservatively when visiting Arab areas, ultra-orthodox Jewish neighbourhoods, and religious and holy sites of any creed. Though light, loose-fitting cottons are excellent for the summer heat, you should bring some sort of jumper whichever season you visit, and cold weather gear if visiting Jerusalem at Christmas.

Conduct

Without descending into stereotypes, there are aspects of the Israeli psyche that often take foreign visitors some getting used to. A rare thing in Israel is a polite standard of service in shops, post offices, banks, and even some tourist information offices and hotels. Likewise, queuing at bus stops, holding doors open and saying 'please' are just not part of the Israeli make-up. There are lots of witticisms floating around that are supposed to sum up the Israeli personality (eg two Israelis in a room means three different opinions), though the reference that native-born Israelis prefer for themselves is sabra – the cactus fruit that is tough and thorny on the outside but remarkably sweet on the inside.

The rules of conduct that most affect foreign visitors to Israel concern visits to holy places, ultra-orthodox Jewish neighbourhoods and Arab areas. The modest dress that you should adopt when visiting such places is discussed elsewhere, though there are a few other rules of etiquette that should be remembered. When visiting mosques, remember to remove shoes before entering. Women are generally permitted entry, though they should cover their heads. In synagogues, both men and women are required to cover heads. In churches, it's hats off for men. Public displays of affection at any religious site should be completely avoided.

Photography

Ultra-orthodox Jews dislike having their photograph taken. Ask first, and be prepared for a refusal. Carrying cameras in certain areas on Shabbat is 'forbidden' (Western Wall, Mea She'arim, Safed). Arab women also dislike being photographed. Again, ask first and be prepared to be disappointed. Soldiers in uniform are an exception to this rule; however, be wary of taking photos of Israeli soldiers in confrontational situations with Palestinians.

Essentials A-Z

Accident and emergency
Medical emergency: T101 (Hebrew) or T911 (English). A special medical helpline for tourists can be reached on T177-0229110. The Jerusalem Post carries a daily list of late-night and all-night pharmacies. **Police**: T100. **Fire**: T102.

Customs and duty free
Persons over the age of 17 are each allowed to bring in duty free 1 litre of spirits, 2 litres of wine, 250 cigarettes or 250 g of tobacco, and personal gifts up to the value of $200. You may have to declare video equipment, personal computers and diving equipment, and pay a deposit, which is refunded when you re-export the goods. Do not lose the receipt.

There are no restrictions on the amount of foreign and local currency that you can bring into Israel.

Prohibited items
It is prohibited to bring fruit and vegetables, plants, fresh meat, animals and firearms into Israel.

Electricity
220 volts, 50 cycle AC. Plugs are of the round 2-pin variety. Adapters can be bought, though they are probably cheaper in your home country.

Embassies and consulates
For a full list of all foreign embassies and consulates in Israel, and Israeli embassies abroad, go to www.embassy.goabroad.com.

Health
See your GP or travel clinic at least 6 weeks before departure for general advice on travel risks and vaccinations. Make sure you have sufficient medical travel insurance, get a dental check, know your own blood group

and, if you suffer a long-term condition such as diabetes or epilepsy, obtain a Medic Alert bracelet/necklace (www.medicalert.co.uk). Also, get advice from your doctor and carry sufficient medication to last the full duration of your trip. You may want to ask your doctor for a letter explaining your condition. If you wear glasses, take a copy of your prescription.

Travellers should consider carrying a small first-aid kit that contains such basic items as headache treatments (eg Paracetamol), preparatory treatments for diarrhoea such as Loperamide (eg Imodium, Arret), oral rehydration proprietary preparations (ORS), plus sticky plasters and corn plasters (eg Band Aid). A good insect repellent may also come in handy, particularly those with around a 40-50% concentration of Diethyl-toluamide (DET). There are also repellents available that use more natural ingredients. All of these items are available in Israel, though you will probably find that they are cheaper at home.

Vaccinations
Confirm your primary courses and boosters are up to date. It is advisable to vaccinate against diphtheria, tetanus, poliomyelitis, hepatitis A and typhoid. Other vaccinations that may be advised are hepatitis B and rabies.

Health risks
The standard of healthcare in Israel is very high (it leads the world in some fields). There are no special health precautions that visitors should take, except to avoid **dehydration** and **sunburn/stroke**. A wide-brimmed hat plus high-factor sun-cream should be worn as protection against the sun, whilst 4 litres of water should be drunk per day to avoid dehydration. Dark-coloured urine, perhaps coupled with a feeling of lethargy, is often a sign of dehydration. Tap water in Israel is safe, though the delivery system in the Old City of Jerusalem may

be questionable. Bottled water is widely available. Sunglasses with 100% UV protection are a must. Note that not all clothes offer protection against the sun. As a general rule of thumb, if you can see through it when you hold it up to the light, then you can burn through it.

Travellers continuing on to countries such as Egypt should arrange **malaria** prophylaxis (prevention) before leaving home. Remember that most courses must be started 2 weeks before arriving in the infected area, and continued for 4 weeks after leaving. Consult your doctor or travel clinic.

If swimming or diving in an area where there are poisonous fish such as stone or scorpion fish (also called by a variety of local names), sea urchins on rocky coasts, or coral, tread carefully or wear plimsolls. The **sting** of such fish is intensely painful but can be helped by immersing the stung part in water as hot as you can bear for as long as it remains painful. This is not always very practical and you must take care not to scald yourself. It is highly recommended that you take immediate local medical advice in order to ascertain whether any coral or sting remains in the wound. Such injuries take a long time to heal and can be liable to infection. The main diving resorts in Israel (and across the Egyptian border in Sinai) have medical facilities equipped to deal with diving accidents.

If you get sick

Contact your embassy or consulate for a list of doctors and dentists who speak your language, or at least some English. Doctors and health facilities in major cities are also listed in the Directory sections of this book. Make sure you have adequate insurance (see below).

Useful websites

www.btha.org British Travel Health Association.
www.cdc.gov US government site that gives excellent advice on travel health and details of disease outbreaks.

www.fco.gov.uk British Foreign and Commonwealth Office travel site has useful information on each country, people, climate and a list of UK embassies/consulates.
www.fitfortravel.scot.nhs.uk A-Z of vaccine/health advice for each country.
www.numberonehealth.co.uk Travel screening services, vaccine and travel health advice, email/SMS text vaccine reminders and screening returned travellers for tropical diseases.

Insurance

It is strongly recommended that you take out insurance, in particular health insurance. Health care in Israel is of a high standard, and the costs are equally high. Receiving the bill from a night's stay in hospital may induce an instant relapse! Check exactly what your medical cover includes, eg ambulance, helicopter rescue or emergency flights back home.

When you take out travel insurance, make sure that it is a policy that suits your needs. Whilst many policies that cover theft appear to offer comprehensive coverage, they have very low ceiling limits on individual items (often limited to £250). If you are carrying expensive equipment you may need to get separate cover for those items unless they are covered by existing home contents insurance.

Check for exclusions such as diving, skiing, mountain biking and even hiking. Also check the payment protocol. You may have to pay first before the insurance company reimburses you. Always carry with you the telephone number of your insurer's 24-hr emergency helpline and your insurance policy number.

A policy where the insurance company pays the bill direct (rather than you paying, then claiming back the fees later) is probably a better deal, though generally more expensive. Keep all receipts for any treatment that you receive.

Language

If the State of Israel represents the in-gathering of the Jewish people from the Diaspora, then the Hebrew language represents one of the main unifying factors. In fact, the very pronunciation of modern Israeli Hebrew (a compromise between Sephardi and Ashkenazi elements) symbolizes its unifying influence.

For several thousand years Hebrew was just used for Jewish liturgy. Indeed, there are some elements in Israeli society (most notably the ultra-orthodox community from Eastern Europe) who believe that it is blasphemous to use Hebrew outside of liturgy, and thus they continue to use native tongues (frequently Yiddish). The modern usage of Hebrew was revived largely through the efforts of Eliezer Ben Yehuda (1858-1922), with the modern Hebrew movement becoming appended to the early Zionist movement. Theodor Herzl is alleged to have wistfully remarked, "Can you imagine buying a train ticket in Hebrew?".

Hebrew is a West Semitic language related to Assyrian and Aramaic. As a general rule, an Israeli could read a Hebrew Bible with relative ease, whilst someone brought up on biblical Hebrew would have some difficulty reading an Israeli newspaper.

The second most widely spoken language in Israel and the Palestinian Territories is Arabic. It belongs to a branch of the southwestern branch of the Semitic language group, though there are a number of different dialects.

Road signs in Israel are almost always written in Hebrew and English, and in most areas Arabic too. English is widely spoken and understood, particularly by those involved in the tourist industry. The Diaspora experience is reflected in the number of other languages spoken in Israel, including Ethiopian, German, Yiddish, Polish, Romanian, Hungarian, Spanish, and notably Russian.

Money

Currency ➔ *€1 = 5.11 NIS, £1 = 5.82 NIS, US$1 = 3.52 NIS (Aug 2011)*

The unit of currency in Israel is the New Israeli Shekel, written as NIS. It has in fact been 'new' for over 20 years. The Hebrew plural of shekel is shekelim, though the generally used expression is 'shekels' (or 'sheks'). The new shekel is divided into 100 agorot. There are notes of 200, 100, 50, 20NIS, plus coins of 10, 5, 2 and 1NIS. There are also coins of 50 and 10 agorot. .

Note that by paying in foreign hard currencies (preferably US dollars) for hotel accommodation, car hire, airline tickets and expensive purchases, you avoid paying the 17% Value Added Tax (VAT). For details on VAT refunds, see page 23. Though almost all foreign hard currencies are accepted, US Dollars remain the best option. It is always useful to have some hard currency cash with you, particularly when you are crossing borders. A mix of high and low denomination US dollars is probably the best bet.

Credit cards

Credit cards are accepted pretty much everywhere in Israel (though not everywhere in the West Bank). Banks with ATMs are found in even the smallest towns. Debit/credit card withdrawals are the easiest and best way to access your travelling funds.

Changing money

Travellers' cheques can be cashed at banks and money-changers, though commission charges are excessive. Good places to exchange TCs are post offices (which all offer commission-free foreign exchange at good rates). You will need to bring your passport.

Licensed Arab money-changers inside Jerusalem's Damascus Gate (and in most Palestinian towns) may give you marginally better than bank rates for cash and TCs. They are also a good source of Jordanian dinars and Egyptian pounds for those travelling beyond Israel (something worth considering).

If you need to transfer money, most main post offices act as agents for Western Union. Commission charges are high, though. For further details, see www.westernunion.com.

Cost of travelling

Public transport in Israel is reasonably good value. As an example, the 1-hr bus ride from Tel Aviv to Jerusalem is $5 (20NIS), whilst the country's longest bus journey, the 6 hrs from Haifa to Eilat, is $20. For further details on getting around see page 11.

Your daily budget will be influenced by how much sightseeing you intend doing. Israeli museums, galleries, religious sites, national parks and general sights charge anywhere between nothing and $10 for admission, though the average is around $5. Don't let admission fees deter you from visiting; if you are on a very tight budget, then pick and choose carefully.

With careful budgeting it should be possible to eat, sleep and see something of the country on $40-$50 per day. You do meet some people surviving on $20 a day or less, though they invariably seem to be miserable and tend to leave Israel having seen next to nothing of the country.

Opening hours

Few first-time visitors to Israel are prepared for the impact of Shabbat, or the Jewish Sabbath. Beginning at sun-down on Fri and finishing at sun-down on Sat, it sees all Israeli offices, banks, post offices, and most shops, restaurants and places of entertainment close down completely. Almost everywhere, both the inter-city and urban transport systems grind to a complete halt. If you don't want to go hungry or get stranded somewhere, plan in advance for Shabbat. Note that in many work environments, the 'weekend' is now adding Fri to the Sat day of rest. The picture is further confused by the fact that shops and businesses in Muslim (Arab) areas observe Fri as their Sabbath, whilst Sun is the day of rest for Christians. Anyone who claims their

religion to be 'monotheism' (as opposed to just Judaism, Christianity or Islam) should in theory be entitled to a very long weekend! The following are a general guide only:

Banks Sun, Tues and Thu 0830-1230 1600-1700, Mon, Wed and Fri 0830-1200.

Post offices Sun-Thu 0700-1900, Fri 0700-1200 (though branch offices generally close 1230-1400).

Government offices Sun-Thu 0800-1300 and 1400-1730, Fri 0900-1400.

Shops Mon-Thu 0800-1300 and 1400-1900, Fri 0900-1400.

Post

Outgoing mail from Israel is notoriously slow, taking 4-5 days to Europe and 7-10 days to North America and Australia. Incoming mail is rather quicker. Almost all post offices offer poste restante (doar shamur), and holders of Amex cards and TCs can use the American Express Clients' Mail service at their offices. Post offices also offer commission-free foreign exchange at good rates for TCs.

Safety

There are a number of security and safety considerations that should be borne in mind when visiting Jerusalem. Though acts of terrorism have been rare in recent years, it remains a volatile city and violence can flare up as a result of any political provocation. Recently, incidents have centred on the Haram Al-Sharif/Temple Mount area and you might find access to the Western Wall Plaza denied if trouble is anticipated. Attacks on Jews in East Jerusalem and the Old City are very unusual and security forces are much in evidence, however choice of wearing a kippa or making other outward displays of Jewishness is something that ought to be considered (though of course there is the argument that you shouldn't be intimidated by racist attacks). Likewise, tourists who wander around in 'amusing' IDF t-shirts should not be surprised if they are greeted with hostility (or worse) when wandering around the Muslim Quarter. Note that not all terrorist attacks in Jerusalem are committed against Jews/Israelis by Palestinians; you need to be equally vigilant in the vicinity of institutions (bus stations, government offices, places of worship) where the likely targets of any attacks are Palestinians.

Women may experience varying levels of harassment in the East Jerusalem/Old City area, ranging from disparaging or suggestive remarks to actual physical touching. The Old City should be considered unsafe for lone females at night (who might feel quite vulnerable and isolated after dark). Wandering around the Old City (particularly the Muslim Quarter) at any time whilst dressed in skimpy clothes remains a bad idea; wearing baggy and androgynous clothing can make for a more stress-free experience. It may seem like a fine idea to wear your shorts when you get on the bus at Eilat or Tel Aviv but, by the time you have reached the Old City and are wandering around looking for a hostel, you will realize your mistake. Beware of pressing crowds when the human traffic jams on Tariq Khan es-Zeit reach their peak.

As with any city that attracts huge numbers of tourists, Jerusalem (and the Old City in particular) has its share of pickpockets and confidence tricksters. On the whole, however, despite the religious and political tensions, Jerusalem is considerably safer than most cities in the 'West' (and of course has a considerable 'security presence'). Being sensible and vigilant, though not over-paranoid, is the best way to approach the issue of safety in Jerusalem.

Taxes

Departure tax for foreigners flying out of Israel is incorporated within the ticket price, but leaving Israel for Egypt by land, foreigners must pay 98.5NIS departure tax at the Eilat/Taba crossing. Leaving Israel for Jordan by land, foreigners pay 98.5NIS departure tax at the Jordan Valley and Arava crossings, and 163NIS at the Allenby/King Hussein Bridge.

Tax refunds

Though there is a 17% Value Added Tax on many goods in Israel, tourists are entitled to a VAT refund on certain products (generally not electrical, photographic or computer equipment). Shops that participate in the scheme generally have a large sign in the window, also see www.cpl.co.il. You should get a 5% discount on the marked price of the goods. Make sure that the VAT paid is marked clearly on the invoice (in shekels and US dollars). The goods should then be placed in one of the special clear-sided bags, with the invoice prominently displayed. You cannot open the bag prior to leaving Israel. At Ben-Gurion Airport, a booth in the 'departures' lounge will stamp the invoice and pay the refund, minus a commission.

Telephone

Telecards are available at post offices, shops and kiosks. Telecard-operated public phone boxes can be used for international direct dial (IDD) calls. The standard international access code of 00 has been replaced with the access numbers of three private firms, 012, 013, 014.

Peak rates are Mon-Fri 0800-2200. There is a 25% discount Mon-Fri 2200-0100 and all day Sat and Sun. There is a 50% discount Mon-Sun 0100-0800.

Mobile phones can be rented on arrival at Ben-Gurion Airport, or see www.israelphones.com for rental phone delivery anywhere in Israel. Calls cost about 1.20NIS per minute. Most foreign providers operate here (but it's worth checking your mobile package from home). To buy a SIM card, plus activation, usually costs 200NIS. In Israel, Cellcom and Orange both offer fixed-line (local user) and pay-as-you-go services.

Time

Israel is 2 hrs ahead of Greenwich Mean Time (GMT+2); 7 hrs ahead of American Eastern Standard Time; 8 hrs behind Australian Eastern Standard Time. Clocks go forward 1 hr for daylight-saving ('summer time') in Mar, and back again at Rosh Hashanah (usually Sep).

Tipping

In common with many other countries in the world, bar staff, waiters and waitresses in Israel receive fairly low wages, relying on tips to top up their salaries. If service is good then add 10%, if not leave nothing. It is not customary to tip taxi drivers. Tipping guides and tour bus drivers is a matter of personal choice. If someone cleans your room the right thing to do is leave a tip (5NIS per day is perfectly acceptable).

Tourist information

Visit www.visitisrael.gov.il, www.goisrael.com and www.peacecentre.org. The best source of online information for the Territories is www.thisweekinpalestine.com. **Municipal Tourist Offices**, *Jaffa Gate, T02-6271422, www.tour.jerusalem.muni.il, Sat-Thu 0830-1700, Fri 0830-1330*. Usefully located, make this your first point of call to pick up one of the detailed maps of the Old City, which clearly shows every street. They also have brochures, information, audio-guides, etc. The Municipality also run free walking tours every Saturday at 1000 (English and Hebrew) to various Jerusalem sites and areas, recommended particularly for long-stay visitors (leaving from Safra Square, Jaffa Street: meet near the palm trees; full list of destinations on website). The Municipality hotline is T106 (from outside Jerusalem T02-5314600). **Christian Information Centre**, *Jaffa Gate, T02-6272692, www.cicts.org, Mon-Fri 0830-1730, Sat 0380-1230*. Come here for information relating to churches for all denominations, throughout the Holy Land. **Jewish Student Information Centre**, *5 Beit-El, Jewish Quarter, T02-6282634, www.jeffseidel.com*. Free tours, hostel accommodation and more for Jewish youth. Also see Tour Operators, page 153, and www.holypass.co.il, which can save up to 25% on sightseeing around many of the Old City sights.

Visas and immigration

On arrival (by air, land or sea) you will be requested to fill in a landing card. If you request (but only if you specifically ask), the immigration official will stamp this card and not your passport. This card is then surrendered to an official before collecting your baggage. The lack of a stamp will only cause you difficulties when crossing the border into Egypt or Jordan, when officials may delay you while they check everything is in order. This usually just involves a few phone calls being made. Also, you may face questions when entering/exiting the West Bank. Note that you may have to provide evidence of a return ticket, though this is very rare.

Passports

All visitors require a passport that is valid for 6 months beyond the date of their entry into Israel. You should carry your passport with you (in a secure place) at all times. You may be required to show it when checking in to hotels. You will be asked for your passport at checkpoints if travelling around the West Bank.

Visas

Almost all nationalities are granted a free 3-month **tourist visa** on arrival, whether via land or air. The exceptions to this rule include most African countries, Arab/Muslim nations, India and many of the former Soviet republics. Be aware that at a land border you may be asked how long you intend to stay; then the exact figure you state could well be what you are issued with. Tourist visas do not permit you to work. They can be extended (see below). Visas expire on exit from Israel. For further details on arrival protocol see page 6.

If you are intending to work on a kibbutz or moshav, it is possible to apply for a 6-12 month volunteer visa once you are already inside Israel with the help of your kibbutz or moshav. Applicants should be aware that this visa is non-transferable, so if you move kibbutz you need a new visa.

A 12-month **student visa** is available to those who have been accepted by a university/education institute, though it is non-transferable and does not allow you to work. It is recommended to apply for the visa before arriving in Israel from an Israeli embassy abroad, though it is possible to obtain after arrival in the country if necessary. You require a letter of acceptance and proof of sufficient funds to cover tuition and living costs.

Work visas are arranged either before arrival through an Israeli embassy abroad, with a letter from your employers in Israel, or when already in Israel with a tourist visa. When in Israel, employers arrange working visas on your behalf, certified by the Ministry of the Interior. A work permit is non-transferable between jobs or employers and you will be liable for tax and national insurance contributions.

Jewish visitors considering returning to Israel permanently may be eligible for **temporary residence**. It is advisable that you contact one of the relevant agencies to guide you through this process: Association of **Americans and Canadians in Israel** (AACI), Jerusalem, T02-5661181, www.aaci.org.il; **British Olim Society**, 37 Pierre Koenig, Talpiyyot, Jerusalem, T02-5635244; 76 Ibn Gvirol, Tel Aviv, T03-6965244, www.ujia.org.il.

Visa extensions

Tourist visas can be extended for further 3-month periods at offices of the Ministry of the Interior. Appointments must be made in advance by calling *3450 Sun-Thu 0800-1200, with later shifts on Wed and Sun (1600-1900), though there can be a 2-week wait before you can even get an appointment. You should remember that granting visa extensions is at the discretion of the Ministry of the Interior and you are in no position to begin demanding your rights.

It costs 145NIS for an extension (plus 75NIS for multiple entry) plus one passport photo. It pays to dress smartly and act in a polite manner, and it's recommended to bring proof of sufficient funds. Having an itinerary of places that you still wish to visit in Israel may assist your application.

The **Ministry of the Interior** can be found at: 24 Hillel, Jerusalem, T02-6294726; 125 Menachem Begin, Tel Aviv, T03-5193305; Municipality Building, HaTemarim Blvd, Eilat, T08-6381333; 23 Zaki Elkhadif, Tiberias, T04-6729111. It is a nightmare renewing a visa at one of the main offices (even getting an appointment is an ordeal). Better to go to one of the regional offices, such as Netanya, Rishon LeTzion or Ramat Gan. You will need a hotel receipt that shows an address in the place where you are renewing your visa. Then it is possible to obtain a renewal in 1 day.

Many people feel it is simpler to leave Israel just before your visa expires (eg go to Sinai, Egypt, or Jordan) and get a new visa upon re-entry. However, crossing into Egypt for an hour, then returning, tends to raise the suspicions of immigration officials. Spending a weekend in Amman is a workable option (for cheap package deals to Jordan see **Flying Carpet**, www.flying.co.il). There is now a Jordanian consulate in Ramallah which can provide a Jordanian visa so that you can cross at the Allenby/King Hussein Bridge Crossing, rather than travelling all the way to the Rabin Crossing in Eilat.

Expired visas

There can be severe penalties for overstaying your visa, though how rigorously they are enforced appears to be a rather hit-or-miss affair. You may be obliged to pay a monthly charge for each month (or part thereof) that you have overstayed. Some travellers who have over-stayed their visa report being interrogated for hours at the airport/land border with the possibility of a deportation order being issued at the end. Others who have over-stayed by only a few days report no fines and no such problems. If you attempt to leave Israel at a land border with an expired visa you will almost certainly be refused exit and referred back to the Ministry of the Interior. Be polite and repentant. If you overstay your visa, you may be blacklisted and denied re-entry to Israel for 5-10 years (though this normally only applies to those who overstay by 6 months or more).

Women travellers

Women travelling alone face greater difficulties than men or couples. Despite the fact that levels of conventional crime are considerably lower in Israel than in parts of North America and Europe, women travellers in Israel occasionally experience a degree of sexual harassment. Instances of physical assault are thankfully very rare, though verbal harassment or suggestive comments more commonplace. It is probably best to steadfastly ignore rude comments directed at you but aimed at boosting the caller's ego, though if you feel yourself to be in any immediate danger, don't be afraid to shout and make a scene. Dressing conservatively certainly minimizes the hassle and is in any case required for visiting holy sites, so it is perhaps a good habit to get in to. In many parts of Israel you are free to wear whatever you like, as young Israeli women in Tel Aviv and Eilat so clearly demonstrate. Note, however, that going topless on the beach is still quite rare and can attract unwanted attention.

Working in Israel

Without the proper work permits, it is not really possible for foreign travellers to get work in Israel, since authorities started cracking down on illegal employment around 2006. There is a dependency on foreign workers in the construction and agriculture sectors, as there are difficulties in attracting Israelis to these menial and low-paid manual labour jobs, and Palestinians can no longer get work permits very easily. Therefore, construction workers, home-helps, agricultural workers, etc, are granted a 5-year period that is strictly regulated,

and illegal workers are actively tracked down. Most foreign workers in the cities are Chinese, Filipino or Indian, while in moshavim you will see large numbers of Thai farmers working the land.

Kibbutz

Several points need to be made about the kibbutz system straight away. You won't make much money, and it is doubtful whether it is a great way to conserve your travelling funds either (with many volunteers drinking away their savings). It is also not a good way to get to see Israel since you have to work six days a week, your day off is on the day that the buses don't run, they are usually situated in remote locations and you generally have to stay for more than 3 months to qualify for the kibbutz outings. However, it will offer a unique experience, and, according to what your expectations are and what sort of people you share the experience with, it may well be a memorable one. (**NB** The concept and functioning of the kibbutz and moshav is discussed below).

To join a kibbutz as a volunteer you have to be aged 18 to 32, in good mental and physical health, have proof of health insurance (not always asked for) and be willing to submit to a HIV/Aids test (not always enforced). Your work regime will be 6 days per week, 8 hours per day (generally starting very early in the morning), and you will be expected to accept whatever task is assigned to you. There is every reason to believe that volunteers are given the most menial and tedious chores on the kibbutz. Gardening is considered to be a good job. Getting up at 0430 to pick up all the dead chickens that died overnight is not.

In return for your labour you will receive free accommodation (usually in a special volunteers' block well away from the regular kibbutzniks), meals, a number of basic requisites such as toiletries, plus a personal allowance of around US$100 per month. Volunteers generally have access to all the recreational facilities at the kibbutz. You may believe that with all your basic needs provided for it would be possible to save your monthly personal allowance – not necessarily true. It's very easy to drink away both your monthly allowance and your travelling funds that you're holding in reserve. On the positive side, like-minded kibbutz volunteers can become lifelong friends (and partners).

You can organize a kibbutz placement in your home country (begin preparations for this at least 1 month in advance) or wait until you arrive in Israel. A list of kibbutz representatives overseas and in Israel is provided below.

To organize a kibbutz placement when already in Israel go to the kibbutz representative in Tel Aviv, 6 Frishman (cnr with HaYarkon), T03-5246154/6, www. kibbutz.org.il, but as you will need a volunteer visa you may end up waiting a while. July/August is a bad time to try this approach as student numbers are high, whereas harvest period is a good time. Acting like a sober, diligent, hard worker is a good way of getting a placement. It is also possible to apply directly to an individual kibbutz; many offer advice for volunteers on their websites.

Kibbutz representatives

overseas **Austria**, Schimmelgasse 16, 1030 Vienna, T0676 83181466, pnina schreiber@chello.at. **Belgium**, Bureau de Volontaires, 68 Ave Ducpetiaux, 1060 Bruxelles, T0475-891324. **France**, T01-48040866, paris@hachomer.net. **Germany**, Schadowstr 9, 60596 Frankfurt, T69-61993460, lydia.boehmer.gmx. de. **Netherlands**, Oppenheim Travel, Cronenburg 164, Amsterdam 1081GN, T20-4042040, arjan@oppenheim.nl. **UK**, Kibbutz Representatives, 1A Accommodation Rd, London NW11, T020-84589235; Kibbutz Representatives, 222 Fenwick Rd, Glasgow, T0141-6202194; Kibbutz Representatives, Harold House, Dunbabin Rd, Liverpool, T0151-7225671; Kibbutz Representatives,

11 Upper Park Rd, Salford, Manchester M7 0HY, T0161-7959447; Project 67, 10 Hatton Garden, London EC1N 8AH, T020-78317626. **USA** and **Canada**, 114 West 26th Street, New York, T212-4622764, www. kibbutzprogramcenter.org.

Moshav

Whilst many kibbutzim are diversifying into light industry and tourism, agriculture remains the backbone of the moshav system. Moshav volunteers are usually assigned to one particular farmer, and the success (or otherwise) of your moshav experience will almost certainly depend upon this relationship. Moshav farmers generally have a reputation for being slave-driving bullies. Moshav work tends to be far harder than that on a kibbutz ('back-breaking' is an often-used term), though the financial rewards are greater. Overtime is often compulsory, though getting paid for it can be a problem. The after-hours social scene varies considerably from moshav to moshav; you may be billeted with other volunteers, though don't be surprised if you are on your own. Moshav volunteers generally provide their own food (better get used to tomatoes), though if your farmer supplies your meals expect wages to be halved.

Moshav volunteers have to be aged 18 to 35 and have medical insurance. Don't apply unless you are physically fit and prepared for hard manual labour. To join a moshav go to the representatives office at 19 Leonardo de Vinci St, Tel Aviv, T03-5258473 (bus 70 from central bus station). Good luck!

Archaeological digs

If you want to work on an archaeological dig in Israel, contact the Israeli Antiquities Authority as early in the year as possible and request their list of forthcoming excavations that are open to volunteers (see www.antiquities.org.il, and look under 'public information'/'join a dig'). Bear in mind that you will have to pay for this experience. The **Institute of Archaeology** at the Hebrew University, Mount Scopus, (http://archaeology.huji.ac.il) provide a similar opportunity. Half-day digs are available at Beit Guvrin National Park through **Archaeological Seminars**, T02-5862011, www.archsem.com, price $30 for adults, $25 children (between the ages of 5-14 years), does not include entrance fee to the National Park.

Volunteering in the Palestinian Territories

A number of organizations arrange volunteer opportunities inside the West Bank. A registration fee is normally required if arranging the placement from overseas, as well as proof of medical insurance. You pay your own flight and transport costs, though accommodation and meals are usually provided.

Organizations offering such placements include: **Canadian and Palestinian Cultural Exchange**, (CEPAL), volunteers work and live in camps in cooperation with CEPAL's Palestinian NGO partners, 323 Chapel Street, Ottawa, Ontario, Canada, www.cepal.ca. **Cinema Jenin**, Jenin, an interesting project to re-open the cinema, www.cinemajenin. org. **International Voluntary Service** (IVS) GB, Thorn House, 5 Rose Street, Edinburgh, EH2 2PR, T0131-2432745, http://ivsgb.org/info. The **Israeli Committee Against House Demolitions (ICHAD)**, Jerusalem-based direct action organization, www.icahd.org. **Palestine Red Crescent Society**, medical volunteers for a recommended minimal stay of three months, non-medical volunteers for a recommended minimal stay of six months, PO Box 1928, Jerusalem, T02-628.6694, www.palestinercs.org. **Universities Trust for Educational Exchange with Palestine (UNIPAL)**, short-term summer teaching English assignments and other work/activities as needed, BCM UNIPAL, London, WC1N 3XX, www.unipal.org.uk. **Project Hope**, Nablus, opportunities for skilled/unskilled volunteers, www.projecthope.ps . Also see www.sciint.org and www.volunteerabroad.com for further volunteer opportunities in Palestine and Israel.

Contents

Contents

Footprint features

Jerusalem

Ins and outs

Getting there and away Coming from Ben Gurion Airport, sheruts (shared mini-bus taxis) can drop you off at your destination/hotel in Jerusalem. Many visitors arrive from Tel Aviv by bus, to the multi-storey Central Bus Station to the west of the New City centre, from where buses connect to the Old City. Sheruts from Tel Aviv's Central Bus Station arrive in the New City at Zion Square within walking distance of the Old City. There are also two bus stations in East Jerusalem: Suleiman Street bus station (outside Damascus Gate) serves destinations in East Jerusalem and Ramallah; Nablus Road bus station (also near Damascus Gate) serves southern destinations in the West Bank; usually you must change in Bethlehem.

Trains run between Jerusalem and Tel Aviv in 1½ hours, 10 per day, but the station is inconveniently located in Malha suburb to the southwest of the city. The express train line that will connect Jerusalem to Ben Gurion Airport in less than 30 minutes is not expected to be completed until 2017.

Jerusalem: overview

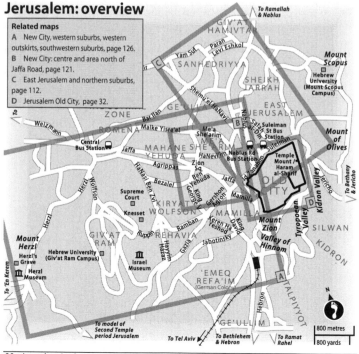

Related maps
A   New City, western suburbs, western outskirts, southwestern suburbs, page 126.
B   New City: centre and area north of Jaffa Road, page 121.
C   East Jerusalem and northern suburbs, page 112.
D   Jerusalem Old City, page 32.

Old City

Start your visit to Jerusalem with these highlights: a wander around the walled Old City, taking in the Citadel, Church of the Holy Sepulchre and the Via Dolorosa; the Temple Mount/Haram al-Sharif area, featuring the Western (Wailing) Wall and Dome of the Rock; and the Mount of Olives, for its views and important Christian sites.

Old City Walls and Gates

Amongst Jerusalem's most striking features are the pale-yellow stone walls that encircle the Old City: for many visitors, the first vision of these walls is a lasting one. They are equally impressive close up, where you can fully appreciate the sheer size of some of the masonry slabs, or from afar, most notably from one of the surrounding hills such as Mount Scopus or the Mt of Olives.

Ins and outs
A complete circuit of the city walls is highly recommended, including sections where you can walk along the top of the walls themselves ('Rampart Walk'). Jerusalem's city walls run for 4.02 km and are breached by eight gates (seven of which are open to passage). Visitors should note that each gate has three names: an Arabic/Muslim version, a Hebrew version, and an Anglicized version that is in common usage (and used here).

Old City overview: gates & quarters

Background
Relative to Jerusalem's long and ancient history, the city walls and gates that you see today are a recent addition, having been completed by **Sulaiman the Magnificent** (Sulaiman II) between 1537 and 1541. The previous city walls had been dismantled in 1219 by al-Malik al-Mu'azzam in order to discourage the reoccupation of the city by the Crusaders. However, certain stretches of the walls follow the course of far older fortifications, dating back to Crusader and Ayyubid, Byzantine, Herodian/Roman and even Hasmonean times, and in places the earlier defences can still be seen.

Ramparts Walk
① *Sat-Thu 0900-1600 (-1700 in summer), Fri 0900-1400. NB on Fri only southern ramparts open. Tickets cannot be bought on*

Jerusalem Old City: sights, sleeping & eating

Sleeping
1 American Guesthouse
2 Al-Arab
3 Austrian Hospice
4 Golden Gate Inn
5 Christ Church Guesthouse
6 Citadel
7 Gloria
8 Hashim
9 Lutheran Guesthouse
10 East New Imperial
11 New Swedish
12 Notre Dame de France & La Rotisserie restaurant
13 Notre Dame de Sion Ecce Homo Convent
14 Petra
15 Hebron Hostel

Eating
1 Abu Shukry
2 Abu Sair Sweets, Jaffar Sweets
3 Abu Shukri
4 Armenian Tavern
5 Papa Andreas
6 Quarter Cafe
7 Felafel/ hummus places
8 Versavee Bistro Bar
9 Gate Café

Sat or holidays: buy the day before. Adult 16NIS, student 8NIS, valid for two days. You also can buy a combination ticket for 55NIS, allowing entry to the Ramparts Walk, Jerusalem Archaeological Park, Zedekiah's Cave and the Roman Plaza, valid for 3 days (saving 18NIS). The main ticket office is by Jaffa Gate, T02-6277550, www.pami.co.il, but you can also buy tickets and enter from Damascus Gate or the entrance beyond the Citadel. Exit-only points are at Herod's Gate, New Gate, Zion Gate, Dung Gate and Lions' Gate, but (confusingly) after 1600 you cannot exit from Jaffa, Damascus or the Citadel.

Some sections of the ramparts are closed, notably between Lions' Gate and Dung Gate, and the section within the Citadel. The route is split into two sections: the southern ramparts (Jaffa-Dung, 30 minutes) and the northern ramparts (Jaffa-Lions, 1-1½ hours). It is particularly nice to walk in late afternoon sunlight, and is of human as well as historical interest, giving glimpses into the hidden everyday life in the Old City.

Warnings The stone path along the ramparts is particularly slippery when wet. And, although all sections are securely fenced, vertigo sufferers might be affected. Security staff patrol the area between Damascus and Lions' Gate (in case children throw stones) until around 1500; however, we have not received any reports of problems by tourists when walking alone after that time.

Northern Ramparts Walk (Jaffa Gate to Lions' Gate)

Jaffa Gate Though Sulaiman II's original 1538 gate remains, and is still used for pedestrian access, a section of the curtain wall to the south was demolished in 1898 (and the moat filled in) to allow Sultan 'Abd al-Hamid II's guests, the German **Kaiser Wilhelm II** and his wife, to drive into the city in the splendour of their carriage. **General Allenby** also entered the city with the victorious British Army at this point in December 1917, though he consciously chose humbly to proceed on foot (following the cabled recommendation of the British War Office: "Strongly suggest dismounting at gate. German emperor rode in and the saying went round 'a better man than he walked.' Advantages of contrast will be obvious"). This also contrasts with the entry into Jerusalem of Gustave Flaubert in 1850, who commented: "We enter through the Jaffa Gate and I let a fart escape as I cross the threshold very involuntarily. I was even annoyed at bottom by this Voltaireanism of my anus" (*Les oeuvres complètes de Gustave Flaubert: Vol.19, Notes de voyage*, edited by L. Conrad, Paris 1910).

The gate is referred to by Arabs as *Bab el-Khalil*, or 'Gate of the Friend'; a reference to Abraham, the 'Friend of God', whose tomb lies south of here in Hebron. The Hebrew name, *Sha'ar Yafo*, reflects the gate's orientation towards Jaffa (Yafo). The two graves just inside the gate (behind the railings near the tourist office) are said to belong to two of Sulaiman II's architects, executed for displeasing him with their penny-pinching (see Jaffa Gate to Zion Gate, page 37).

Jaffa Gate to New Gate One point along this stretch of the walls is labelled "Watchtower"; a reference to the period between 1948 and 1967 when Jordanian soldiers stationed here looked down upon the no-man's land that divided the Jordanian-controlled Old City from Israeli-held Jerusalem. Amos Elon recounts an amusing incident when a nun on the Israeli side of the line managed to 'cough' her dentures into the no man's land: "A brace of blue-helmeted UN truce supervisors, brandishing white flags, combed the debris-covered terrain where few persons had ventured for years and fewer still had come back alive. The false teeth were successfully retrieved" (Jerusalem: City of Mirrors, 1989).

Just before New Gate, inside an angle in the wall, is the small Ottoman-period (16th-century) **al-Qaymari mosque**. Also at this northwest corner, just outside the Old City walls, are the remains of a substantial tower (35 m by 35 m) built of re-used Herodian blocks, though almost certainly dating to the Crusader period. The north wall of the tower is best seen in the small 'archaeological garden' outside the Ottoman period walls, whilst parts of the huge internal piers are preserved within the Christian Brothers' College (viewing is discretionary, and by appointment only). The structure is commonly referred to as **Tancred's Tower**, after the Crusader knight who assisted Godfrey of Bouillon in capturing Jerusalem in July 1099. A medieval legend claims this as the spot where David slew Goliath (*I Samuel 17*), with the tower referred to in some sources as the *Castle of Goliath* (Arabic: *Qasr Jalut*). A further identification is with Herod Agrippa I's *Psephinus Tower* (described by Josephus in his *Jewish War V: 160*), though not only is the archaeological evidence against such an interpretation, the written evidence is also contrary (Josephus describes an octagonal, as opposed to square, tower). The tower was probably razed in 1219 by al-Malik al-Mu'azzam, nephew of Salah al-Din.

New Gate to Damascus Gate As its name suggests, New Gate (Arabic: Bab al-Jadid, Hebrew: Sha'ar He-Hadash) is a relatively recent access point into the walled city, cut in 1887 by the Ottoman Sultan 'Abd al-Hamid II in order to facilitate communications with the expanding 'New City' to the northwest. It remained sealed from 1948 until 1967. The stretch of wall from New Gate to Damascus Gate is particularly fine Ottoman period work, though excavations suggest that Sulaiman II's architects followed the line of the third- or fourth-century CE Byzantine walls.

Damascus Gate The most impressive gate in the city walls, Damascus Gate (Bab al-'Amud in Arabic, Sha'ar Shechem in Hebrew) is also considered to be one of the best examples of Ottoman architecture in the region. Flanked by two defensive towers, it is solid yet highly decorated with elaborate *crenellation* (battlements) above. It is not unknown for the *machicolations* above the gate, originally designed for dropping molten lead or boiling oil on to attackers, to have been used for dispensing tear gas canisters! The gateway is set back within a pointed arch of carved wedge-shaped blocks (known as *voussoirs*) and is reached via a bridge built in 1967 as a temporary structure. The entrance passage to the gate makes a double turn before leading into the heart of the Muslim Quarter. The street inside the gate and the plaza outside are used as informal market places (though the majority of the fruit vendors have recently been relocated, more's the pity). Still, it's a lively and busy thoroughfare and arguably the most interesting way to enter the Old City. The steps are certainly one of the best place to sit and absorb the atmosphere of Jerusalem, particularly in the hour before Shabbat.

Sulaiman II's structure is built precisely upon the lines of the former Roman period gate, with excavations in the area revealing remains from most periods of Jerusalem's history. To view closely the Roman and Crusader remains (and for access to the Roman Plaza Museum and Ramparts Walk), take the steps that go under the bridge (to the right of the entrance as you look at Damascus Gate from the outside).

Beneath the modern bridge (now a scruffy café) it is possible to observe the kerbstones of the medieval roadway that entered the gate on precisely the same line as the modern entrance, though at a lower level. The Byzantine and Roman gates also stood at this spot, again at a lower level still, with Roman remains evident in the building bearing the mark of the **Tenth Legion** (**Fretensis**).

Emerging on the east side beneath the modern bridge, the remains of the **East Tower** and **East Gate of the Triple Gate** are clearly distinguishable. This round-arched triple gate flanked by two towers is thought to have been built by the emperor Hadrian in 135 CE at the north end of the cardo maximus of his city of Aelia Capitolina. The fact that no traces of any first-century CE walls have been found goes far to support the theory that this triple gate was more a triumphal arch than a defensive structure. However, there is enough archaeological evidence to support the view that **Hadrian** merely rebuilt a gate begun by **Herod Agrippa I** (c. 40-41 CE) as part of the 'Third North wall', possibly reusing some of the drafted stones from the Temple (destroyed in 70 CE). Hadrian's gate opened on to a **monumental paved plaza** at the top of the cardo maximus, at the centre of which stood an honorific column, probably bearing a statue of his likeness. In fact, the Arabic name for Damascus Gate, *Bab al-'Amud*, actually means 'Gate of the Column', though like everything in Jerusalem, the interpretation is not straightforward. Murphy-O'Connor reminds observers (*The Holy Land*, 1992) that Ottoman-period gates invariably take their name from something outside them, and consequently the 'column' in question may refer to the huge column drums found within St Stephen's Church, about 200 m to the north. In the Crusader period the gate was referred to as St Stephen's Gate, with tradition associating the stoning to death of the first Christian martyr just outside. Following the defeat of the Crusader's Latin Kingdom in 1187, Christian pilgrims were forbidden from gathering close to the vulnerable north wall of the city, so the name was conveniently 'moved' to the gate on the east side of the city (see page 37). The Hebrew name for the gate, *Sha'ar Shekhem*, refers to the gate's orientation towards Shechem (Nablus).

Within the Roman Triple Gate is the **Roman Plaza** ① *Sat-Thu 0900-1600 (summer -1700), closed Fri, adult 10NIS (or with combined ticket, see page 30)*. In the eastern guard tower, first used by Roman soldiers, there are the remains of an oil press from the early Arab period. Venturing further below brings you to a small excavated section of the Roman/Byzantine plaza with polished stone slabs bearing the carved markings of a gaming-board similar to the ones found at the Convent of the Sisters of Sion (page 64). There is also a copy of the sixth-century CE Madaba Map, and photos and diagrams of the Damascus Gate through the ages. But you don't get much for your money, to be honest.

Damascus Gate to Herod Gate Between Damascus Gate and Herod Gate the bed-rock is exposed at the surface. At the mid-point between the two gates, an ancient quarry extends beneath the city walls, known as **Zedekiah's Cave** or **Solomon's Quarry** ① *Sat-Thu 0900-1600 (summer -1700), closed Fri, buy tickets a day in advance for Sat. Adult 16NIS (or a combined ticket, see page 30)*. It is generally well-lit, though you might want to bring a torch to explore more thoroughly. Discovered in 1854 by an adventurous dog, the origins of the cave are still open to debate. The malaki limestone found here was almost certainly exploited by Herod the Great and/or Herod Agrippa I, and may well be the 'Royal Caverns' that Josephus mentions (*Jewish War V: 147*). However, it is not unreasonable to speculate that the tradition associated with Solomon (*I Kings 5:17-18*) is also plausible. The cave complex extends for, well, who knows? It's certain that the main passageway leads some 230 m from the cave entrance, though Jewish tradition relates how Zedekiah escaped the besieging Babylonian army in 586 BCE through this hidden network of passages all the way to Jericho! The size of the quarry is remarkable, as is the concept of walking deep beneath the Muslim Quarter. As the cave descends, the shapes hewn from the rock vividly bring the blocks of the Temple wall to mind. The main hall has been used to hold Freemasons ceremonies, a notion pioneered by Sir Charles Warren.

Herod Gate This small gate in the north wall originally took its name from the rosette panel above the arch (*Bab al-Zahra*, or Gate of Flowers). Some time in the 16th or 17th century, Christian pilgrims mistakenly confused a nearby medieval house, *Dair Abu 'Adas*, with the palace of the man who condemned Jesus, Herod Antipas (Abu 'Adas/Antipas?), since when the name Herod Gate has stuck. Like Lions' Gate, this gate has been modified to allow direct access.

Herod Gate to Lions' Gate It was through a breach in the medieval-period walls just to the east of where Herod Gate is now located that the Crusaders first entered Jerusalem, at noon on 15 July 1099. The northeast corner of the Old City has always been considered to be Jerusalem's weak spot since the terrain is relatively flat and the protective ravines that defend the other sides are absent. Attempts have been made to improve the defences on this side by digging a deep ditch from the rock, and building a large number of insets and off-sets into the walls (thus increasing the field of fire). The northeast corner is occupied by the Stork Tower (or Burj Laqlaq), one of the more impressive towers in the ramparts.

Lions' Gate Built in 1538 by Sulaiman II, the name that he gave, *Bab al-Ghor* or Gate of the Valley (of Jordan), has never caught on, though the Hebrew name, Sha'ar ha-'Arayot or Lions' Gate (referring to the carved lions that adorn either side of the arch) has. Many Muslim sources still call the gate by its Arabic name, *Bab Sitti Maryam*; an obvious reference to the Church and Tomb of the Virgin Mary just to the east. During the Crusader period the name changed from the 'Gate of Jehoshaphat' to 'St Stephen's Gate' for reasons given above (see under 'Damascus Gate', on previous page), and is often still referred to as such. The gate was modified during the British Mandate period to allow access to motor vehicles. It was through Lions' Gate that the Jordanian Arab Legion entered the Old City in 1948, but also through here that Colonel 'Motta' Gur led an Israeli parachute brigade in capturing the city on 7 June 1967. Lions' Gate is the end point of the northern section of the walls, and the starting point for the tour of the Muslim Quarter (page 60).

Southern Ramparts Walk (Jaffa Gate to Dung Gate)
Jaffa Gate to Zion Gate To the south of Jaffa Gate is the Citadel (see page 39). Ascend to the Ramparts Walk at the stairs 100 m south of Jaffa Gate by the Citadel (signed). There are a number of points of historical interest along the stretch of wall between the Citadel and the southwest corner (before the wall turns east towards Zion Gate), though most of these features are best seen from outside (as opposed to on top of) the city walls.

This section of the city walls follows the line of far older defensive fortifications. Sections of the Hasmonean **city walls** (c. 164-63 BCE) are clearly visible in places, as are the slightly later **Herodian tower and walls**. One tower along this stretch is particularly noteworthy, featuring bulging Herodian stones at its base, medieval blocks above, and Ottoman-period work at the top. It was just to the south of here, close to the first-century CE city gate, that the Roman army finally broke through into the Upper City in 70 CE, during their suppression of the Jewish Revolt (see Josephus' *Jewish War VI: 374-99*).

At the southwest corner of the Old City walls, just beyond the remains of what must have been an impressive medieval tower, the line of the walls turns sharply east towards Zion Gate. Legend has it that Sulaiman II's walls should have been extended south to encompass the supposed site of the Tomb of David on Mount Zion. However, to save time and money this extension of the walls was not undertaken; a decision taken by the architects that is said to have cost them their lives when a furious Sulaiman II found out.

Zion Gate Completed in 1540, Sulaiman II's *Bab al-Kabi Da'ud* (or 'Gate of the Prophet David') was severely damaged in the 1948 battle for the city: in fact, when the Jewish Palmach forces breached the gate with over 70 kg of explosives on the night of 18/19 May 1948, they did something that according to Collins and Lapierre "no Jewish soldier had done since the days of Judas Maccabeus [c. 164 BCE] – they had breached the walls of Jerusalem" (*O Jerusalem*, 1972). Their success was short-lived, however, with the Palmach forces being forced to withdraw almost immediately. Zion Gate still bears the scars of the 1948 fighting, and some of the ornamentation seen here is not original.

Zion Gate to Dung Gate Extensive excavations have taken place along the stretch of wall between Zion Gate and Dung Gate, with visible remains from most periods of Jerusalem's history. Some of the main points of interest are within the line of the current city walls, though most are outside.

Continuing east from Zion Gate, it is possible to see part of the **Ayyubid tower** built in 1212, but dismantled just seven years later. To the east of the Ayyubid tower, inside the city walls, is a short section of wall dating to the Crusader period, whilst further east still is the **Sulphur Tower** (Arabic: *Burj al-Kibrit*). An inscription on the south side dates it to 1540, though the mixed remains of the tower projecting beneath it date to the medieval period. Close to the Sulphur Tower can be seen a section of the first-century BCE **aqueduct** that brought water from Solomon's Pools near Bethlehem to the Temple at Jerusalem. With various repairs, including the insertion of the ceramic pipes in the early Ottoman period, the aqueduct remained in use until early in the 20th century!

Just beyond the angle in the wall lie the remains of a sixth-century CE building, possibly a hospice, that is thought to be connected with the **Nea Church** just inside the walls, whilst further along the wall itself a small section of the Nea Church's southeast apse protrudes beyond Sulaiman II's walls (see page 87). The massive size of the four revealed courses (the upper of which has been restored) hint at the monumental size of this structure, and serve to confirm its status as the largest basilica in Palestine.

The rest of the section between here and Dung Gate is occupied mainly by rock-cut **cisterns** and **ritual baths** that formed part of first-century CE houses. Flanking Dung Gate to the west is a large **medieval tower** that is usually associated with the Crusader *Tanner's Gate*, or *Gate of the Leatherworkers*. Its foundations rest upon a section of **paved Byzantine road** that led down to the Pool of Siloam (see page 140).

Dung Gate This was probably a small Ottoman postern gate (built 1540-1541), but was greatly enlarged between 1948 and 1967 by the Jordanians to allow motor vehicles to enter the Old City (Jaffa and New Gates being sealed during this period). The name in common usage (Hebrew: *Sha'ar ha-Ashpot*) is said to refer to its proximity to a former waste dumping site, though its official name of *Bab al-Maghariba* (Gate of the Moors) is derived from its position close to the former Moorish (North African) colony.

Dung Gate to Lions' Gate For details of the southeast section of the Old City, where it abuts the south wall of the Haram al-Sharif/Temple Mount, see under the **Jerusalem Archaeological Park**. Unfortunately, the sensitive religious and political nature of the Haram al-Sharif/Temple Mount means that it is impossible to visit the Golden Gate on the east side of the Old City. Details of this structure are included within the Haram al-Sharif/Temple Mount section (see page 43).

The Citadel (Tower of David)

ⓘ *T02-6265333, 24-hr information T02-6265310, www.towerofdavid.org.il. Sep-Jun: Sun-Thu 1000-1600, Fri closed, Sat and hols 1000-1400. Jul-Aug: Sat-Thu 1000-1700, Fri 1000-1400. Adults 30NIS, student 20NIS, children 15NIS. Entrance fee includes a free guided tour, English: Sun-Thu at 1100, (in Jul/Aug also Fri at 1100); French: Tue at 1100. Personal audio guides available in English at the ticket office. There is a wheelchair route, though it does not reach all of the viewpoints and museum displays. Cafés, toilets. There's also a sound and light show: The Night Spectacular, adult 50NIS, students/children 40NIS; combined tickets for the Citadel and the Night Spectacular: adults 65NIS, students/children 55NIS. Book in advance on website or 24-hr tel no, although it's possible to get tickets on the night. A bit overpriced for only 45 mins, but children especially will enjoy the clever lighting effects giving a potted history of Jerusalem, and the optical illusions set against the Citadel walls are memorable. Bring warm clothes (even in summer); no photography.*

Located on high ground on the west side of the Old City (just south of Jaffa Gate), the Citadel of Jerusalem has been the city's stronghold for around 2000 years. Built largely upon the site of Herod the Great's first-century BCE palace/fortress and incorporating the substantial remains of one of three massive towers that he built, successive rulers of

Citadel (Tower of David)

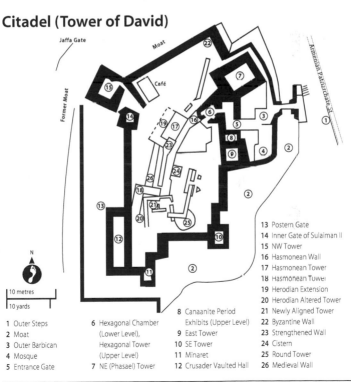

1 Outer Steps
2 Moat
3 Outer Barbican
4 Mosque
5 Entrance Gate
6 Hexagonal Chamber (Lower Level), Hexagonal Tower (Upper Level)
7 NE (Phasael) Tower
8 Canaanite Period Exhibits (Upper Level)
9 East Tower
10 SE Tower
11 Minaret
12 Crusader Vaulted Hall
13 Postern Gate
14 Inner Gate of Sulaiman II
15 NW Tower
16 Hasmonean Wall
17 Hasmonean Tower
18 Hasmonean Tower
19 Herodian Extension
20 Herodian Altered Tower
21 Newly Aligned Tower
22 Byzantine Wall
23 Strengthened Wall
24 Cistern
25 Round Tower
26 Medieval Wall

Jerusalem from the Romans, Arabs, Crusaders, Mamluks and Ottomans all rebuilt, modified and reused this defensive stronghold. Following the capture of Jerusalem by the Israelis in 1967, the Citadel was turned into a magnificent museum, and tells the history of the city through a superb assembly of scale models, maps, paintings, photographs, holograms, video footage and artefacts found during numerous excavations. Given the superb views from the ramparts, and the clear and concise museum presentation, the Citadel is an ideal place to begin a visit to Jerusalem. A thorough visit takes 1½-2 hours.

Ins and outs
Getting around There are three marked 'theme-routes' around the Citadel, of which the **Exhibition** tour (**red**) provides an excellent introduction to the city and gives the greatest rewards when undertaken in chronological order. The tour described here begins with the Exhibition (red) tour, and tries to provide background details on the building within which each exhibit is displayed rather than merely repeating the historical information provided by these museum displays. The **Panorama** (**blue**) tour around the towers and battlements requires little explanation, with noticeboards posted at key vantage points. The tour of the Citadel concludes by descending to the garden in the centre for a closer examination of the **Excavations** (**green**). Note, however, that in order to gain some perspective on this "jumble of masonry" it is wise to take advantage of the aerial perspective provided from the top of the Northeast (Phasael) tower (**7**). Bold numbers in brackets refer to a point marked on the map.

Background
Early history Evidence suggests that the site here was used as a stone quarry as early as the seventh century BCE, but was included within the northwest angle of the city walls by the late second century BCE. The dating of this 'First Wall' (which can be seen in the garden on the 'Excavation' tour) remains contentious, though the weight of opinion is behind the argument that it was built by the **Hasmoneans**, probably John Hyrcanus (134-104 BCE).

What is clear, however, is that **Herod the Great** built three monumental defensive towers here in the first century BCE to protect the magnificent palace that he constructed for himself just to the south. The base of Herod's **Phasael Tower**, named after the king's brother who had fallen in battle, can still be seen today on the northeast side of the Citadel, though there is the possibility that this could be the **Hippicus Tower** named after Herod's great (dead) friend. The latter tower is described by Josephus as being "superior in size, beauty, and strength to any in the whole world" (*Jewish War, V: 162*). The third tower was named after Herod's wife **Mariamme**, whom the king "had himself killed through passionate love" (*ibid*).

Josephus provides us with a flowery description of Herod's **palace**, repeatedly referring to its "magnificence", "splendour" and "beauty", concluding that "no words are adequate to portray the Palace" (V: 176). Parts of the palace were destroyed at the outbreak of the Jewish Revolt in 66 CE, when the rebels gained access by undermining one of its towers and torched the building (*Jewish War II: 430-440*). The Roman garrison took refuge in the three great towers and, having agreed to surrender, were then treacherously murdered by the Jews (*Jewish War, II: 431-56*). Josephus suggests that by this act "the city was stained by such guilt that they must expect a visitation from heaven if not the vengeance of Rome" (*ibid*).

Excavation in the 'Armenian Garden' to the south of the Citadel suggest that the palace would have stretched almost to the line of the present south wall of the Old City. Following **Titus'** conquest of Jerusalem in 70 CE, this area became for the next 200 years part of the camp of the Tenth Legion Fretensis.

Of course, much of the interest in Herod's palace lies in its relevance to the Christian tradition of the Crucifixion. Most experts now believe that the Roman Procurator of Palestine, in this case **Pontius Pilate**, would have stayed here in Herod's palace (as opposed to the Antonia fortress on the opposite side of the city, see page 63) whilst visiting from the Roman capital at Caesarea. Thus, this would be the site of the **Praetorium** where Pontius Pilate judged Jesus (for example *Mark 15:1-15*). If so, as is probably the case, this completely undermines the authenticity of most of the modern route of the Via Dolorosa.

Later history Remains are scant from the Early Arab period of occupation (638-1099 CE), though parts of an **Umayyad** palace have been excavated here (and in the 'Armenian Garden' to the south). When Jerusalem fell to the **Crusaders** in 1099, the **Fatimid** garrison in the Citadel withstood the attack and negotiated their surrender and safe passage from here. The Citadel was subsequently rebuilt into the fortress-palace of the newly established Crusader kings of Jerusalem, but was surrendered to **Salah al-Din** (Saladin) when he took the city in 1187. The fortifications were rebuilt and then dismantled a number of times in the ensuing years, but only when it was clear that the Crusaders were not going to return imminently did the Muslim rulers feel comfortable about extensively refortifying the city. By this time the **Mamluks** had replaced the Ayyubids as the rulers of Palestine, and it was the Mamluk sultan **al-Nasir Mohammad** who gave the Citadel much of its present form (c. 1310-11). Further additions were made between 1531 and 1532 by the Ottoman ruler **Sulaiman II** ('the Magnificent'), who was later to build the Old City walls that you see today. In recent years the Citadel has been used as barracks by the Jordanian army (1948-67) before being turned over to its present use as a museum following the Israeli capture of the city during the Six Day War.

The museum's full title, **The Tower of David Museum of the History of Jerusalem**, perpetuates the use of the popular name for the Citadel that arose in the fourth century CE when Byzantine Christians incorrectly identified the site as the palace of David. The Crusaders revived this erroneous identification, with their reused Herodian tower referred to as the 'Turres David'. In the 19th century the minaret (still standing) of the mosque became known as the **Tower of David**, and the name is now generally applied to the whole Citadel complex.

Sights
The current **entrance** to the Citadel is on the northeast side, a short way inside Jaffa Gate. The **outer steps** (1) here are those from which the British commander General Allenby declared the liberation of Jerusalem from Turkish rule in 1917. This ornamental entrance dates to the period of Sulaiman II's rebuilding project (1531-1532) and bears his name in a number of inscriptions. A bridge passes over the medieval **moat** (2) and enters the **outer barbican** (3) that the Mamluks, and then Sulaiman II, adapted from the original Crusader gate system. On the left is the **open air mosque** (4) built by Sulaiman II, whilst to the right a series of steps lead down into the moat and café.

The main **entrance gate** (5) dates to the 12th century and comprises a guardroom (complete with original stone benches), a portcullis, and the usual L-shaped right-angled turn that was designed to slow down enemy attackers. This Crusader gate complex was also restored by the Mamluk sultan al-Nasir Mohammad. The entrance gate leads into a **hexagonal chamber** (6) built in the 14th century, where the main ticket office is located. It is possible to proceed into the courtyard garden from here, though it is recommended that you follow the blue and red arrows up the stairs to the top of the **Northeast (Phasael)**

tower (7). A small room within this tower shows the Italian artist Emannuele Luzzati's 14-minute animated film "Jerusalem" (every half an hour between 1010 and 1640; Hebrew with English translation).

The base of this tower is solid all the way through, with the original Herodian construction comprising eight courses above the bedrock rising to just under 19 m. The smaller masonry at the top of the tower dates to al-Nasir Mohammad's building efforts in the early 14th century.

Exhibition (red) tour From the top of the **Northeast tower** follow the red arrows down to the adjacent roof of the 14th-century Mamluk **hexagonal tower (6)**. The top of this tower provides a good aerial perspective of the mixed remains in the garden below, with an information board indicating the key points of interest.

To the south of the hexagonal tower, on the same level and still outdoors, there is some information on Jerusalem in the *Canaanite period (c. 3000-1200 BCE)* **(8)**. To the south of this exhibit is the **East tower (9)**, probably built during the Mamluk period on Crusader foundations. The chamber that you enter on this level is devoted to the *First Temple period (c. 1000-586 BCE)*, and features among other things a model of the City of David in the 10th century BCE. The lower level of the east tower (follow the red arrows) is devoted to the *Hellenistic, Hasmonean and Second Temple period (332 BCE-70 CE)*, featuring an excellent model of Robinson's Arch.

Continue to the **Southeast tower (10)**, also built between 1310 and 1311 by al-Nasir Mohammad and restored between 1531 and 1532 by Sulaiman II. The chamber inside is devoted to the *Late Roman and Byzantine periods (131-638 CE)*, with an interesting model of Queen Helena's Church of the Holy Sepulchre.

Exiting the tower, follow the line of the south wall (at either ground or ramparts level) to the southwest corner of the Citadel, passing the 14th-century mosque with its (possibly) 16th-century **minaret (11)** to your left. The southwest corner of the Citadel is occupied by a **Crusader vaulted hall (12)**, with a now-blocked **postern gate (13)** at its northwest corner. In the 14th century the upper level of the vaulted hall was converted into a mosque by al-Nasir, with repairs made by Sulaiman II between 1531 and 1532 noted in an inscription above the minbar (pulpit chair). The exhibition in this upper chamber is devoted to the *Early Islamic period (638-1099 CE)*, the *Crusader and Ayyubid period (1099-1291)* and the *Late Arab period of the Fatimids and Mamluks (1291-1516)*. The lower level of the Crusader vaulted hall occasionally has exhibitions.

Exit the Crusader vaulted hall **(12)** and continue along the west wall to the *Mamluk (1260-1517 CE)* and *Ottoman (1517-1917 CE)* exhibition in the middle level of the northwest tower. This middle level also contains information on Jerusalem in the *British Mandate period (1917-1948)* and the establishment of the State of Israel (1948). Exit into the Archaeological Garden, where a red arrow points down into a former deep cistern below the **inner gate of Sulaiman II (14)**. Here is a superb 1:500 scale model of Jerusalem in the mid-19th century CE, built by the Hungarian artist Stefan Illes in 1872 for the World Fair in Vienna. Lost for many years, the model was rediscovered in Geneva in 1984 and is now here on an extended loan. It is possible to exit the Citadel from the Northwest Tower. The red Exhibition tour finishes here.

Excavations (green) tour Though it is possible to wander into the courtyard garden in the centre of the Citadel to examine the excavations up close, it is advisable to view them first from from the roof of the **hexagonal tower (6)**.

The second-century BCE **Hasmonean wall** (16) makes a sweeping curve through what Prag describes as a "jumble of masonry" (*Blue Guide*, 1989). Defended by two **towers** (17) (18) from the same period, this is almost certainly the 'First Wall' described by Josephus (*Jewish War, V: 142-5*). Its continuation can be seen at the start of the tour of the Jewish Quarter (see page 83). The periods of Hasmonean building can be distinguished from later periods by the general use of smaller blocks. The rooms abutting the Hasmonean wall (16) became buried beneath the podium that Herod built to support his palace. He also built an **extension** (19) to one of the Hasmonean towers, whilst reducing the size of the other (20). For some unexplained reason this tower had to be rebuilt early in the first century CE, on a slightly different alignment (21). Evidence of the damage caused to the palace during the Jewish attack of 66 CE was identified just here.

To the north side of the Northeast (Phasael) tower is a section of the **Byzantine wall** (22) added in the fourth century CE; perhaps part of Herod Agrippa's Third North Wall. The original Hasmonean wall (16) was also strengthened (23) and the Herodian tower (21) rebuilt. The **cistern** (24) also dates to this period. Later additions include the **round tower** (25), generally thought to be part of an eighth-century CE Umayyad palace, and the stretch of medieval wall (26). If you have any time left at the end, it is recommended to do the Panoramic tour for the excellent views.

Temple Mount/Haram al-Sharif

ⓘ *Entry hours are restricted to Sun-Thu 0730-1030 and 1330-1430. During the holy month of Ramadan visiting is only Sun-Thu 0730-1000, and the Haram al-Sharif may be closed completely during certain Islamic festivals. Non-Muslims can only enter the Haram al-Sharif through the Bab al-Maghariba (Gate of the Moors, via the covered ramp leading up from the Western Wall Plaza), though you can leave by any of the functioning gates. Non-Muslims are not permitted to enter the Dome of the Rock nor Al-Aqsa Mosque, and this is very unlikely to change in the near future. The Islamic Museum, on top of the mound, remains shut.*

The Temple Mount/Haram al-Sharif is an artificially raised platform built upon a low hill on the eastern side of the Old City. Whilst representing the architectural and visual focus of Jerusalem, it could also be said to be one of the most contested pieces of real estate on earth. The site of the First and Second Jewish Temples, the latter where Jesus taught, it is now home to a shrine and mosque that make it the third most important place of pilgrimage within the Islamic world. Whilst the status of Jerusalem divides Israelis and Palestinians like no other matter, the custody of the Temple Mount/Haram al-Sharif provides a vivid and terrifying focus to this confrontation. When trouble flares up in the Old City, it invariably is centred around this area, and consequently the Western Wall Plaza will be closed to visitors. Though there are no standing remains of the Temple, Jews still visit the Western (Wailing) Wall to mourn its destruction. The central Islamic buildings stand on the Haram al-Sharif/Temple Mount itself and include Jerusalem's main congregational mosque (al-Aqsa Mosque), plus one of the world's most beautiful architectural monuments, the Dome of the Rock. Non-Muslims are not permitted entry to either structure.

Ins and outs

Getting there and away There are any number of ways of approaching the Temple Mount/Haram al-Sharif, though most arrive via the Western Wall Plaza (on foot from just about any direction in the Old City, or by buses 1, 3 or 38). There is (free) 24-hour access to the Western Wall Plaza.

Temple Mount or Haram al-Sharif?

Even for a guidebook that is attempting to be non-partisan, problems arise when it comes to deciding by which name to refer to certain contested sites.

In the main, the name commonly used in Western sources has been selected, based largely on the premise that most of the readership is drawn from here and thus the 'common' name used will strike a chord of familiarity. Thus, there is a chapter called 'West Bank' and not 'Judea and Samaria' or 'Occupied Territories'. With regard to the platform on which the Jewish Temple once stood, but is now occupied by the Dome of the Rock, al-Aqsa Mosque, and a number of Muslim shrines, when referred to in a Jewish context this Handbook will use the term Temple Mount; and when referred to in a Muslim context, it will be referred to as the Haram al-Sharif. In a general context the Handbook will call it the Temple Mount/Haram al-Sharif (though the placing of 'Temple Mount' before 'Haram al-Sharif' signifies nothing). The Hebrew name for the Temple Mount is *Har Ha-Bayit*, though it is sometimes referred to as *Har Ha-Moriyya* (Mt Moriah) or *Beth Ha-Maqdas* (the Holy House). The Arabic name Haram al-Sharif means 'Noble Sanctuary', though *Bait al-Maqdis* (the Holy House) is occasionally used.

Getting around It is important to dress modestly when visiting both the Muslim and Jewish holy places around the Temple Mount/Haram al-Sharif. This means no shorts (on men or women), with women in particular being reminded to wear loose, non-revealing clothes. Some form of head covering is advisable for both sexes (paper kippas are provided at the male entry point to the Western Wall). Photography is not permitted in the Western Wall Plaza on Shabbat or Jewish holidays (and should be treated as a privilege and not a right at other times), nor is smoking, using mobiles or taking notes. Decorous behaviour is also essential in both the Jewish and Muslim areas, with public displays of affection being wholly inappropriate. Al-Qasr Mosque and the Dome of the Rock are off-limits to non-Muslim visitors, and so are some other areas of the Haram al-Sharif (there are no signs indicating where you can and cannot go, though someone will soon tell you). Anyone offering to be your guide is definitely best avoided.

Background
Mount Moriah Tradition links the low hill upon which the Temple Mount/Haram al-Sharif stands with the Mt Moriah upon which **Abraham** offered his son Isaac as a sacrifice, as a sign of his obedience to God (*Genesis 22*). There are at least two other versions of this story, with Muslims believing that it was Ishmael, and not Isaac, who was offered by Abraham, whilst Samaritans believe that the biblical description of the sacrifice site – "Abraham lifted up his eyes, and saw the place afar off" (*Genesis 22:4*) – better fits Mt Gerizim (near Nablus) than the low rise here in Jerusalem. Tradition also places here the "threshing floor of Araunah the Jebusite" that **David** purchased in the 10th century BCE as the site upon which to build an altar to God (*II Samuel 24:18-25*). Other traditions central to Judaism, Christianity and Islam appear to have been placed at this spot retrospectively, with the rock at the spiritual centre of the Temple Mount/Haram al-Sharif also being associated with the place where God took the dust for the creation of Adam, where Adam was buried, where Cain and Abel offered their gift to God, and where Noah raised an altar after leaving the ark.

Solomon's Temple Though it was David who brought the symbol of the Israelites covenant with God (the Ark of the Covenant) to Jerusalem, it is generally claimed that his militaristic past meant that he had too much blood on his hands to build the first Jewish Temple, and thus the task was left to his son **Solomon**. Johnson (*A History of the Jews*, 1987), however, suggests that this argument does not stand up since "war and the Israelite religion were closely associated", citing as an example how the Ark of the Covenant was sometimes carried into battle like a flag or standard. He argues that David chose not to build the Temple since this would have changed the essential nature of the balance between state and religion, and he wished to avoid turning Israel into a royal temple-state.

Work began on Solomon's Temple c. 961/960 BCE, taking seven years to complete, and though no trace remains it is possible to make a tentative reconstruction from the description in the Old Testament (*I Kings 5-8*). It was built of stone and timber, with the Phoenician king of Tyre, Hiram, sending both cedars and stonemasons to assist in its construction (*I Kings 5:1-18*). He also sent experts in casting bronze to make the ceremonial vessels. The Temple was tripartite in plan, with an inner **Holy of Holies** housing the Ark of the Covenant. Whether the Ark stood on the 'rock', or the 'rock' served as an altar in the Holy of Holies is unknown. The entrance to the Temple was to the east, flanked by two free-standing columns named for unknown reasons *Jachin* and *Boaz* (*I Kings 7:21*). The Temple was looted of its treasures on a number of occasions before being destroyed in the **Babylonian** sack of Jerusalem in 586 BCE. However, it is important to note that the building style of the Temple, similar to Canaanite temples excavated at Lachish and Bet Shean, would have been "put up and equipped in a manner quite alien to the Israelites" (Johnson, *ibid*). In fact, Johnson goes on to argue that "What is clear is that Solomon's Temple, in its size and magnificence, and its location within the fortified walls of a royal upper city or acropolis, had very little to do with the pure religion of Yahweh which Moses brought out of the wilderness" (*ibid*). What Johnson is suggesting is not that Solomon was building a pagan place of worship, but that he was introducing a religious reform that was based upon royal absolutism. This centralization of religious power and cult worship did not survive the death of Solomon, leading to the dissolution of the United Monarchy and the return to the northern (Israel)/southern (Judah) rivalry.

Post-Exilic Temple Following the return from Exile, the Temple was rebuilt by **Zerubbabel** c. 537-515 BCE, probably on the same plan as Solomon's effort but without the ornamentation. The Ark of the Covenant, however, had been lost. **NB** Though the Post-Exilic Temple in reality represents the second Temple built on this site, the term 'Second Temple' is generally used to refer to Herod the Great's creation (see below).

Herod's Temple The decision of **Herod the Great** to construct a grand new temple on the Temple Mount says much about his character as a propagandist and a showman. The fact that he built the Antonia fortress (page 63) and the three great towers (Phasaeal, Hippicus and Mariamme, see page 38) before commencing work on the Temple further illustrates Herod's standing amongst a suspicious Jewish population. With his Idumean background, his Hellenizing reforms and his dependence for legitimacy on his Roman backers, Herod had to be very careful in how he went about building his Temple since this would require the dismantling of the Post-Exilic Temple then standing on the Temple Mount. He did this by summoning a national council of religious leaders in 22 BCE and laying his plans before them. At every step of the way he was extremely sensitive to charges of desecration, even going so far as to train up to 1000 priests as builder-craftsmen to work in areas forbidden to the ritually impure. Though the temple structure itself took less than two years to complete, such was the monumental scale of the entire complex that it was barely finished when the Romans tore it down in 70 CE.

In order to fulfil his ambitions of creating a temple that would not only rival Solomon's effort but also exceed it in splendour, it was necessary to enlarge the Temple Mount platform. This was done by bridging the valleys surrounding the Mt Moriah of Solomon's Temple, and filling them in. The Herodian Temple Mount enclosure was shaped like an uneven rectangle, with the following dimensions: west wall 485 m, east wall 470 m, north wall 315 m, south wall 280 m. Thus, the enclosure covered an area in the region of 144,000 sq m; a remarkable achievement.

The magnificence of Herod's building project can still be appreciated, despite the fact that no trace of the Temple building itself actually remains standing in place. Large sections of the retaining wall can still be seen, rising in various numbers of courses above the bedrock. The most easily visible, and famous, section of Herod's retaining wall is preserved at the so-called Western Wall, where seven courses rise above the level of the present plaza with more courses reaching down to bedrock below. See the line drawing on below to help you visualize the scene. The southeast corner of the mound perhaps best displays the scale of the enclosure, with 35 original courses extending 42 m above the bedrock.

A fairly accurate picture of the Temple building and the enclosed plan has been reconstructed by examining the fragments found on or near the site, the subterranean features remaining in situ, and the detailed descriptions found in contemporary accounts (most notably Josephus' *Jewish War V, 1-226* and *Antiquities XV, 380-425*). Standing on a vantage point overlooking the Temple Mount and reading the relevant passage in *The Jewish War* is an enlightening experience. The Temple enclosure probably had nine gates, and was surrounded on three sides by a portico, with a *double (Royal) portico* to the south. It is suggested that this is where the moneychangers and usurers, whose tables Jesus upset, would have been located. The outer *Court of the Gentiles* could be entered by non-Jews, though entry to the sacred area was prohibited on pain of

Herod the Great's Temple: the Second Temple

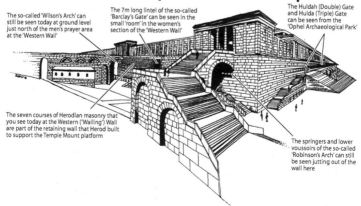

The so-called 'Wilson's Arch' can still be seen today at ground level just north of the men's prayer area at the 'Western Wall'

The 7m long lintel of the so-called 'Barclay's Gate' can be seen in the small 'room' in the women's section of the 'Western Wall'

The Huldah (Double) Gate and Hulda (Triple) Gate can be seen from the 'Ophel Archaeological Park'

The seven courses of Herodian masonry that you see today at the Western ('Wailing') Wall are part of the retaining wall that Herod built to support the Temple Mount platform

The springers and lower voussoirs of the so-called 'Robinson's Arch' can still be seen jutting out of the wall here death (parts of two tablets, one in Latin and one in Greek, declaring this fact have been found). Within the sacred area itself, the *Beautiful Gate* led from the *Court of the Women* to that of the men (*Court of Israel*), and from thence into the *Court of the Priests*. This is perhaps where the young Jesus was presented (*Luke 2:22-39*). Like the Solomonic Temple, Herod's construction was on a tripartite plan, with the inner chamber veiled by a purple curtain (that tradition says was rent in two during the Crucifixion: *Matthew 27:51*; *Mark 15:38*; *Luke 23:45*). The curtain concealed the inner *Holy of Holies*. Though the exact location of the Holy of Holies is unknown (a factor which prevents religious Jews from visiting the Temple Mount for fear of violating it), it is generally assumed that it stood on the site of the rock that is now enshrined within the Dome of the Rock. The destruction of the Second Temple by the Romans in 70 CE is vividly brought to life by Josephus (*The Jewish War VI, 230-442*).

The 12th-century CE rabbi and sage Maimonides ruled that, despite the destruction of the Temple, the site still retained its sanctity and hence any Jew wishing to visit had to be ritually pure. Unfortunately, this is not that simple. The ritual purification process is laid out explicitly in The *Fourth Book of Moses, Called Numbers* and features, amongst other things, the "ashes of the burnt heifer of purification for sin" (*Numbers 19:17*). The heifer had to be red and "without spot, wherein is no blemish, and upon which never came yoke", and if only two hairs of the heifer were not red, it couldn't be used. As a further complication, the preparation had to be carried out by Eleazar, the heir apparent of Aaron. Thus, when the Temple was destroyed, no new ashes could be produced, and so purification is not possible until the Messiah arrives to prepare a new supply. As a result, rabbinical consensus is of the opinion that all Jews are now ritually impure.

Haram al-Sharif The Temple platform appears to have been largely neglected and ignored by the Byzantines, and it is with the arrival of the Arab armies in 638 CE that the course of the enclosure's history is irreversibly changed. The holiness of the site to Muslims is immediately apparent from the early decision of the caliph Omar to build a mosque on the Temple Mount platform, within a year of the Arab conquest of Jerusalem. The mosque is described as a simple crude affair by the Christian pilgrim Arculf (c. 670 CE), perhaps reusing the columns from Herod's ruined Royal Portico. However, many right-wing Israelis suggest that the Arab conquerors of the city 'invented' the religious significance to Muslims of the site as a means of superseding the influence of previous Jewish or Christian claims to Jerusalem (see box on the next page).

By the end of the seventh century CE/start of the eighth century CE, the Muslims had built the Dome of the Rock (c. 691-2 CE) and the al-Aqsa Mosque (c. 705-15 CE) on the Temple Mount platform, renamed the enclosure the Haram al-Sharif, and banned non-Muslims from entering it. Subsequent centuries saw the Crusaders occupy the Temple Mount/Haram al-Sharif, turning the Dome of the Rock into a Christian prayer hall and the al-Aqsa Mosque into a palace for the king, and then the headquarters of the Templars. Salah al-Din's conquest of Jerusalem in 1187 saw the main buildings revert to their former use, followed by the continuous additions of Muslim shrines and monuments through the Mamluk and Ottoman periods. Despite the capture of all of Jerusalem by the Israelis in 1967, the Haram al-Sharif has remained in Muslim hands since the 12th century.

Sights
Dome of the Rock The Haram al-Sharif, like most views of Jerusalem, is dominated by the graceful lines of the Dome of the Rock (Arabic: *Qubbat al-Sakhra*). The building's dimensions

Haram al-Sharif / Temple Mount overview

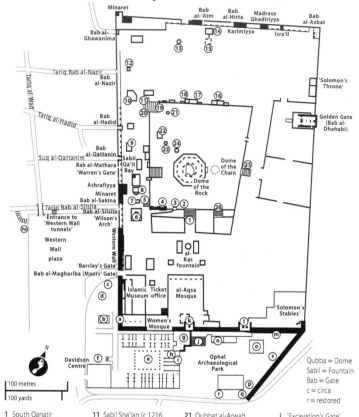

1 South Qanatir (c 10th cent)

2 Minbar of Burhan al-Din (c 1388, r 1843)

3 Qubba Yusuf (c 1681)

4 Qubba Nahwiyya (c 1207)

5 SW Qanatir (c 1472)

6 Qubba Musa (Dome of Moses) (c 1249)

7 Mastabat al-Tin (c 1760)

8 Sabil Bab al-Mahkama & Birka Ghaghanj (c 1527)

9 Mihrab 'Ali Pasha (c 1637)

10 Sabil al-Shaikh Budayr (c1740)

11 Sabil Sha'lan (c 1216, r 1429, 1627)

12 Sabil Basiri (c 1456)

13 Qubbat Sulaiman (c 1200)

14 Sabil al-Sultan Sulaiman (c 1537)

15 Pavilion of Sultan Mahmud II (c 1817)

16 NE Qanatir (c 1326)

17 N Qanatir (c 1321)

18 Cell of Muhammad Agha (c 1588)

19 NW Qanatir (c 1376, r 1519,1567)

20 Qubbat al-Khadir (c 16th cent)

21 Qubbat al-Arwah (c 16th cent)

22 Masjid al-Nabi (c 1700)

23 Qubbat al-Mi'raj (c 1200)

24 Qubbat al-Nabi (c 1538, r 1845)

25 E Qanatir (c 10th cent)

26 SE Qanatir (c 1030, r 1211)

a 'Robinson's Arch'

b Pier

c Herodian Street

d Umayyad Courtyard

e Umayyad Palace

f Umayyad Hospice?

g Medieval Tower

h Byzantine House

i 'Excavation's Gate'

j Herodian Plaza

k Double Gate

l Triple Gate

m Single Gate

n Mikvehs (Ritual Baths)

o Byzantine Building

p 7th–6th century BCE remains

q Herodian Building

r Byzantine Homes

s Byzantine City Wall

Qubba = Dome
Sabil = Fountain
Bab = Gate
c = circa
r = restored

rest upon a mathematical precision that is related to the piece of rock that it encloses. If it does, as some believe, stand at the centre of the world, then it is a fitting monument. Not only is it the first great building of Islam, it is an architectural masterpiece in its own right.

It was built between 688-692 CE by the fifth Umayyad caliph, 'Abd al-Malik, following the Arab capture of Jerusalem (638 CE). Though Muslims emphasize that the Dome of the Rock was built to commemorate the prophet Mohammad's night ascent to heaven (*Sura XVII*), there are several less-divinely inspired considerations that must have been in 'Abd al-Malik's mind. In fact during the succeeding (and rival) Abbasid caliphate, attempts were made to discredit the Umayyad caliph 'Abd al-Malik by suggesting that he built the Dome of the Rock in order to lure the lucrative pilgrim trade away from the Ka'ba at Mecca. There is an element of truth in this, though it is generally believed that 'Abd al-Malik was seeking to consolidate a rival political, as opposed to religious, centre in the Jerusalem-Damascus region. However, there are fairly strong grounds to believe that 'Abd al-Malik was seeking to build a striking monument that would reaffirm Islam as the successor to its imperfect predecessors.

This point is underlined by the founding inscription around the ambulatories inside the building, quoting a verse from the Qur'an: "O you People of the Book, overstep not bounds in your religion, and of God speak only the truth. The Messiah, Jesus, son of Mary, is only a Messenger of God, and his Word, which he conveyed into Mary, and a Spirit proceeding from him. Believe therefore in God, and his prophets, and say not three. It will be better for you. God is only one God. Far be it from his glory that he should have a son" (Sura IV, verse 169). The emphasis on this rejection of the Christian Trinity is aimed at the Byzantine church that had been established for almost four centuries in Jerusalem. The magnificence of the Dome of the Rock was certainly a conscious effort to 'out do' the Christian religious buildings long-since established in the city, though it may have been aimed as much at wavering Muslims as towards Christians.

The architects of the Dome of the Rock are unknown, though the architectural style is a successful synthesis of a number of influences, reflecting the spread of Islam and the consequent use of craftsmen and traditions from these conquered lands. Though numerous repairs have been carried out over the centuries, the basic form remains largely unchanged.

The base is an **octagon** (c. 53.75 m in diameter) built of local limestone courses. The walls are faced with marble panels, though the original seventh-century CE glass mosaic coverings were replaced in the 20th century using polychrome glazed tiles made in Kütahya, Turkey. The predominant colour is a beautiful turquoise-blue, with white, green, black and yellow tiles adding to the overall effect. The stylized floral motifs closely resemble the original patterns, though the colours are far more vivid. Of particular note is the band of blue and white tiles that extends all the way round the octagon, and features verses from the Qur'an (*Sura XXXVI*). Each face of the octagon features five grilled windows, allowing light to penetrate inside.

The original dome collapsed in 1016 and was rebuilt in 1022, though many repairs have been made since. The original lead casing proved to be too heavy, leading to instability, and was replaced in 1961 with the brilliant gold-coloured anodized aluminium that you see today. When the Crusaders occupied the Temple Mount/Haram al-Sharif following their capture of Jerusalem in 1099, the Dome of the Rock became the *Templum Domini* (Temple of Our Lord), and a tall cross stood at the pinnacle of the dome. It was replaced with a crescent by Salah al-Din in 1187.

Inside, a single line of Kufic script, the 'founder's inscription', runs along the top of both sides of the inner octagon. It originally featured 'Adb al-Malik's name, the founding date

(AH 72, or 691 CE), and *Sura IV*, verse 169 (see above), though the later Abbasid caliph al-Ma'mun (813-830 CE) inserted his name instead, but without altering the founding date. The interior of the drum is lavishly decorated, with al-Zahir (c. 1027), Salah al-Din (c. 1198) and al-Nasir Mohammad (1318) all leaving their mark.

At the centre of the inner octagon is the **Holy Rock**. The rock is associated with Abraham's sacrificial offering (*Genesis 22:2-19*), and the place where David built an altar to God (*II Samuel 24:18-25*), and thus is generally believed to be the site of the Holy of Holies in the Solomonic Temple where the Ark of the Covenant stood. Muslims believe that Mohammad began his Night Ascent from this rock, and his footprint has been left in the rock in the southwest corner. Tradition relates how the rock attempted to follow Mohammad on his journey, and thus the handprint next to the footprint is where the angel Gabriel held down the rock. During the Crusader period the footprint was venerated as that of Christ, with the result that visiting pilgrims chipped away parts of the rock to keep as souvenirs or sell as relics. By the late 12th century the rock had to be paved with marble, and a beautiful wrought-iron screen built around it to keep the souvenir-hunters away.

At the southeast angle of the rock a Crusader-period marble entrance gives way to a **cave** beneath. Muslim tradition holds that the rock overlies the centre of the world, lying above a bottomless pit whilst the waters of Paradise flow beneath the cave. The spirits of the dead can supposedly be heard here awaiting Judgement Day, and hence the popular name of the **Well of Souls** (Arabic: *Bir al-Arwah*). Similar themes can be found within the Jewish Talmud.

Dome of the Chain Immediately to the east of the Dome of the Rock is a small dome supported by 17 columns (all of which can be seen from any point). Referred to as the Dome of the Chain (Arabic: *Qubbat al-Silsila*), built from 691 to 692 CE by 'Adb al-Malik, the function of which is still a matter of scholarly debate. Much has been made of the fact that it, and not the Dome of the Rock, stands at the centre of the Temple Mount/Haram al-Sharif platform, and it has been speculated that it stood above the Solomonic (and then Herodian) sacrificial altar. Its position on the platform has also been used to suggest that it marks the *omphalos*, or navel of the world. In all likelihood it was built to house the treasury of the Haram al-Sharif, though the traditions surrounding it may have created a sense of sacredness that may have acted as a deterrence to would-be thieves. The popular name derives from the tradition that a chain once stretched across the entrance, hung there by either David, Solomon, or God. Those who swore falsely whilst holding the chain were either struck by lightning, or a link would fall, thus giving judgement on them as a liar.

Platform of the Dome of the Rock The Dome of the Rock stands on a **platform**, with eight **staircases** ascending from the esplanade. At the top of each staircase is a *qanatir*, a series of arches or arcade. They are popularly referred to by Muslims by the Arabic word *mawazin*, meaning 'scales'; a reference that derives from the tradition that on the Day of Judgement, scales will be hung from them to weigh the souls of the dead. The oldest is the west qanatir, dating to 951-52 CE, with the rest dating to the 10th, 14th and 15th centuries (with later refurbishments). Also of interest on the dome platform itself is the **Qubbat al-Mi'raj**, or Dome of the Ascension of the Prophet. Murphy-O'Connor proposes that the "mere existence of this structure shows that the original purpose of the Dome of the Rock was not to commemorate the Ascension of Mohammad" (*ibid*), though this argument can be challenged on two counts. Firstly, as Prag points out (*Blue Guide*, 1989), this commemorates not the spot from which Mohammad ascended, but rather where he prayed prior to his Ascension. Secondly, the identification of the Temple Mount/

Haram al-Sharif with *al-Masjid al-Aqsa al-Mubarak*, "the furthermost Blessed Mosque" where Mohammad made his Night Ascent, is very old, with the pilgrim Arculf describing a rudimentary mosque here by 680 CE, and the Dome of the Rock being constructed a little over 10 years later. The Qubbat al-Mi'raj, by contrast, dates to 1200-01, and thus any tradition surrounding it is far later. Also of note on the dome platform is the exquisite **Minbar of Burhan al-Din**, next to the south qanatir, a 14th-century pulpit (restored in 1843) which is associated with praying for rain.

Al-Aqsa Mosque Whilst the Dome of the Rock is a shrine and place of pilgrimage, **al-Aqsa Mosque** serves as Jerusalem's Jama'i Masjid, or main Friday congregational mosque. Though not an unattractive building, it loses out in inevitable comparison with the Dome of the Rock, though the two do rather complement one another. However, its architectural history is far more complex than that of its near neighbour and, as a result of its numerous restorations, its original form is far more difficult to discern.

The date of the first mosque built on the former Temple Mount platform is uncertain. It is not entirely clear whether the caliph **Omar** built a mosque here following the Arab capture of the city in 638 CE, though the Christian pilgrim Arculf describes a rudimentary mosque standing in the ruins of Herod's Royal Stoa (portico) in 680 CE. A mosque certainly was standing here by 715 CE, presumably built by the Umayyad caliph **al-Walid I**. This mosque may well have formed the basis of the plan of the mosque seen today. By c. 775 CE the mosque had been enlarged to a fifteen-aisled basilica-like structure, though whether the work was carried out by the Umayyads or the Abbasid caliph **al-Mahdi** (775-785 CE) is also uncertain (though the general consensus is that the work was Umayyad). The main entrance to the mosque was via the Double Gate and the passage beneath the mosque (see Jerusalem Archaeological Park, page 56). The steps down can be seen outside the main entrance to the mosque, though they are not open to the public. Two major earthquakes in 74//48 CE and 774 CE caused extensive damage, though every set-back saw repairs swiftly made. By the ninth century the mosque probably had seven aisles on either side of a central nave, a central door in the north wall, with a marble portico along the north façade, and a large lead-sheathed dome.

The earthquake of 1033 devastated the mosque, with the relative impoverishment of the city at this time meaning that al-Aqsa was restored as a more modest five-aisled building. Crusader rule in Jerusalem saw the mosque used first as a palace of the king, then as a headquarters of the **Order of the Knights Templar**. They made a number of structural alterations, including the construction of the Templar Hall to the west (now occupied by the Women's Mosque and Islamic Museum). In 1187 **Salah al-Din** restored the building to its original purpose, making a number of changes including endowing the mosque with a beautiful **minbar** (pulpit) of carved, inlaid and gilded cedar wood. In 1969, a mad Australian started a fire in the al-Aqsa and the pulpit was destroyed (see box, page 57).

Other features on the Haram al-Sharif

There are a number of other points of interest on the Haram al-Sharif, though not all are accessible to tourists. The **Golden Gate** (Arabic: *Bab al-Dhahabi*), date unknown, has links with Eudocia (mid-fifth century CE) and the triumphant entry into Jerusalem by the Emperor Heraclius (631 CE), though there are architectural features that are distinctly Umayyad. It is very similar in style to the Double Gate in the south wall, which is generally believed to be Herodian with Umayyad (amongst others) modifications. Its north entrance is often referred to as the **Gate of Mercy** (Arabic: *Bab al-Rahma*), and the south entrance the **Gate of Repentance** (Arabic: *Bab al-Tawba*). The gate, blocked in the eighth century CE, is the source of a number of traditions. It is variously believed that the just will enter through this gate on the Day of Judgement – hence its popularity as a burial site. A Muslim tradition seems to suggest that a Christian conqueror will enter through this gate; perhaps a byproduct of the tradition that Jesus entered this gate on Palm Sunday, and will appear here at the Second Coming. The theory has also been proposed that the purpose of the Muslim cemetery is to deter any Jewish or Christian messiah!

Just to the north of the Golden Gate is '**Solomon's Throne**' (Arabic: *Kursi Sulaiman*), a small rectangular structure with twin shallow domes. A Muslim tradition holds that when Solomon died, his body was propped up here so as to conceal his death from the demons, and thus avoid fulfilling the prophecy that said that the Temple would be destroyed following his death. The structure probably dates to the 16th century CE, with the fact that it may have been built by Sulaiman II ('the Magnificent') perpetuating the tradition.

The so-called **Solomon's Stables** complex are in fact part of the subterranean vaulting system that Herod the Great built to support his Temple Mount, and have no connection whatsoever with Solomon. Much of the upper parts and arches were actually built by the Crusaders (who introduced the Solomonic link) when they used the vaulted chambers as a stables for their war-horses. In 1996 the halls were opened as a prayer chamber capable of accommodating 10,000 people, with the 'Solomon's Stables' name being dropped in favour of the **Marwani Mosque** title. Over 200 architectural units have been recorded on the Haram al-Sharif. Amongst the minor features that can be inspected close, the most interesting include the following three. The **Sabil Qa'it Bay**, to the west of the Dome of the Rock, is an attractive structure built in the late 15th century CE, but largely restored in 1883. Though it is built in the style of a funerary monument, it is in fact a public fountain drawing water from what may well be a Herodian cistern below. This is possibly the same cistern that is described in relation to the 'cave' synagogue close to Warren's Gate (see 'Western Wall Tunnels' tour, page 54). The isolated structure to the north of the Dome of the Rock is the **Qubbat Sulaiman**, possibly an Ayyubid-modified Crusader building (c. 1200 CE) that tradition links with the spot at which Solomon prayed after completing the Temple. Also of note between al-Aqsa Mosque and the Dome of the Rock is **al-Kas**, the main fountain at which Muslims perform their ritual ablutions before praying at al-Aqsa.

Western Wall ① *Access 24 hrs, every day of the year (free), www.thekotel.org.* The focus of Jewish prayer and pilgrimage, the Western Wall (Hebrew: Ha-Kotel Ha-Ma'aravi) is not part of the Temple building itself, but an exposed stretch of the retaining wall that Herod the Great constructed c. 20-17 BCE to support the platform on which the Second Temple was built. Approximately 60 m of the 485-m-long western retaining wall is exposed here, allowing Jews and non-Jews alike to appreciate something of the monumental scale of Herod's building project. See the line drawing on page 46 to put the scene before you into historical and archaeological perspective.

Though seven courses of Herodian masonry are visible, there are in fact a further 19 courses below the level of the current pavement. The Herodian blocks are characterized by their carefully drafted edges and are cut with such precision that they are set without mortar. Though most of the stones are around 1 m high and weigh around 1,800-4,500 kg), there are some notable exceptions: one stone of the 'mastercourse' in the southeast corner is estimated to weigh 90,000 kg, whilst another stone to the north of the Western Wall area (and visible on the tour through the Western Wall Tunnel, page 54) is 13.6 m long, 3.5 m wide, 3.5 m high, and estimated to weigh around 570,000 kg! Above the seventh Herodian course the stones are Umayyad (c. seventh century CE), whilst the smaller ones at the top are part of the restoration effort that followed the 1033 earthquake.

It is not entirely clear when Jews first began to gather here to lament the destruction of the Temple, though it is reasonable to assume that it may well have closely followed Hadrian's death in 138 CE. By the third to fourth century CE it was certainly common practice, though following the Arab conquest in 638 CE and the subsequent construction of Islamic monuments on the platform itself it appears that the Western Wall itself became the focus of Jewish pilgrimage. Because of the Jewish lamentations here, it became known as the **Wailing Wall**. Though only a small section of the Wall was available to Jews, as the Jewish population of Jerusalem increased in the 19th century they attempted to change long-standing practices at the Wall (such as bringing chairs for the elderly to rest, and putting up a temporary screen to divide the male worshippers from the women). Though these introductions seem innocent enough, the Muslim leaders opposed any change in the status quo for fear that they would lead to further concessions. Matters were brought to a head on Yom Kippur in 1928 when, following complaints from the Supreme Muslim Council, British policemen forcibly removed a screen from the Wall. Complaints were made to the League of Nations and the British parliament by leading Zionist officials, with Chaim Weizmann writing an open letter to the Yishuv (Jewish community in Palestine) stating that the only solution to this problem of access was to "pour Jews into Palestine". As the Muslims had feared, the matter had moved from being a religious one to a political and racial question, and they were quick to link the confrontation at the Wall with the greater question of Jewish designs on Palestine. In mid-August 1929 members of Betar, the youth organization of Jabotinsky's Revisionist party, marched on the wall, raising the Zionist flag and singing the Zionist anthem. The following day at Friday prayers Muslims were exalted to defend the Haram al-Sharif. The following Friday (23 August 1929) saw a full scale riot ensue in which Jewish quarters in Jerusalem, Hebron and Safed were attacked. Zionist groups responded, and by the end of the week 133 Jews and 116 Arabs had been killed, with many more injured.

The square, or **Western Wall Plaza**, in front of the Wall took its present form after the Israeli capture of the whole of Jerusalem in the Six Day War of 1967. Until this time the houses and buildings of the Magharibi or 'Moors Quarter' virtually abutted the western retaining wall of the Temple Mount/Haram al-Sharif platform. These, including the 12th-century CE mosque and shrine of Shaikh 'A'id (the Afdaliyya Madrasa), were bulldozed in June 1967 to allow greater Jewish access. The Western Wall is now divided into two distinct areas for prayer: men have the larger area to the north, whilst women are separated by a screen to a smaller area to the south. At the southern end of the women's prayer area (and accessible only to modestly dressed women) is the so-called Barclay's Gate. Erroneously identified with the Kiponos Gate of the Mishnah, Barclay's Gate allowed access to the Temple Courts on the Temple Mount platform via a ramp from the street below. All that can be seen today is part of the 7-m-long lintel of the gate, made from a single stone.

The 1990s saw hostile confrontations between orthodox and liberal Jews, as a group of women attempted to assert their rights at the Western Wall. The 'Women of the Wall' gathered here to sing from the Torah for an hour or two per month, maintaining that no halachic ruling stated that the Wall belongs only to men. However, the Supreme Court in 2002 voted against their right to worship as they please by the actual Western Wall, and a special prayer hall for women was created by Robinson's Arch (where the sounds of their chanting from the Torah cannot be heard).

Just to the north of the men's prayer area (and accessible only to modestly dressed men), a gateway leads to a further prayer area beneath the so-called **Wilson's Arch** (see drawing on page 46). This structure (described in further detail as part of the 'Western Wall Tunnels' tour, below) is generally agreed to be easternmost of the series of arches that supported the causeway spanning the Tyropneon Valley, linking the Upper City with the Second Temple.

Western Wall Tunnels ⓘ *Sun-Thu 0700-evening, Fri 0700-1200. Advance bookings must be made with the Western Wall Heritage Foundation, T1599-515888, have a credit card ready. Tickets are collected from a pre-paid booth by the entrance, no refunds (though it is possible to enter at a later time if you miss your slot). Yarmulkes (provided) or some form of head-covering must be worn. Modest dress is essential. The first section is wheelchair accessible, though some prior arrangements should be made. During daylight hrs the tour emerges in the Muslim Quarter; the guide will escort those who feel that they need this service back to the Western Wall Plaza. Or after darkness, visitors walk the tunnels in reverse to exit via the main door (recommended if you want to spend longer inside). Tours take about 1 1/4 hrs.*

The Western Wall Tunnels complex features a number of places of major archaeological, historical, religious and (arguably) political interest. The key sites date to several important periods in Jerusalem's history, most notably the Hasmonean and Herodian eras, though a number of questions still need to be answered and further excavations are necessary. Unfortunately, fear of desecration (by Jews and Muslims), and the fact that the complex has been turned into a political issue (by Israelis and Palestinians), means that any excavations here cause invariably prompt unrest. However, some of the more fanciful legends and traditions surrounding the 'tunnels' may be rendered obsolete or mundane if archaeology wins the day, so it is perhaps best that some of the questions remain unanswered.

Tour The entrance to the Western Wall Tunnels complex is on the northwest side of the Western Wall Plaza (marked by the 'Western Wall Heritage' sign). Turning right you enter a **vaulted passage** (named the 'secret passage' by Warren) that passes a series of arches and vaulted chambers. This is in fact the route of the causeway over the Tyropneon Valley that connected the Temple with the Upper City on the Southwestern Hill. The original causeway leading to the Temple was destroyed by the Hasmoneans in their defence against Pompey in 63 BCE, rebuilt by Herod the Great when he constructed the Second Temple, and then destroyed again in 70 CE as the Jewish Zealots retreated into the Temple in the face of the Roman advance (see Josephus' *Jewish War II, 344; Antiquities XIV, 58*). The present vaults support Tariq Bab al-Silsila (the Street of the Chain), though their date of construction is uncertain. According to some tour guides, it took six people 24 years to excavate this section, since they worked with their hands only for fear of alerting the Muslim householders above!

Towards the end of this passage, to the right, a low window-grille reveals a vaulted chamber at a lower level. Warren explored this so called **Masonic Hall** in 1867, suggesting that it was at least as old as the Western Wall (in other words Herodian), though possibly older (Hasmonean). Measuring 14 m by 25.5 m, it is well built with a paved floor and a single central column (now broken but still visible) supporting the vaulted roof. Its original function is unknown, though it is said to have been used by Masons who connected it with Solomon's works in the Temple.

At the point where the causeway meets the Temple Mount/Haram al-Sharif platform, it is supported by **Wilson's Arch**. Explored and described by Wilson in 1864, it is very similar to 'Robinson's Arch' to the south (see page 56), and excavations appear to confirm

Wilson's assertion that its lower courses and pier at least date to the Second Temple period. The upper courses are probably Umayyad. There is a prayer room here for women that offers a good perspective on Wilson's Arch, while men can get a better view via the small entrance to the north of the men's prayer area at the Western Wall.

Turning north, the narrow passage opens out into a high **cruciform chamber**. The hall is part of four interlocking vaults that were built by the Mamluks (c. 14th century CE) as the substructure supporting the buildings above. The purpose of these vaults was to raise the street level to such an extent that their buildings would be on the same level as those inside the Haram al-Sharif. There is some evidence to suggest that these substructures were used as cisterns. Dominating this hall today is a mechanical **model of the Second Temple** which brilliantly illustrates the levels of construction around the Western Wall area. From this hall a series of steps lead down to a **section of the Herodian Western Wall**. The 'mastercourse' can be examined here, including one monster stone (c. 13.6 m by 3.5 m by 3.5 m) said to weigh 570 metric tons! Though quarried locally it is not known how it was moved into position, particularly considering that there are a further 15 rows to the wall that are hidden below ground level.

Continuing north alongside the Western Wall, at a point a little over 40 m north of Wilson's Arch is **Warren's Gate**, which was discovered by Charles Warren in 1867 whilst exploring a cistern on the Temple Mount esplanade. The cistern was in fact originally an underground staircase leading from street level outside the platform, up to the esplanade, and there is reason to suppose that it served the Jewish population as a synagogue during the Early Arab period (638-1099 CE). Its location was chosen due to its presumed proximity to the site of the **Holy of Holies** (which is generally thought to have stood on the west side of the Temple Mount and explains why Jews pray at the west, as opposed to the other walls). In fact, at a point just to the north of Warren's Gate is a section of the wall that is continually wet. Jewish tradition suggests that the wall is crying over the destruction of the Temple. People stop here to post notes into the cracks of the wall or sometimes to pray. A little further to the north of here is another Mamluk period **cistern** that utilizes the space created by the substructure supporting the buildings above.

As the tour continues north, the so-called **Western Wall Tunnel** exposes the entire length of Herod's magnificent Western Wall of the Temple Mount platform. At a point nearing the northwest angle, the retaining wall moves out by some 2 m as the **bedrock** is exposed. Part of an open **Hasmonean cistern** can be seen, protected by a large stone serving as a **guard-rail**. Beyond this a number of **Herodian columns and paving stones** that belong to the Herodian street that ran along the outside of the western retaining wall remain in situ. It is also possible to see a section of a **quarry** from which stone for the retaining wall was cut.

The tour continues down the narrow canyon-like **Hasmonean aqueduct**. Though certainly used by the Hasmoneans to channel water to the Temple from a source in the vicinity of where Damascus Gate now stands, the aqueduct may be older (though links with Solomon are highly unlikely). It was certainly last used by the Hasmoneans since Herod's construction of the Antonia fortress (c. 37-35 BCE) cut off its source of supply. The tunnel now terminates at the **Struthion Pool**, a second-first-century BCE rock-cut storage pool. The pool appears to have taken its present form in the second century CE during Hadrian's construction of Aelia Capitolina. The pool is split by a dividing wall, the rest of it falling within the property of the Sisters of Sion to the north (see page 64). The Roman blocked steps to the west lead up to a grocery store in the Muslim Quarter, whilst the exit (to the right) emerges on to the Via Dolorosa in the Muslim Quarter beneath the steps that lead to the Umariyya Boys' School (see page 63).

Generations Centre ① *Book via T*5958 or T02-6271333, www.thekotel.org, Sun-Thu 0800-evening, adults 20NIS, children 10NIS, 1-hr guided tour included. Headphones available for languages other than English and Hebrew.*

A trip through time, the "Chain of Generations" traces 2000 years of the Jewish national story. It's pretty kitsch with glass sculptures, illuminations and sound-and-light visuals.

Jerusalem Archaeological Park ① *T02-6277550, www.archpark.org.il, Sun-Thu 0800-1700, Fri and hol eves -1400, adult 30NIS, student 16NIS (or combined ticket including Ramparts Walk, Roman Plaza and Zedekiah's Cave 55NIS). For guided tours in English (1 hr, 160NIS, includes 'Virtual Reality' of life in the Second Temple period) phone ahead. Audio guide included (recommended).*

Excavations to the south and southwest of the Temple Mount/Haram al-Sharif enclosure have revealed remains from several key periods in the city's history. The whole area, variously referred to as the Jerusalem Archaeological Park or the Davidson Centre, has elevated walkways, explanatory signs, and a marked walking route making it more tourist friendly. The excellent Davidson Centre, which uses computers, artefacts and films to bring archaeology to life, is recommended as a first stop before touring the area. The tour outlined below highlights areas which are not mentioned by the audio tour.

From the entrance to the park head to the southwest angle of the Temple Mount/Haram al-Sharif platform. About 12 m north of this corner, look up towards the small section of Herodian masonry jutting out from the face of the wall. These are the springers and lower *voussoirs* (wedge-shaped stone blocks that form an arch) of the so-called **Robinson's Arch** (a) (named after the American who discovered them in 1835). The discovery of the **base of a pier** (b) to the west, and a careful study of Josephus (*Antiquities XV, 410-11*), suggests strongly that the arch supported a series of monumental staircases that led south to the Lower City. In the piers that supported Robinson's Arch four Herodian shops were discovered, opening on to the Herodian street that ran beneath the arch. A neatly preserved section of the **Herodian street** (c) can be seen running in front of the wall. Also to be seen here is an Umayyad period **courtyard** (d) that stands over a former pool from a Byzantine house. As some indication of the quantity of debris that built up here, Robinson's Arch, originally 17.5 m above the level of the Herodian street, was virtually at ground level in 1968.

Much of the Archaeological Park is covered by the remains of an eighth-century CE **Umayyad palace** (e) (85 m by 95 m), made more interesting by the fact that it does not appear to be mentioned in any written source. The plan of the palace featured a central open court, probably partly paved and partly planted with trees, whilst covered porticoes ran around the outside of the court. It is generally agreed that a building with an identical plan, though smaller, stood directly to the west of the Umayyad palace, possibly serving as an **Umayyad hospice** (f). It appears that these buildings were badly damaged in the Abbasid period, the masonry being reused for construction elsewhere in the city (as is the constant theme in Jerusalem).

To the east of the Umayyad palace, built against the south side of the al-Aqsa Mosque, is what appears to be a **medieval tower** (g). Possibly built in the 12th century by the Crusaders, it may have been refurbished by Salah al-Din (c. 1191) before finding its present form under the Mamluks (15th century). A flight of modern steps provides a good perspective of the excavations in the Park. Spiral steps descend to the remains of a partly reconstructed Byzantine house (h), whose mosaic floors have been preserved in several rooms.

Passing through the '**excavation gate**' (i) in the wall, to the left is a section of restored pavement and steps cut from the rock belonging to the **Herodian plaza** (j). The retaining

Plots against the Haram al-Sharif

The Temple Mount/Haram al-Sharif is more than just a symbol of nationalism between the Israelis and the Palestinians, whilst those who have played a part in trying to alter the status quo have not necessarily been Jewish or Muslim. In August 1969, a 29-year-old Australian by the name of Denis Michael Rohan set fire to al-Aqsa Mosque, and then proceeded to take photos of his handiwork. By the time Rohan was apprehended the mosque had been badly damaged and the 12th century CE minbar presented by Salah al-Din completely destroyed. He was to claim later that the "abominations" on the Temple Mount were delaying the rebuilding of the Temple, and thus putting the Second Coming on ice. Rohan's aim was to see the Jewish Temple rebuilt "for sweet Jesus to return and pray in". In an oft-quoted aside, then Prime Minister Golda Meir's comment to her cabinet colleagues that "we must condemn this outrage" was met by Menachem Begin's "yes of course, but not too much".

wall of the Temple Mount/Haram al-Sharif platform can be examined in some detail here. A continuous section of the Herodian 'master-course' can be traced all the way to the southeast corner of the platform. Of particular note in this south wall of the Temple Mount/Haram al-Sharif platform are the three gates. About two-thirds of the **Double Gate (k)** is obscured by the medieval tower (**g**), though a section of its eastern part can still be seen. This is certainly the western *Huldah Gate* (Arabic: *Abwab al-Akhmas*) of Herod's Temple, one of the main entrances from the Lower City, though much of the one that you see today is Umayyad. In the third course above the arch's cornice is a reused statue base (upside-down) that mentions the second-century CE Roman emperor Hadrian, or possibly his adopted son Antoninus. The **Triple Gate (l)** marks the position of Herod's original eastern Hulda Gate, and part of the western door jamb can still be seen, though again this gate largely dates to the Umayyad period. Further east is the **Single Gate (m)**, a postern gate cut by the Crusaders but blocked by Salah al-Din since 1187. It leads to one of the chambers within 'Solomon's Stables' (see page 52). The southeast angle of the Temple Mount/Haram al-Sharif platform, perhaps originally 41 courses of Herodian masonry high (26 above ground, 15 below), is traditionally linked with the *Pinnacle of the Temple* (*Matthew 4:5; Luke 4:9*).

Immediately to the south of the wall between the Double and Triple Gates are a number of Herodian or Roman period **mikvehs (n)**, or Jewish ritual baths. The large building to the southeast of the Triple Gate is Byzantine (**o**); a number of vessels that obviously belonged to a Byzantine church, including a bronze cross and door knocker, were discovered here. Other remains that can be seen in this section of the Park include a tower, gate and **storerooms (p)** dating to the seventh-sixth centuries BCE (being excavated); a **Herodian building (q)** doubtfully linked with Queen Helena of Adiabene (see page 116); further **Byzantine houses (r)** and sections of the **Byzantine city wall (s)**.

Via Dolorosa and the Stations of the Cross

The Via Dolorosa, or 'Way of Sorrows', is the traditional route along which Jesus carried his cross on his way from his Condemnation to his Crucifixion. It remains a major draw for Christian pilgrims, many of whom carry crosses and prostrate themselves at the various 'Stations'. Because of the confused, sometimes amusing, process by which the modern route came into being, it is easy to mock the hordes of pilgrims who continue to walk the route. Yet the Via Dolorosa remains a triumph of faith over fact, and if you go with the philosophy that "these are probably not the places where the actual incidents happened, but that is not important: what is important is that the incidents did happen, and that is what we are here to commemorate", then the experience can be a means of renewing a relationship with God.

Ins and outs
The first seven Stations of the Cross fall within the Muslim Quarter of the Old City, and full details of the various sites are described within the description of this quarter beginning below (and see the map on page 60). The VIIIth and IXth Stations are on the 'border' between the Christian Quarter and the Muslim Quarter, with full details of these stations found in the description of the latter beginning on the next page. The final five Stations are all found within the Church of the Holy Sepulchre (see page 73). You can walk the entire route in as little as 30 minutes, though most prefer to spend more time (human traffic jams can also make this walk considerably longer).

Background
The origins of recreating Jesus' steps as part of an act of pious remembrance are very old indeed, with Egeria describing such a procession (from the Eleona Church on the top of the Mt of Olives, via the place of Jesus' arrest at Gethsemane on the evening of Maundy Thursday, arriving at Calvary on the morning of Good Friday) as far back as 384 CE. Though the latter section of the route was largely the one followed today, there were no devotional stops at various 'Stations' marking specific incidents on Christ's journey. Within a couple of centuries such devotional stops had been introduced, though the route itself had substantially changed. However, it was the medieval pilgrims who took up this devotional walk with relish. The various sects into which the Christian church had long since split each provided their own version of the Via Dolorosa, the route of which generally reflected where in Jerusalem their churches were located. Yet it was not just in Jerusalem, or indeed the Holy Land, that the Via Dolorosa was created; by the 15th century cities all across Europe had their own symbolic Via Dolorosas! This was later to become a source of some confusion for visiting pilgrims: they were used to 14 'Stations' or devotional stops and were surprised to find that the Jerusalem Via Dolorosa had just eight. The solution was simple: they added six more! The modern route was established in the 17th century, though some 'Stations' were not fixed at their present point until the 19th.

Whilst the authenticity of the site of the Crucifixion and Tomb of Christ at the Church of the Holy Sepulchre is strongly supported, retracing Jesus' route to Calvary depends entirely upon locating the Praetorium where he was condemned. The modern route is based upon the assumption that Pilate would have stayed at the Antonia fortress (page 63) when visiting the city from the Roman capital at Caesarea. However, most scholars now agree that Pilate would almost certainly have resided at the palace that Herod built just to the south of the present Citadel, on the opposite side of the city (see page 39). Gospel descriptions of the trial setting (*Matthew 27:19; Luke 23:4; John 18:28*) match other descriptions of the Herodian palace, such as those found in Josephus (*Jewish War II, 301*). Thus, a more likely route would involve Jesus heading east along what is now David Street, perhaps turning north towards Calvary at the three parallel souqs at the current junction of David Street, the Cardo and Tariq Khan es-Zeit. In fact, it is a miracle that the trinket salesmen on David Street have not campaigned more rigorously to have this route introduced!

Tour

The following is just a brief summary of the Via Dolorosa; fuller details can be found within the sections on the 'Muslim Quarter' and the 'Church of the Holy Sepulchre'. The route is marked by the dotted lines on the 'Old City: Sights' map on page 60.

Ist Station This commemorates the spot where Jesus was condemned to death by Pilate. The present tradition suggests that this took place at the Antonia fortress, a site now occupied by the 'Umariyya Boys School (page 63).

IInd Station The site where Jesus traditionally took up the cross, this event was previously commemorated in the street outside, though is now more commonly associated with the courtyard of the **Monastery of the Flagellation/Chapel of Condemnation** (page 64). The route then passes beneath what is known as the Ecce Homo Arch (page 65).

IIIrd Station Where Jesus fell for the first time, marked by a small carving outside the **Polish Catholic Chapel** at the junction of the Via Dolorosa and Tariq al-Wad (page 65).

IVth Station Where Jesus met his mother, commemorated by a carving of the event outside the **Armenian Catholic Patriarchate and Church of Our Lady of the Spasm** on Tariq al-Wad (page 66).

Vth Station Jesus falls again and Simon of Cyrene is compelled to carry the cross; the station is marked by a small 'V' at the junction of Tariq al-Wad and Tariq al-Saray (also known as the Via Dolorosa, see page 66).

VIth Station A Roman numeral VI on the door of the **Church of the Holy Face and St Veronica** commemorates the spot where Veronica wiped the face of Jesus with her handkerchief, the imprint of the face remaining on the cloth (page 66). The present location is part of the 13th-century tradition.

VIIth Station At the top of the street, at the junction with Tariq Khan es-Zeit, a small VII above a doorway opposite marks the VIIth Station (page 66). This is sometimes commemorated as the spot where Jesus fell for a second time, though it also marks the **Porta Judicaria** where legend relates that the death decree was posted. This Station was seemingly introduced in the 13th century to prove to confused medieval pilgrims that the Holy Sepulchre site was indeed outside the city walls at the time of the Crucifixion. The door here is sometimes open, revealing an altar set next to a pillar from the Constantine Church of the Holy Sepulchre, as well as a small chapel.

VIIIth Station Located a little way up Aqabat al-Khanqah Street (see page 66) , this Station marks the traditional site where Jesus addressed the women of Jerusalem: "Daughters of Jerusalem, weep not for me", and is is marked by a VIII on the wall of the **Monastery of St Caralambos**. Now return to Tariq Khan es-Zeit and continue along it, ascending the steps to the right just beyond Zalitimo's Sweets. Follow the narrow street to the end.

IXth Station Where Jesus fell for a third time, marked by a IX on the pillar at the entrance to the **Ethiopian Monastery** on the 'roof' of the Church of the Holy Sepulchre (page 67).

From here there are a number of options. If open, you can descend via the Chapel of the Ethiopians to the 'Parvis' (courtyard outside the present entrance to the Church of the Holy Sepulchre). Alternatively, retrace your steps to Tariq Khan es-Zeit, take the first right on to Harat al-Dabbaghin, and this also leads to the Parvis.

Xth and XIth Stations Located in the **Latin Chapel of the Nailing to the Cross** on Calvary (inside the Church of the Holy Sepulchre, page 79), the Xth and XIth Stations commemorate where Jesus was stripped of his robes and nailed to the cross.

XIIth Station The **Greek Chapel of the Exaltation or Raising of the Cross** marks where the cross was raised and Jesus died (inside the Church of the Holy Sepulchre, page 79).

XIIIth Station The **Stabat Mater altar** between the two chapels is where Jesus' body was taken down from the cross and handed over to Mary (inside the Church of the Holy Sepulchre, page 79).

XIVth Station The **Tomb of Christ** at the centre of the Rotunda is the final Station of the Cross (inside the Church of the Holy Sepulchre, page 79).

Muslim Quarter

The Muslim Quarter is both the largest quarter in the Old City (c. 28 ha) and one of the most densely populated parts of Israel (with population estimates of around 25,000 residents). For many visitors it is also their first experience of a truly Middle Eastern city, and a surprisingly vibrant and real experience despite the many tourist shops. Although there are a number of fine Islamic institutions (notably those dating to the Mamluk period), the majority of visitors are primarily interested in the Christian sites associated with the route of the Via Dolorosa.

Ins and outs
Getting in and getting away Most visitors arrive via the Christian Quarter (along David Street from Jaffa Gate), or from East Jerusalem via Damascus Gate. Although many begin their tour of this quarter at the Chapel of the Condemnation on Via Dolorosa/Tariq Bab Sitti Maryam (because it's the Ist Station of the Cross), there are a number of points of interest towards Lions' Gate further east. With most visitors following the route of the Via Dolorosa, the main dilemma comes when you reach the Vth Station of the Cross. The description below follows the most popular choice: it details the rest of the sites along the Via Dolorosa as far as the Church of the Holy Sepulchre (subsequently described in the 'Christian Quarter' on page 73), and then gives details of the various points of interest on Tariq al-Wad, Aqabat Tekieh, Tariq al-Khalidiyya and Tariq Bab al-Silsila (the area to the west of the Temple Mount/Haram al-Sharif, see map on page 60).

Warning The Muslim Quarter is a conservative area and you should dress accordingly: you will probably be denied access to both Muslim and Christian sites if your dress is not deemed to be modest enough (no shorts/bare shoulders/revealing clothes on either sex). **NB** 'bab' = gate; 'tariq' = street; 'madrasa' = Islamic religious school; 'sabil' = fountain; 'ribat' = hospice; 'turba' = tomb; 'hamman' = bathhouse.

Background

During the Umayyad period (seventh to eighth centuries CE), the division of the Old City into well-defined 'quarters' was far less regimented (or political) than today, and there is considerable evidence to suggest that the main Muslim residential and commercial districts lay west and southwest of the Haram al-Sharif (the current Jewish Quarter!). Though there is evidence of continued Muslim activity in this northeast corner of the Old City, by the Fatimid period (10th to 12th centuries CE) this was in fact the Jewish Quarter. Following the arrival of the Crusaders through a breach in the medieval walls near Herod Gate in 1099, the present Muslim Quarter was occupied largely by Christian Crusaders, with several major churches constructed.

This northeast quarter of the Old City can be said to have become firmly Muslim in the 12th century CE, when the Ayyubid Caliphs (12th to 13th centuries CE), and then the Mamluks (13th to early 16th century CE) established large numbers of schools, mosques and foundations in the quarter. The Mamluks in particular developed the areas adjacent to the Haram al-Sharif, building many fine madrasas, tombs and town houses, the exteriors of which can still be viewed today (since most are in private use, it is not generally possible to view the interiors).

The period of Ottoman rule in Jerusalem (1512-1917) saw the establishment of the Ottoman administration in the Muslim Quarter (including the governor's palace), as well as commercial interests (most notably in the caravanserais to the west of the Haram al-Sharif). It also saw the return of many of the Crusader-period buildings (particularly along the Via Dolorosa) to Christian use. The fact that this northeast quarter of the Old City has been the key 'Muslim Quarter' for the last 800 years or so explains why Palestinian Muslims find it so provocative when Jewish groups buy or lease property in the area, then move in to establish a 'Jewish presence'. However, the latter group argue that Jews continued to live in the 'Muslim Quarter' throughout this period, until being driven out by Arab mobs in 1936.

Sights

Around Lions' Gate Immediately inside Lions' Gate is the **Hamman Sitti Maryam**: a bathhouse named for the Virgin Mary and still in use until quite recently. The adjacent **Sabil Sitti Maryam** ('fountain of the Virgin Mary') was built by Sulaiman II in 1537. The doorway just beyond the fountain belongs to the **Greek Orthodox Church of St Anna** and displays a sign claiming it as the "birthplace of the Virgin Mary". For a small donation you will be led down a few steps inside the doorway to the right, and shown a small room with a mosaic floor that is claimed to be the spot in question.

Bethesda Pools ⓘ *Daily 0800-1200 and 1400-1800, winter-1700, adult 7NIS (entrance to the Church of St Anne is free). Small souvenir shop and toilets.*
Entering this Greek Catholic complex, you emerge into an attractive square court containing a number of fragments of masonry excavated in the vicinity, set amongst flower beds that are carefully tended by the French White Fathers who occupy the seminary. The bust at the centre of the court is of Cardinal Lavigerie, founder of the order. Beyond this medieval cloister is the Greek Catholic Church of St Anne (details below) and the Bethesda Pools (but don't expect to find any water in them).

A pool here is thought to have been first cut around the eighth century BCE to channel rainwater to the First Temple, and may well be the '**upper pool**' referred to in the Bible (*II Kings 18:17*). The high priest Simon the Just is thought to have added the second pool c. 200 BCE. By the Early Roman period healing properties had been attributed to the pools, with additional baths and pools having been dug from the bedrock just to the east. The sick, blind, lame and paralysed gathered here awaiting the 'disturbing of the water', as recounted in John's gospel, and this was the scene of Jesus' miracle that so infuriated the Jewish elders since it was performed on the Sabbath (*John 5:1-12*, see box above).

Hadrian's paganizing of Jerusalem (into Aelia Capitolina) in 132-135 CE saw the construction of a small temple/shrine to Serapis (Aesculapius) featuring five colonnades, which Origen described following his visit c. 231 CE (though he mistakenly believed that he was describing the five 'porches' mentioned in the gospel account). By the mid-fifth century CE a small church on the site commemorated the miracle, whilst shortly afterwards the tradition developed linking this spot with the birthplace of the Virgin Mary (with a subsequent church taking her name). The early church was probably destroyed during the Persian invasion of 614 CE, though ninth-century CE records record some form of church on the site.

The church seems to have survived the anti-Christian edicts of the Fatimid sultan al-Hakim in the early 11th century CE, and there appears to have been a church standing on the site when the Crusaders arrived in 1099 (though it may not have been serving a Christian purpose). A small chapel was erected on the site of the Byzantine church and a convent church for Benedictine nuns was also built. In fact, the Crusader king Baldwin I placed his repudiated Armenian wife Arda into the care of the Benedictine nuns here. The Crusader period saw the revival of the tradition concerning the birthplace of the Virgin Mary, and the house of her parents Anne and Joachim. In the early 12th century CE the Church of St Anne that you see today was constructed.

Greek Catholic Church of St Anne Many commentators consider the Greek Catholic Church of St Anne to be the finest example of Crusader ecclesiastic architecture in the Old City, and it is easy to see why. In spite of an extension to the church that saw the façade shifted west by 7 m (you can clearly see the 'join'), the church retains the clean lines of classic Romanesque architecture. The rather plain and austere interior is also renowned for its superb acoustics. There is a fine entrance portal, above which remains the inscription of Salah al-Din that records the conversion of the church into the Salahiyya Madrasa in 1192. Franciscans were granted permission to continue to hold Mass in the madrasa on the annual Feasts of the Immaculate Conception and the Nativity.

The present church was probably built sometime around 1140, in a basilica style with three naves. From the south aisle a number of steps lead down into the crypt of the earlier Byzantine chapel that tradition holds was built over part of Joachim and Anne's home (the parents of the Virgin Mary). One of the small chambers holds an altar above which stands a statue of the Virgin Mary, whilst a second chamber contains an icon depicting the 'Nativity of the Virgin'.

By the mid-19th century, the property was all but abandoned, with some sources saying that the Muslims believed it to be haunted. In 1856 the Ottoman Sultan 'Abd-al-Majid I offered the site to Napoleon III in recognition of French support for the empire during the Crimean war. The building had previously been offered to Queen Victoria for similar services rendered, though she chose to take Cyprus as a gift instead: much to the continued regret of the Anglican Church!

Mamluk-period buildings around Tariq Bab Sitti Maryam At the top of Tariq Bab Hitta (at its junction with Tariq Bab Sitti Maryam) is the **Ribat al-Maridini**, a mid-14th-century hospice built to house pilgrims from Mardin (now in southeast Turkey). Further down Tariq

Bab Hitta on the same side of the street is the **al-Awhadiyya**, the supposed tomb of Salah al-Din's great-great-nephew al-Malik al-Awhad (d. 1298). The recessed arch entrance is guarded by two recessed re-used Crusader columns, now painted with graffiti. Opposite is the **al-Karimiyya**, a madrasa built in 1319 by a former Inspector of the Privy Purse in the Mamluk administration. A Copt converted to Islam, Karim was responsible for a number of religious endowments in Cairo and Damascus, though he was later disgraced and forced to leave office (supposedly for protecting Christians). The road finishes at the *Bab Hitta* (Muslims only).

Continuing west along Tariq Bab Sitti Maryam, the vault spanning the road belongs to the former **al-Mujahidin mosque**, built in 1274. As recently as the 1860s a square Syrian-style minaret was still standing, as depicted by C.W. Wilson in his *Picturesque Palestine* (1880). Only its base can now be seen. Attached to the north side of the mosque is the **Mu'azzamiyya madrasa**, established in 1217.

Under the vaulted arch, a vaulted street (Tariq Bab al-'Atm, sign-posted as 'King Faisal Street') leads left (south) towards the al-'Atm Gate to the Haram al-Sharif (*Bab al-'Atm*). At the top of the street on the left is the al-Sallamiyya madrasa, built by an Iraqi merchant c. 1338. It is noted for its attractive recessed entrance doorway with typically Mamluk style red-and-cream door jambs, and for the three grilled windows of the assembly hall (another architectural feature typical of the period). Further down the street on the same side is the al-Dawadariyya Khanqah, now a day-centre for disabled youth (visitors welcome). Built in 1295 by a Mamluk amir who served under six different sultans, this is amongst the finest Mamluk buildings in the quarter although recent modernisation has changed its appearance somewhat. The road finishes at the *Bab al-'Atm* (Muslims only).

Continuing west along Tariq Bab Sitti Maryam, it is possible to take a short diversion north along Aqabat Darwish Street, though in reality there is very little to see at the three main sites on this diversion: **Church of St Mary Magdalene** (Ma'muniyya School), **St Agnes Church** (Mawlawiyya Mosque) and **Greek Orthodox Church of St Nicodemus** (handpainted sign reads "Apostle Peter's Prison") but the street itself is very attractive and is blissfully free of traffic.

Antonia fortress The site upon which the Antonia fortress used to stand, (now occupied by the 'Umariyya Boys' School), has been of military significance since the time of Nehemiah at least (c. 445 BCE), and may have been the location of his 'tower of Hananeel' (*Nehemiah 3:1*). It is also likely that a stronghold existed on this site during the overlapping periods of Ptolemic (304-30 BCE), Hasmonean (152-37 BCE) and Seleucid (311-65 BCE) rule. The Antonia fortress was built some time between 37 and 35 BCE by **Herod the Great** in order to protect, but perhaps also to control, the Temple. It was named on behalf of his patron Mark Anthony and is described in some detail by Josephus: "[it] was built on a rock 75 feet high and precipitous on every side ... the interior was like a palace in spaciousness and completeness ... it was virtually a town, in its splendour a palace ... in general design it was a tower with four other towers attached, one at each corner; of these three were 75 feet high, and the one at the SE corner 105 feet ... the city was dominated by the Temple and the Temple by Antonia ... " (*Jewish War V: 237-245*). Captured by the rebels in 66 CE, the conquest of Antonia became a priority for Titus and was one of the principal foci of attack for the Roman Fifth and Twelve Legions. Josephus graphically describes the bitter two-month campaign that finally led to its capture on 24 July 70 CE (*Jewish War V: 466*; 523; *VI: 5*). Titus ordered his soldiers to "lay Antonia flat" (*VI: 93*) to allow his troops easy access to the Temple, and now all that remains is a section of the 4-m-thick south wall.

Christian tradition identifies Antonia with the **Praetorium** (seat of Roman procurators in Jerusalem) where Pilate judged and sentenced Jesus (*Mark 15:1-15*), though archaeologists generally dispute this claim. However, the former site of the Antonia fortress marks the traditional **First Station of the Cross**.

NB A window from the upper terrace of the 'Umariyya Boys' School commands possibly the best view Dome of the Rock in the whole city. Entrance is via the steps up the outside wall. The iron door in the alcove under the flight of steps is the exit to the 'Western Wall Tunnel' (see page 54). Entrance is via the steps up the outside wall, and visits are possible outside of school hours.

Chapels of the Flagellation and Condemnation ① *T02-6280271/6282936, daily Apr-Sep 0800-1145 and 1400-1800, Oct-Mar 0800-1145 and 1300-1700, free.*
Within this complex stands the Chapel of the Flagellation (to the right, east), the Chapel of the Condemnation (to the left, west) and the Monastery of the Flagellation (straight ahead, north). The latter is an eminent Franciscan school of biblical and archaeological studies and houses a small museum with a number of interesting finds.

It remains unclear as to when Christian tradition first placed events in Christ's Passion at this site, though Crusader churches commemorating the Flagellation and Condemnation certainly once stood here. During the Ottoman period it is reported that the buildings were being used as stables, and later as a private house, until the whole complex was given to the Franciscans by Ibrahim Pasha in the early 19th century.

The current **Chapel of the Flagellation** was built between 1927 and 1929 to a design by the Italian architect Antonio Barluzzi. A simple single-aisled chapel, the gold dome above the altar features a representation of the crown of thorns (*Matthew 27:29; Mark 15:17*), plus images of Jesus being scourged at the pillar (*Mark 15:15; John 19:1*), Pilate washing his hands (*Matthew 27:24*), and the release and triumph of Barabbas (*Matthew 27:26; Mark 15:15; Luke 23:24-25*).

The **Chapel of the Condemnation** is an early 20th-century structure built upon the site of a medieval three-aisled chapel. The most interesting feature of the chapel is a section of pavement that continues under the wall into the property of the Sisters of Sion next door. This is part of the *lithostrotos* (Greek for 'pavement', *Gabbatha* in Aramaic, see *John 19:13*) upon which Pilate is said to have set up his judgement seat. You can see games carved into the flagstones by bored Roman soldiers. For full details of the *lithostrotos*, see the 'Convent of the Sisters of Sion', below.

The Chapel of the Condemnation is the **First Station of the Cross** in the Franciscan's procession, whilst the **Second Station of the Cross**, where Jesus took up the Cross, is the courtyard outside. Every Friday at 1500 the Franciscans lead a procession carrying a heavy wooden cross from here along the route of the Via Dolorosa.

Convent of the Sisters of Sion ① *T02-6277292, Mon-Sat 0830-1230 and 1400-1700, adult 8NIS. Toilets. NB this place is an absolute nightmare when packed with several tour groups; however, in the late afternoon you may be alone.*
The Convent of the Sisters of Sion contains several very interesting items connected to the tradition of this area as the site of the Passion of Christ. These include the Struthion pool, sections of the pavement (*lithostrotos*) laid over the pool that have an earlier connection with Christ's condemnation, and a lateral section of the 'Ecce Homo Arch' that passes over the Via Dolorosa outside. There is also a small museum that you will pass through during the visit.

Struthion pool The Struthion ('sparrow') pool is a rock-cut cistern that dates to the end of the second/beginning of the first century BCE. Originally an open pool measuring around 52 m by 14 m, it was fed by a channel from the region of what is now Damascus Gate, itself supplying the Temple via a Hasmonean aqueduct. The construction of the Antonia fortress from 37 to 35 BCE cut the aqueduct to the Temple and led to a change in the plan of the pool.

The pool was roofed over in the second century CE, with the outstanding barrel vaults that supported Hadrian's pavement above still clearly visible. It was discovered during the construction of the convent in the early 1860s, though until 1996 it was only possible to view a small section of the pool. The controversial decision to extend the 'Western Wall Tunnel' by excavating the former Hasmonean aqueduct means that it is now possible to view the whole pool: though you have to visit two different sites to do so!

Lithostrotos This impressive pavement of large smooth slabs is associated with the Christian tradition of Pilate's condemnation of Jesus: "When Pilate therefore heard that saying, he brought Jesus forth, and sat down in the judgement seat in a place that is called the Pavement, but in the Hebrew, Gabbatha" (*John 19:13*). The fact that incised gaming-boards of a dice game called 'King's Game' are carved into the *lithostrotos* recalls to Christians the scene of the Roman guards' mockery of Jesus (*John 19:2-3*) and the casting of lots for his garments after his crucifixion (*John 19:23-24*). The flaw in this argument is the fact that this pavement was laid by the emperor Hadrian in 135 CE as part of the eastern forum for his city of Aelia Capitolina. However, some sources suggest that Hadrian's pavement may have used re-cut and re-laid Herodian flagstones, and thus there is still hope that Jesus may have walked on these stones.

Ecce Homo Arch The arch spanning the Via Dolorosa outside the Convent of the Sisters of Sion is popularly known as the 'Ecce Homo Arch'. Christian tradition has it that this is the spot at which Pilate presented Jesus in his crown of thorns and purple robe to the baying crowd, and declared "Behold the man!" (in Latin, *Ecce Homo*, see *John 19:5*). However, it is not claimed that this is the actual arch from which Pilate made his declaration. The arch that you see spanning the Via Dolorosa today is part of the central arch of a triple-arched gate that is attributed to Herod Agrippa I (41-44 CE). The northern lateral arch of what was probably Herod Agrippa I's east gate to the city can be seen within the Basilica of the Ecce Homo. To see this section, pass under the Ecce Homo Arch on the Via Dolorosa and climb the steps on your right to the Basilica. A glass screen allows sightseers to view the northern lateral arch without disturbing proceedings within the Basilica, while a map on the wall puts things into context.

Greek Orthodox Prison of Christ ⓘ *Mon-Sat 0900-1600, Sun 0900-1300.*
Just to the west of the Ecce Homo Arch is the Greek Orthodox Prison of Christ, which serves as the **Ist Station of the Cross** in the Orthodox Church's Easter procession. Visitors are shown three 'cells' (one for Jesus, the other two for the criminals he was crucified with).

Polish Catholic Chapel (IIIrd Station of the Cross) ⓘ Just to the south of the junction of the Via Dolorosa and Tariq al-Wad is the **Polish Catholic Chapel** (so named because it was restored in 1948 with donations from Polish soldiers who had served in the Palestine campaigns of World War II). The tiny chapel outside, marked by two fallen pillars, commemorates the **IIIrd Station of the Cross** where Jesus fell for the first time. The scene is depicted in a small carving above the chapel.

IVth Station of the Cross About 25 m south of the Polish Catholic Chapel is the **Armenian Catholic Patriarchate and Church of Our Lady of the Spasm**, marking the **IVth Station of the Cross** where Jesus met his mother. A small bas-relief of Mary touching Jesus' face recalls the scene.

Vth Station of the Cross At the junction of Tariq al-Wad and the street variously known as Tariq al-Alam or Tariq al-Saray (though invariably referred to and signposted as the Via Dolorosa), a Roman numeral 'V' marks the modern site of the **Vth Station of the Cross** where Simon of Cyrene took up the cross. Before turning along here, if you look ahead down Tariq al-Wad, the house built over the road was referred to as the 'House of the Rich Man' in the 14th century. Next door, the 'House of the Poor Man' was the site of the 14th-century Vth station.

    NB The rest of this section on the Muslim Quarter first details the rest of sites along the Via Dolorosa as far as the Church of the Holy Sepulchre, and then returns to the points of interest on Tariq al-Wad, Aqabat Tekieh, Tariq al-Khalidiyya and Tariq Bab al-Silsila.

VIth Station of the Cross Continuing up the slight incline on the Via Dolorosa, at the point where a vault stretches over the street, the Roman numeral 'VI' on the left indicates the **VIth Station of the Cross**. Tradition claims this as the site of the home of St Veronica, who used her veil or handkerchief to wipe the face of Christ. A medieval tradition claims that an imprint of his face was left on the cloth, which has subsequently been involved in a number of miracles and is now the property of St Peter's in Rome (though the Greek Orthodox Patriarchate in the Christian Quarter also has one!). The identification of this site as the VIth Station is medieval. Bullfighting fans will know that a 'Veronica' is a pass made with the cape, so called because the cape is grasped in two hands in the manner in which St Veronica is shown in religious paintings as holding the veil/handkerchief with which she wiped the face of Christ. The **Church of the Holy Face and St Veronica** ① *Mon-Sat 0930-1300*, just beyond the 'VI' is another example of Antonio Barluzzi's work (restoring the 19th-century chapel), with fine stained-glass windows and vaulted ceilings.

Porta Judicaria (VIIth Station of the Cross) The point where the Via Dolorosa meets Tariq Khan es-Zeit is one of the most congested spots in the Old City, with a crush of Palestinian shoppers meeting hoards of bewildered and disorientated tourists walking the Via Dolorosa. The junction marks the **VIIth Station of the Cross**, though views vary as to which event this station commemorates. Some hold that this is where Jesus fell for a second time, whilst others refer to it as the **Porta Judicaria** (or 'Gate of Judgement') where the death sentence notice would have been posted. The latter argument was seemingly introduced in the 13th century to remind pilgrims that this was the former city limit in the first century, thus confirming that the place of crucifixion ('Golgotha') was outside the city walls.

VIIIth Station of the Cross Located a little way up Aqabat al-Khanqah on the left, the VIIIth Station is marked by a small 'VIII' on the wall of the **Monastery of St Caralambos**, and commemorates Jesus addressing the women of Jerusalem: "Daughters of Jerusalem, weep not for me". It is possible to to view the interior from the rear, through a window.

    Returning to Tariq Khan es-Zeit, you come to a wide stone staircase on the right. In the angle beneath the stairs is a private shop selling traditional Arab sweets: **Zalatimo's Sweets** *(no sign, daily 0700-1400)*. Within the storeroom here lies the superb remains of Constantine's massive doorway between the propylaea and east atrium of his fourth-century CE Church of the Holy Sepulchre (see page 73). **NB** It is customary to make a purchase if seeking permission to view the doorway, or pay 5NIS (he'll ask for 10NIS).

IXth Station of the Cross Ascending the staircase, follow the winding street (Aqabat Dair al-Sultan) to its dead end. The column on the left marks the IXth Station of the Cross where Jesus is said to have fallen for the third time. Passing through the gate on to the 'roof' of the Holy Sepulchre, you encounter the **Ethiopian Monastery** ① *gate open 0800-1800, winter -1700*, occupying the ruins of the 12th-century Canons' Cloister (itself built upon the ruins of the Constantine basilica). Unable to fulfil their tax obligations to the Ottoman sultan in the 16th-17th centuries, they lost their ownership to various parts of the Holy Sepulchre to the Copts, and were forced up to these small cells on the 'roof'. The dome that you see at floor level is the same one that you see from the Chapel of St Helena below.

A doorway in the southwest corner of the roof leads into the narrow **Chapel of the Ethiopians**, from where steps descend via the Coptic Chapel of St Michael to the courtyard (Parvis) outside the Church of the Holy Sepulchre. This is probably the most interesting and affecting way to enter the Church of the Holy Sepulchre, where the last five Stations of the Cross are all found. If the gate to the roof is closed, retrace your steps to Tariq Khan es-Zeit, continue south to the next right turn (Harat al-Dabbaghin), and follow this street to the Parvis.

Coptic Orthodox Patriarchate and Coptic Church and Cistern of St Helena ① *Daily 0900-1630 or 1700. A small donation may be requested.*
Next to the pillar marking the IXth Station of the Cross is the Coptic Orthodox Patriarchate, whilst opposite is the Coptic Church of St Helena. From this tiny church, about 70 steps descend to the large (and generally full) '**Cistern of St Helena**'. The wonderfully spooky cistern has not yet been dated. It's a must.

St Alexander's Chapel and Russian Excavations ① *Daily 0900-1800, adult 5NIS. Prayers are said for Tsar Alexander III on Thu at 0700 in the chapel. Women will be given a skirt to wear; bags must be left at the entrance; no photos allowed.*
Located at the junction of Tariq Khan es-Zeit and the main Muslim-Quarter souqs is the so-called St Alexander's Chapel and Russian Excavations (also known as the Russian Mission in Exile). Beneath this 19th-century building lay a number of remains from Constantine's fourth-century CE church, as well as Hadrian's second-century CE building. The site was acquired by Russia in 1859 (for the very fact that it contained elements of the original Holy Sepulchre), with the present structure built to protect them, following the visit of the Grand Duke Sergei Alexandrovitch in 1881. The building subsequently became known as the Alexandrovsky Hospice (of the Orthodox Palestine Society). There is a small museum on the right-hand side as you enter the building.

Tour The column (1) at the bottom of the stairs (2) is part of a poorly built triumphant arch built by the (poor) Christian community of Jerusalem to show their gratitude to Constantine Monomachos for his 11th-century rebuilding efforts. It was probably modelled on the far more impressive Hadrianic arch that previously marked this spot, part of which can still be seen (3). Some of the walls of Hadrian's monumental structure can still be seen (4). These utilized some Herodian blocks, and were in turn reused in Constantine's basilica. According to legend, the gate (5) ahead was the gate through which Jesus was led out of the city on his way to Golgotha (hence the protective glass over the sill), though it is in fact a Constantinian entrance to the south cloister (that may previously have been a

Hadrianic arch). At a later date this gate was modified, possibly being enlarged by cutting back the walls on either side and inserting the two blocks (6). Beyond this gate was the pavement of Hadrian's cardo maximus (7), flanked by a row of columns of which part of two remains (8). To the left (west) is a door (9) that Constantine cut through the Hadrianic wall (4) as a minor entrance into the basilica. The main entrance lies (10) just to the north and can be seen within Zalatimo's Sweet shop (see page 66). From the modern chapel (11) a medieval arch (12) led to the Canons' Cloister, now occupied by the Ethiopian Monastery (see page 67)

Muslim Quarter souqs Jerusalem's most atmospheric **bazaar** stands at the junction of the Muslim, Christian and Jewish Quarters, at the point where Tariq Khan es-Zeit, David Street, Tariq Bab al-Silsila and the Cardo converge. Three parallel streets are linked by narrow lanes along the route of the Roman-Byzantine town's cardo maximus, though much of the structure that you see here is Crusader. For much of the 12th century, the central street of the covered market was the property of St Anne's Church (see page 62), and the monogram 'SA' appears in the masonry above some of the arched entrances to the shops. When St Anne's Church was converted into the Salahiyya Madrasa by Salah al-Din in 1192, he also transferred the title deed. The other two streets on either side were waqf of al-Aqsa Mosque. The street on the west was the vegetable market in Crusader Jerusalem, but it is now the **Souq al-Lahhamin** (or 'Street of the Meat Sellers'). Visiting tourists tend to find this street particularly nauseous. The central street is the **Souq al-'Attarin** ('Street of the Spice Sellers'), though it previously fulfilled all the Crusaders' drapery needs. The east street is **Souq al-Khawajat** ('Street of the Merchants'). If you continue south on the most westerly of these souqs (Habad, see 'Old City: Sights' map on page 60), a flight of iron steps to the left leads up to the **rooftops** above these souqs. There are excellent views from here (as well as some peace and quiet).

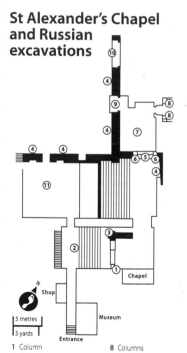

St Alexander's Chapel and Russian excavations

1 Column
2 Stairs
3 Pier of 2nd century Arch
4 Walls of Hadrian's Platform
5 Gate
6 Blocks
7 Pavement of Cardo Maximus
8 Columns
9 Door cut by Constantine
10 Main Entrance (Zalatimo's Sweets)
11 Modern Chapel
12 Medieval Arch

Muslim Quarter: area to the west of the Haram al-Sharif
Dar al-Sitt Tunshuq ('Palace of the Lady Tunshuq') Considered by some to be one of the finest Mamluk monuments in the city, it is in some need of restoration though it is still possible to admire some typical features of Mamluk building style.

The entrance portals are of particularly good work, notably the now-blocked east door, whilst some of the inlaid work is well executed. Little is known about 'Lady Tunshuq', except that she died in 1398 ten years after the palace was built. It is suggested that she fled to Jerusalem to escape the campaigns of Timur (Tamerlane), though to be able to build such a palace, she was no ordinary refugee. In later years (c. 1552) the building was incorporated within a charitable foundation ('Imaret of Khassaki Sultan') established by a wife of Sulaiman II, and was then used in the 19th century as the residence of the Ottoman governor. Part of the palace was subsequently used as an orphanage. Opposite the palace is the **Mausoleum of Sitt Tunshuq**, which also features some nice detail, and now houses a wood-workers.

Maktab Bairam Jawish Though an early Ottoman structure, built in 1540 by the Amir Bairam Jawish as either a school or pilgrim hospice, the inference is that the architects and craftsmen were Mamluk trained since it incorporates so many features from this earlier period. Its most notable points are the lead plates that bond the courses (the source of the madrasa's name 'Rasasiyya'), and the decorative arch. This building is at the east end of Aqabat Tekiek, at its junction with Tariq al-Wad.

Sights along Tariq Bab al-Nazir From the Aqabat Tekieh/Tariq al-Wad junction, proceed straight ahead (east) into the narrow street opposite that leads to the Haram al-Sharif. The top of this street is marked by a **fountain** built by Sulaiman II in 1537 (called 'Sabil Tariq Bab al-Nazir' or 'Sabil al-Haram'). The street leads to the Bab al-Nazir ('Gate of the Inspector': hence the street name), though confusingly this gate is sometimes referred to as the Bab al-Habs ('Gate of the Prison') and hence the street has a second name (Tariq Bab al-Habs).

Fifty metres down Tariq Bab al-Nazir, on the left, is the **Hasaniyya madrasa**, built by Husam al-Din al-Hasan in 1434. Next door is the Ribat **'Ala' al-Din Aydughdi al-Basir**, built as a pilgrim hospice around 1267, and probably the oldest Mamluk building in the city. An official in the Mamluk administration, such was the reputation of 'Ala' al-Din Aydughdi that, despite his blindness in later years, he was referred to as 'al-Basir' ('the clear sighted'). Following the loss of his vision he was made Superintendant of the Jerusalem and Hebron Harams ('sanctuaries'). The building was later used as quarters for the Sudanese Muslims who guarded the Haram al-Sharif, and then during the Ottoman period as a prison (hence the gate/street name).

Opposite, occupying much of the south side of Tariq Bab al-Nazir, is the **Ribat al-Mansuri**. This was also built as a pilgrim hospice (c. 1282), but later used as barracks for the Haram guards, and then as a prison. Many North African Muslim families still live here, and though an invitation into their home is a rarely extended privilege, it is a fascinating experience. The road continues to the Bab al-Nazir (Muslims only).

Sights along Tariq al-Hadid About 50 m along quiet Tariq al-Hadid, at the point where the path divides, located on the right is the **Hanbaliyya madrasa**, founded in 1380 by the Mamluk official Baidamur al-Khwarizmi. Taking the left fork, the lane runs all the way to the *Bab al-Hadid* (Muslims only). Just before the gate on the right is the impressive **Jawhariyya madrasa and ribat** that is now occupied by the offices of the Administration of Waqfs and Islamic Affairs. It was built in 1440 by an Abyssinian eunuch by the name of Jawhar al-Qunuqbayi who later became Steward of the Royal Harem. The entrance portal has the now familiar red and cream masonry, whilst the upper windows are well worked. The upper storey extends above the adjacent **Ribat Kurt al-Mansuri** (hospice built in 1293 by the renowned soldier Sayf ed-Din Kurt who died fighting the Tartars in 1299), linking it to the Haram al-Sharif complex itself. Other buildings from the period close to the Bab al-Hadid include the **Arghuniyya madrasa** (c. 1358), with striking carving above the door and windows, the **Khatuniyya madrasa** (c. 1354) and the **Muzhiriyya madrasa** (c. 1480).

Souq al-Qattanin (Market of the Cotton Merchants) This superb 95-m-long Mamluk covered bazaar has been substantially restored, and is an impressive sight featuring 50 or so shops, two bathhouses and a caravanserai. Unfortunately, only half of the shops are open for trade (others are used for storage), and at times it has a somewhat abandoned feel. Burgoyne, who extensively surveyed the Mamluk buildings in the Muslim Quarter between 1968 and 1975, believes that the arcade represents two distinct construction periods, going as far as to suggest that the east section was built merely to fill the space between the market and the walls of the Haram al-Sharif. Even to the untrained eye it is easy to see that this is the case, though the block to the east is in no way inferior. It is now generally assumed that the west half was originally a Crusader market (the lower four courses of masonry are certainly Crusader) that was repaired at the same time that the east section was built. The 'join' in the middle is particularly well executed. The market is generally attributed to **Tankiz al-Nasiri**, with a number of inscriptions in the structure mentioning his gift, including on the doors of the *Bab al-Qattanin* at the east end and on the lintel above these doors. Two of these inscriptions indicate 1336 as the date of construction.

To the north side is the vaulted hall of the **Khan al-Qattanin** (a caravanserai) founded c. 1453-1461. Further along the north side, about half-way, stairs provide access to the living accommodation above the shops. At the east end the steps lead up to the elaborate *Bab al-Qattanin* (Muslims only) through which you can get a stunning view of the Dome of the Rock.

On the south side of the bazaar is the entrance to the **Hamman al-Shifa** (closed), a bathhouse built in 1330 in the Roman-Byzantine style. A 26-m-deep well-shaft draws water from a source below, though it is renowned for its poor quality. Also on the south side of the bazaar, between bays eight and nine, is the entrance to the Khan Tankiz, which is now the Al-Quds University Centre for Jerusalem Studies which runs Arabic language courses (see page 158) and excellent tours.

The **Hamman al-'Ain** is a typical Mamluk bath built c. 1330, also accessed via Al-Quds University. It has been partially restored, though progress was halted. Just to the south of the bathhouse entrance on Tariq al-Wad is the **Sabil Tariq al-Wad**, a fountain constructed by Sulaiman II in 1536.

Crusader Church of St Julian Diagonally opposite Souq al-Qattanin is a street heading west called Aqabat al-Khalidiyya. Just 15 m along the street on the right is a small workshop/furniture maker's showroom. Examination of this structure in 1978 by Bahat and Solar tentatively identified it as the **Crusader Church of St Julian** (though some other sources claim that it may have been dedicated to St John the Evangelist). Despite a number of structural changes throughout the years, this is still identifiable as a three-aisled basilica with three apses.

Tariq Bab al-Silsila This historic street has remained the main east to west artery of the Old City throughout history. The eastern part follows the course of the Hasmonean causeway that crossed the deep Tyropneon valley (the ravine that ran along the side of the Temple Mount/Haram al-Sharif but has now been filled by centuries of construction). Herod the Great enlarged the vaulted causeway (sections of the Hasmonean/Herodian causeway can be seen in the 'Western Wall Tunnels', page 54), and the Mamluks built over it further. In between time, the current Tariq Bab al-Silsila formed one of the main east to west routes in Hadrian's Aelia Capitolina, and the Street of the Temple during Crusader rule. It now leads to one of the main gates to the Haram al-Sharif, Bab al-Silsila (usually Muslims only). There are several noteworthy buildings located just outside the gate, including the ornate **Tomb of Turkan Khatun** (c. 1352), the **Tomb of Sa'd al-Din Mas'ud** ('al-Sa'diyya', c. 1311), and the splendid **al-Tankiziyya madrasa** (c. 1328), though a checkpoint denies access to these on Friday and Saturday.

The **Tashtamuriyya** is an interesting complex on Tariq Bab al-Silsila that was built c. 1382 by Sayf al-Din Tashtamur, a former First Secretary of State to the Mamluk sultan. Not only a residence, the Tashtamuriyya was also built as a tomb, religious school and charitable institution. It's now divided into a number of private residences (some Jewish) and, though not open, it is still possible to admire the impressive façade.

Further along the street on the same side is the **Tomb of Baraka Khan**. A chief of one of the Tartar Khwarizmian tribes that swept through Syria and Palestine in the early 13th century, he ended his days with his severed head impaled on the citadel gate at Aleppo (c. 1246). His memory was rehabilitated when one of his daughters married the Mamluk sultan Baibars. One of his sons is thought to have built this tomb some time between 1265 and 1280. A number of structural alterations have been made to the building, including its conversion into the Khalidi Library in 1900 (home of many ancient Islamic texts), and little remains of its original splendour bar the façade. Almost next door you can see the arched entrances to the **Dar al-Qur'an al-Sallamiyya**, a Koranic school built in 1360. Note the British Mandate period post-box in the wall. The building opposite, at the junction with Tariq al-Wad, is the **Tomb of Baybars al-Jaliq**, a Mamluk official who died c. 1281, though the windows are blocked preventing you from peering inside.

Other minor sights The **Khan al-Sultan** (just off Tariq Bab al-Silsila) is a former Crusader caravanserai that was restored in 1386 by the Mamluk sultan al-Zahir Sayf-al-Din Barquq, and continued to be used in this role during the Ottoman period (with some structural modifications). It still pretty much retains this function, with the lower floors used for storage (though no longer as stables), and the upper floors providing living accommodation.

The **Madrasa al-Lu'lu'iyya** (on Aqabat al-Khalidiyya) was built c. 1373. The street that it stands on is noted for some fine views back to the Dome of the Rock.

Christian Quarter

The Christian Quarter is the second largest of the four divisions of the Old City (c. 18 ha), with a permanent resident population estimated at around 5,200 (3,850 Christian, 1,200 Muslim, 150 Jewish). Spiritually (though certainly not physically or aesthetically) it is dominated by the central shrine of Christendom, the Church of the Holy Sepulchre – revered as the scene of Christ's Crucifixion and Resurrection. The quarter contains numerous other Christian institutions (churches, hospices, convents, patriarchates, seminaries, etc) built to serve the various Christian sects. Today, in excess of 20 different major Christian denominations compete for influence within the quarter, often displaying a distinct lack of Christian brotherly love in the process. Meanwhile, the predominantly Muslim traders along two of the Old City's main shopping streets, David Street and Christian Quarter Road, compete for the tourist dollar.

Ins and outs

Getting there and away Most visitors arrive through Jaffa Gate, though many enter from the Muslim Quarter whilst following the route of Via Dolorosa. **Warning** Given the high tourist flow through this area (notably Omar ibn al-Khattab Square inside Jaffa Gate), it is popular with hustlers offering their services as guides, or trying to tempt you to various shops where you will get a 'special discount' (and they will get a commission). Some of the offers are genuine, and many of the guides are very knowledgeable and speak a number of foreign languages fluently. However, there is no way of sorting the 'wheat from the chaff', and it is wise to err on the side of caution and dispel any offers. **NB** David Street's gently sloping incline, with graded steps and ramps, can be treacherous when wet.

Background

Though the line of Herod Agrippa I's 'Third North Wall' around the first century-CE city is still a matter of speculation, the lack of archaeological evidence for pre-second century-CE construction on the spot now occupied by the Christian Quarter seems to confirm that this whole area was undeveloped until the construction of Hadrian's city of Aelia Capitolina in 135 CE. The Christian Quarter really owes its historical foundation to the rapid expansion of the Christian community in Jerusalem during the Byzantine period, who clustered their institutions around the Holy Sepulchre. This is also true of the Crusaders, who built in this quarter on a monumental scale.

Sights

Pool of the Patriarch's Bath For the best view of this sight you will need to ask permission to climb up to the roof of the **Petra Hostel**. Surrounded on all sides by later period buildings, the Pool of the Patriarch's Bath takes its current name from its medieval function as a source of water for the baths located close to the palace of the Crusader patriarch. However, despite a lack of systematic archaeological investigation, it is clear that the origins of the pool are far older. The area was extensively quarried in the seventh century BCE and a small rain-fed pool could well have existed at that time: hence the alternative name, **Pool of Hezekiah**. It is equally likely that the pool has its origins in the Hasmonean (152-37 BCE) or Herodian (37-4 BCE) quarries that were dug in this vicinity, and it may well be the 'Amygdalon' or 'Tower Pool' mentioned by Josephus in his account of the Roman suppression of the Jewish Revolt in 70 CE (*Jewish War V: 468*). The Crusader period saw the water from the pool used by the patriarch, and later by the nearby bathhouse. Measuring 72 m by 44 m, this large pool is probably only worth seeing if it has recently rained (unless of course you like looking down upon several generations' worth of accumulated trash).

Church of St John the Baptist Visitors to the church are welcome, though it may be necessary to ring the bell in the little courtyard to summon the priest, who may or may not come.

This small church has a complex history, which is not surprising given the fact that it is one of the oldest churches in Jerusalem. Its crypt and foundations date to the fifth century CE, and it is quite possible that it was built to mark the presence in Jerusalem of relics related to John the Baptist. Largely destroyed in the Persian invasion of 614 CE (when the relics were looted and large numbers of Christians massacred), it was restored shortly after, pretty much on the same plan, by the Patriarch of Alexandria. It has what is known as a trefoil shape, with three apses to the north, east and south. The upper storey (ie, bar the crypt and foundations, most of what you see today) belongs to the 11th-century CE reconstruction that was undertaken by the merchant community of Amalfi, Italy. The façade and two small bell-towers are a later addition still.

The Crusader period saw much confusion arise as to the tradition of the site upon which the church is built. The tradition that the church stood on the site of the house of Zechariah, father of John the Baptist, was challenged by the Latins in the 14th century, who claimed that it in fact stood above the former residence of Zebedee, father of St John the Evangelist. The Greek Orthodox, who are now the custodians of the church, have been rejecting this claim since the 17th century.

Whilst the crypt was being cleared of accumulated debris in the 19th century, a magnificent reliquary (an object used to hold religious relics) was located hidden amongst the masonry. Inlaid with precious stones and bound with gilded copper bands, it was made from a piece of rock crystal formed into the shape of a mitre. Amongst the relics it held were 'fragments of the True Cross' and items associated with St Peter, John the Baptist and most of the apostles. It is now held in the Greek Orthodox Treasury of the Church of the Holy Sepulchre.

Christian Quarter Street This thoroughfare features numerous shops selling religious icons and Christian-related souvenirs. Some of the large, smooth **paving stones** along this street date to the Roman/Byzantine city of the third to fourth century CE, and were discovered some metres below the present surface during work on the sewers in 1977.

'Mosque of Omar' NB This is not considered a 'tourist site' by the Muslim community, and non-Muslims are not allowed entry. Do not confuse this mosque with the title 'Mosque of Omar' erroneously applied to the Dome of the Rock on the Haram al-Sharif.

The present mosque was built in 1193 by **Afdal 'Ali** following the defeat of the Crusaders six years earlier by his father Salah al-Din. It takes its popular name from the seventh-century CE story relating to the Caliph Omar's refusal to pray inside the Church of the Holy Sepulchre (see 'Church of the Holy Sepulchre' on page 73), though it was originally referred to as the Mosque of Afdal 'Ali. The original mosque reuses much Crusader masonry from the Muristan (page 82), perhaps from the Hospital of the Knights itself, though much of the work was completed later.

The outer entrance gate dates to the mid-19th century, whilst the minaret had to be rebuilt after the 1458 earthquake (possibly in 1465). The top of the minaret has much in common with its counterpart on the al-Khanqah Mosque (page 83), 100 m to the north; in fact, they are at exactly the same height and a line drawn between them is absolutely parallel to the ground. Further, a line drawn between the two minarets has its mid-point at the entrance to the tomb of Christ in the Holy Sepulchre. Murphy-O'Connor (The Holy Land, 1992) believes that there is no doubt that this was intentional, and may have been a crude effort to 'nullify' the resurrection of Jesus, which Muslims reject.

Church of the Holy Sepulchre
ⓘ *T02-6273314, daily 0400-2000, -1900 in winter, free. For details of service times, contact the Christian Information Centre opposite the Citadel – midnight mass is highly recommended here, with an atmosphere totally different to the camera-clicking disturbances of the daytime.* The Church of the Holy Sepulchre is built upon the traditional site of the Crucifixion and Resurrection of Jesus, and is thus the most important site within Christendom. The church that you see today dates to a number of periods, having been partially destroyed and

rebuilt on a number of occasions, reflecting the Christian experience in the Holy Land. It is admittedly a rather confusing place, and getting to grips with the complexity of not only the setting and history (not least of all the events that it was built to celebrate), as well as the confusing architectural elements, is not easy in the crush of bodies milling around here. If you can, make a series of visits at different times of the day, and it may be an idea to read the account below before entering the church.

Ins and outs There are three approaches to the Church of the Holy Sepulchre, though the only entrance is via the Parvis (courtyard) on the south side (1). Those walking the Via Dolorosa route will, on reaching the Ninth Station of the Cross, have two options. Either to descend to the Parvis via the Ethiopian Monastery on the 'roof' (through the Chapel of the Ethiopians at the upper level, and the Coptic Chapel of St Michael (7) at the lower level). Note that this route is not suitable for large processions (or those carrying crosses), and is probably the most interesting way to arrive. Or to retrace their steps to Tariq Khan es-Zeit, turn right on to Harat al-Dabbaghin, and follow this street through the low doorway into the Parvis. The final approach is from Christian Quarter Road, via Qantarat al-Qiama (St Helena Street), and into the Parvis from the west side. **NB** Modest dress is essential to enter the church.

Church of Constantine Work begun on the Church of Constantine in 326 CE, and it was dedicated on 17 September 335 CE. This truly was a monumental edifice, dwarfing all later efforts including what you see today. It comprised four main elements (atrium, basilica, court and rotunda), and at its longest and widest points it measured around 180 m by 100 m (see plan). The main entrance was from the cardo maximus to the east, into the slightly irregularly shaped **atrium**. This led into the basilica itself, often referred to as the **Basilica of Constantine** or **Martyrium** ('place of witness') which comprised five aisles. The roof was lead, and the ceiling was lined with gold that according to Eusebius "like some great ocean, covered the whole basilica with its endless swell". To the west of the basilica was a porticoed court, with the block of stone venerated as Golgotha in the southeast corner. The court gave on to the Rotunda (or Anastasis, meaning 'Resurrection') around the Tomb of Christ. Construction of this great circular edifice required substantial quarrying and levelling of the rock around the tomb itself, and there is evidence to suggest that it was not completed when the church was dedicated (though certainly by 384 CE, and possibly by 340 CE). A dome (probably wood with a lead covering) capped the **rotunda**, supported by 12 columns 10.5 m high and 8 piers. The exact form of the structure over the tomb (**The Edicule**) is not entirely clear, though attempts have been made to reconstruct it from representations on souvenirs brought back from the Holy Land by early pilgrims.

The **Persian** invasion of 614 CE saw the church burnt, the wooden roof destroyed, the relics looted and the monks murdered. Repairs were undertaken by **Modestus**, Abbot of St Theodosius, though the description of the church given by the pilgrim Arculf in 680 CE varies little from the descriptions of the original Constantine church. The **Arab** conquest of Palestine in 638 CE placed Jerusalem under Muslim control, and led to an amusing, though subsequently fateful, incident in the building's history. Following a tour of the church conducted by the Christian patriarch Sophronis, the Muslim Caliph **Omar** was invited to pray in the church. Omar considerately declined, stating "if I had prayed in the church it would have been lost to you, for the believers would have taken it saying 'Omar prayed here'". Ironically, had it been converted into a mosque it is unlikely that it would have fallen victim to the subsequent desecration at the hands of the Fatimid Caliph **al-Hakim**.

There is evidence that various desecrations of the church took place in the 10th century CE, often at the hands of combined Muslim and Jewish mobs, but the vandalism of 1009 was the most systematic and complete. Al-Hakim ordered Yaruk, governor of Ramla, to "demolish the church of the Resurrection … and to get rid of all traces and remembrance of it". Thus, Constantine's grand church was all but destroyed, though much of the Rotunda remained intact, and the lower levels of the Edicule and much of the rock-cut tomb itself may have been protected from the hammer-wielding vandals by the sheer volume of accumulated debris.

The church rebuilt Until recently it was assumed that the church was rebuilt between 1042 and 1048 by the Byzantine emperor **Constantine Monomachos**. However, it is now clear that the Christian community of Jerusalem began rebuilding the church in 1012, just three years after the al-Hakim- inspired attack. Indeed, as early as 1020 al-Hakim himself had permitted the resumption of Christian liturgies at the site. The subsequent church was a much more modest affair, occupying just the court, Rotunda and some minor chapels and courts of the former building. The original basilica and atrium disappeared (though fragments of these sections of Constantine's church can be seen at 'St Alexander's Chapel and Russian Excavations', page 67, and 'Zalatimo's Sweets', page 66). The columns of the rotunda were cut in half and re-erected (giving the visitor today some sense of the scale of the original Constantine church), and several other modifications made, including the construction of a new apse on the east side. The entrance was as it is today: from the courtyard to the south. This is more or less how the Crusaders found the church when they captured Jerusalem in 1099.

Crusader Church of the Holy Sepulchre There are further misconceptions with regard to dating the Crusader modifications to the church. It has largely been assumed that the 50th anniversary of Crusader rule in Jerusalem was celebrated on 15 July 1149 by the dedication of the modified and restored Crusader Church of the Holy Sepulchre. This assumption has been drawn from the wording of a (now disappeared) Latin inscription above or around the western arch that led to the Chapel of Golgotha (now the Chapel of Adam (**17**). However, it is now clear that this date of dedication refers solely to the Chapel of Golgotha and not the whole **Church of the Holy Sepulchre**. In fact, it is more likely that the Crusader Church of the Holy Sepulchre was not completed until around 1163-1169.
The work undertaken by the Crusader masons was substantial. In addition to rebuilding the chapels around Calvary, they extended the church to the east across Constantine's previously open court by building a choir with an ambulatory and three radiating chapels in the finest late Romanesque style. This was linked to the Rotunda by a crossing covered by a dome and flanked to the north and south by transepts. The principal entrance was (as today) through the portal in the south transept. To the east of the choir, upon the site of Constantine's basilica and atrium, was built the complex needed to house those tending the church.
Although Jerusalem was surrendered to Salah al-Din in 1187, the Church was left unmolested. Pilgrims were permitted to return under the truce signed between Richard Coeur de Lion and Salah al-Din in 1192, and Latin priests were able to join the Syrian priests who had remained since 1187. However, much of the Church was badly damaged in 1244 when the **Khwarismian Turks** rode into the city, and the Edicule itself is said to have been in a particularly parlous state by the time **Boniface of Ragusa** began his restoration programme in 1555.

Recent history A major fire in 1808 had a catastrophic effect on the Church, destroying seven out of ten of the remaining original fourth- and 11th-century columns in the Rotunda, with the collapsing roof badly damaging the exterior of the Edicule. In 1809 the Greek Orthodox community obtained permission from the Ottoman sultan to restore the Church, with the subsequent work being completed in a little over 18 months under the supervision of the Greek architect **Nikolaos Komnenos**. In Biddle's words, "Komnenos' work has not commended itself to non-Orthodox critics" (*ibid*), with the rebuilt Edicule having been described as a "gaudy newspaper kiosk" (Amos Elon). There is even evidence to suggest that the Greeks systematically removed the tombs of the various Crusader kings simply to remove as much trace as possible of the church's Latin past (though it is not really known what state these tombs were in following their looting by the **Khwarismian Turks** in 1244). It should also be noted that Komnenos' restoration was not a structural success either, with the dome of the Rotunda having to be rebuilt in 1868. The whole Church was further weakened by a major earthquake in 1927, and it took until 1959 for a mutually acceptable restoration plan to be agreed by all sides. In the meantime, the Public Works Department of the British Mandatory Government in Palestine (in 1947) had to strap the whole place (including the Edicule) together with iron girders to prevent it collapsing.

Much has been made of the sectarian squabbles within the Holy Sepulchre. The split between the 'Eastern' and 'Western' churches dates to the fifth or sixth centuries, though the theological split subsequently became influenced by political and geopolitical manoeuvres, notably during the Crusades. As a result, the Church of the Holy Sepulchre now finds itself not united by a common belief in Christ's Resurrection, but divided in a territorial battle between Latins, Greeks, Copts, Armenians, Ethiopians and Syrian Jacobites for control of a piece of real estate. Physical fights have broken out over such trivial matters as the positioning of a Greek Orthodox rug a few centimetres into Armenian 'space', or "the sweeping of Greek dust with brooms held by Franciscan hands" (Amos Elon, *ibid*); the wooden ladder seen resting against the outer façade of the main entrance is perhaps the best illustration of such territorial wars (see (**14**) below).

Tour

The exterior The tour of the Church of the Holy Sepulchre begins in the **Parvis (courtyard)** (**1**) on the south side. Standing in the **Parvis** looking towards the entrance doorway of the Holy Sepulchre (north), one can see three Greek Orthodox chapels to your left (west) that were built on the former site of the Constantine baptistery in the 11th century CE. The first (south) is the **Chapel of St James the Less** (**2**), the brother of Christ. In the centre is the Chapel of the Forty Martyrs (**3**), formerly referred to as the Chapel of the Trinity. The north chapel, adjoining the Holy Sepulchre, is dedicated to **St John the Baptist** (**4**). The bell-tower was added in 1170, though it had become so unstable by the early 18th century that almost half of it had to be removed. These three chapels are generally closed.

To your right (east) are entrances to three other buildings. The first, furthest away from the Holy Sepulchre, is the **Greek Monastery of Abraham** (**5**), from where there is (restricted) access to the upper storey of the Holy Sepulchre (including the 'Church of Abraham'). In the centre is the **Armenian Chapel of St James** (**6**) (sometimes open), whilst in the northeast (top right) corner of the courtyard is the **Coptic Chapel of St Michael** (**7**). A staircase inside this chapel leads up to the Chapel of the Ethiopians, the Ethiopian Monastery up on the roof, and the nearby Ninth Station of the Cross (see page 67).

The structure with the small dome in the northeast corner of the courtyard is known as the **Chapel of the Franks** (**8**). This was originally designed as a 12th-century Crusader ceremonial entrance to Calvary/Golgotha, which is on an upper level inside the Holy Sepulchre. It was closed up following the fall of Jerusalem in 1187, though the stairs up (9) can still be seen. The lower storey is referred to as the **Greek Chapel of St Mary of Egypt**, whilst the upper storey is the **Latin Chapel of the Agony of the Virgin**. You can see into the latter from a window in the Latin chapel on Calvary inside (15).

Church of the Holy Sepulchre:
12th century to present day

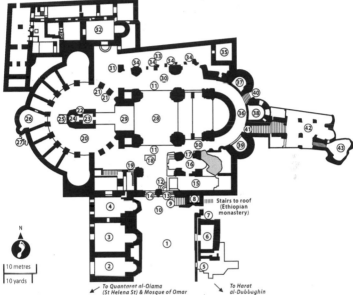

To Quantarat al-Oiama
(St Helena St) & Mosque of Omar

To Harat
al-Dubbughin

1 Courtyard (Parvis)
2 Chapel of St James the Less
3 Chapel of the Forty Martyrs
4 Chapel of St John the Baptist
5 Greek Monastery of Abraham
6 Armenian Chapel of St James
7 Coptic Chapel of St Michael
   (and stairs to Ethiopian
   Monastery)
8 Chapel of the Franks
9 Stairs
10 Tomb of Philip d'Aubigny
11 Redundant wall
12 Steps up to Golgotha
13 Blocked doorway
14 Entrance
15 Latin Chapel of the Nailing to
   the Cross (upper level)

16 Greek Chapel of the Exaltation
   or Raising of the Cross
   (upper level)
17 Chapel of Adam (lower level)
18 Stone of Unction
19 Three Mary's Place
20 Rotunda
21 11th century columns
22 Tomb Monument
23 Chapel of the Angels
24 Chapel of the Holy Sepulchre
25 Coptic Chapel
26 Syrian Chapel
27 Rock-cut Tomb
28 Greek Orthodox Catholicon
29 Arch of the Emperor
   Monomachos
30 Crusader period side aisles

31 Mary Magdalene Altar
32 Chapel of the Apparition
33 North Aisle
34 'Seven Arches of the Virgin'
35 Prison of Christ
36 Ambulatory
37 Chapel of St Longinus
38 Chapel of the Parting of
   the Raiment
39 Chapel of the Derision
40 Doorway to Canon's
   Monastery
41 Step
42 Chapel of St Helena
43 Chapel of the Invention or
   Finding of the Cross

Miracle of the Descent of the Holy Fire

Every year the Church of the Holy Sepulchre is the scene of what Amos Elon describes as "a barbaric ceremony that is part Greek-Dionysiac, part Christian and part Zoroastrian fire worship" (Jerusalem: City of Mirrors, 1989). The origins of the 'Miracle of the Descent of the Holy Fire' are obscure, though it may be derived from the story of Solomon's consecration of the First Temple. On 'Holy Saturday' (the day after the Orthodox Good Friday) the Greek Orthodox Patriarch and an Armenian prelate are locked inside the Tomb of Christ. Then, by miracle, fire descends from heaven, the Patriarch receives it, and proceeds to light a great torch with it before passing it out to the crowd. What this has to do with Christianity is questionable, though it is usually justified by some line about a supernatural event marking the spot of the Resurrection (and is often seen by the Orthodox Church as a symbol of God favouring them).

'Holy Saturday' is arguably the most exciting time to be in Jerusalem. Up to 15,000 people cram into the Church of the Holy Sepulchre on this day, with thousands more locked outside (all streets to the Church are closed off by the Israeli police from about 0700 onwards). If you can't get inside the Church, then Christian Quarter Street or Tariq al-Khanqah are not bad places to spend your day (particularly when the Catholic Scouts and sword swirling Armenians march past). When you eventually manage to get into the Church (often not before 1500), there are still plenty of believers milling around waving dripping candles and struggling get inside the Tomb of Christ.

The ceremony can be a considerable source of tension between the various Orthodox communities: in 1834 over 300 worshippers were said to have died in the mêlée. The whole event, like everything else in the Church, is governed by the 'status quo' agreement of 1757. For example, the spaces between columns 18 and 15 and 11 and 8 of the Rotunda are reserved for Armenians, whilst 14 to 12 and 8 to 5 are for the Greek Orthodox. A knife fight broke out in the Church in 1998 when members of the Syrian Church "displayed religious exuberance" at the Miracle, and were subsequently attacked by Armenians; under the 'status quo' only the Greek Orthodox are allowed to display religious zeal when the Miracle is performed!

Before entering the Holy Sepulchre, it's worth taking a few minutes to admire some of the finer points of the **Crusader façade**, particularly the delicately carved stonework on the upper storeys. The entrance doors are flanked by marble triple columns, topped by carved capitals. You may see Greek Orthodox worshippers kissing the central of the three columns on the left side of the main doorway (14). This tradition relates to the miracle of 'The Descent of the Holy Fire' (see page 78). Seemingly, members of the Armenian community locked the Greek Orthodox Patriarch outside the Church so that only their group would be able to receive the Holy Fire inside the Tomb of Christ. But according to Greek Orthodox tradition, the Holy Fire suddenly burst forth from the central of the three columns outside, lighting the torch of the Patriarch. If you closely examine the column in question you will find that it is blackened by fire!

The right (east) door (13) was sealed shut by the Muslim rulers following the fall of Jerusalem in 1187. The original 12th-century carved marble lintels above the doorway are now in the Rockefeller Museum (see page 113). If you look above the sealed east door, you will see a small wooden ladder. This is probably the most potent symbol of the tension between the different sects that control the Holy Sepulchre. Under the 'status quo' agreement of 1757 (implemented by the Ottomans and reapplied during the British Mandate), existing arrangements within the church cannot be changed. Thus, this ladder which belongs to one sect cannot be removed since it stands on property 'owned' by another sect. In fact, the ladder even appears in the watercolours painted by David Roberts during his tour of the Holy Land in 1839!

The wooden boards just outside the entrance cover the **tomb of Philip d'Aubigny (10)** (d. 1236), discovered by accident in 1867 when a bench concealing it was removed. It thus escaped the fate of the other tombs of the Crusader knights that the Greeks removed during their reconstruction work after the 1808 fire. He was an English knight and councillor to King John at the time of the signing of the Magna Carta, and also Tutor to Henry III.

The interior The entrance (14) to the Holy Sepulchre leads into the south transept of the Crusader church. Notice how the clear view across the church is blocked by the wall in front of you (11). This wall was first constructed shortly after the catastrophic fire of 1808 and was designed to support the badly damaged arch. The Greek Orthodox subsequently used it to hang their icons (and it now features an unimaginative mosaic of Christ's Passion). However, recent restoration of the arch above has made this wall superfluous and it now serves no structural purpose whatsoever. The logical thing to do would be to remove it, allowing the clear view across the church that was originally intended, but then the Greeks would have nowhere to hang their icons! Hence the wall stays. The south transept is dominated by the Stone of Unction (18), though we shall come to this shortly.

Having entered the Holy Sepulchre, the logical route is to take the steps (12) up to **Calvary/Golgotha** immediately to the right. The steps were built subsequent to the blocking of the doorway (13) in the 12th century. They lead to an upper floor that reveals the top of the rock outcrop upon which tradition claims Jesus and the two thieves were crucified – Calvary or Golgotha. The first chapel (south) is the **Latin Chapel of the Nailing to the Cross (15)**, and forms the **Xth and XIth Stations of the Cross** where Jesus was disrobed and nailed to the Cross. Most of the mosaic decoration here is relatively modern, though the ceiling medallion depicting the Ascension is 12th century. It is possible from here to see through the window grille into the Latin Chapel of the Agony of the Virgin (see page 79). The second chapel (north) on Calvary is the **Greek Chapel of the Exaltation or Raising of the Cross (16)**, and represents the **XIIth Station of the Cross**. The slots cut in the rock for the three crosses can be seen in the east apse here, whilst it is also possible to touch the rock itself beneath the Greek altar (leading to some very unholy scenes involving cameras). The Latin **'Stabat Mater altar'** (Our Lady of Sorrows) between the two chapels is said to mark the spot where Mary received the body from the cross, and is the **XIIIth Station of the Cross**.

Descending the stairs from the Greek chapel, it is possible to see further sections of the rock of Golgotha (behind perspex) in the **Chapel of Adam (17)**. Early tradition claims that Christ died where Adam was buried, so hence the name. The concept of the blood of Christ on the Cross dripping on to the first guilty head is particularly strong within the Greek Orthodox, and may explain why many Greek depictions of the Crucifixion feature a skull at the foot of the Cross. You can choose the explanation for the large fissure seen in the rock here according to your personal spiritual leaning. It is either a natural fault in the rock that led the workmen to abandon this section of the quarry prior to its use as a place of execution/burial, or it is the direct result of the earthquake that occured at the time of the

Crucifixion. The tombs of the first two Crusader 'kings' of Jerusalem, Godfrey of Bouillon and Baldwin I, previously lay just inside this chapel, though they were removed by the Greeks during the restoration programme that followed the 1808 fire.

Beyond this chapel, dominating the entrance to the Holy Sepulchre, is the **Stone of Unction (18)**, commemorating the anointing of Jesus' body by Nicodemus prior to its burial (*John 19:38-40*). The previous 12th-century stone was lost in the fire of 1808 and the present limestone slab dates only to 1810. The lamps hanging above it belong to the Armenians, Copts, Greeks and Latins. It is not uncommon to find worshippers prostrating themselves on this 19th-century stone, scooping up the now 'holy' water that they have poured on to it, and wiping cloths and scarves across it.

Ahead, to the left, the small canopy supported by four pillars marks the traditional site where the three Marys are said to have watched the Crucifixion (**19**). The steps lead up to the Armenian Chapel (closed).

From here you enter the **Rotunda** or **Anastasis (20)** that was originally part of Constantine's fourth-century CE church, and later restored in the 11th, 12th and 20th centuries. The columns and piers are thought to closely follow the line of the fourth-century CE supports, whilst two of the columns to the northeast (**21**) are originals from the 11th-century reconstruction. This was originally a single column used in Constantine's church (and possibly reused from Hadrian's structure), cut in half for the 11th-century rebuilding programme. It gives some idea of the scale of second- and fourth- century CE monumental building projects in Jerusalem. In 1997, the walls and columns were restored, along with the dome, which has a 'starburst' on its interior representing the Twelve Apostles and the spreading out of the Church in the World.

At the centre of the Rotunda is the **Tomb of Christ**, covered by the Edicule (**22**) (or tomb monument, see box on page 111) which is surrounded by bunches of burning candles. The entrance to the marble tomb monument is to the east, and the approach is lined by tall electric candles belonging to the Armenians, Greek and Latins. The queue to enter usually goes half way around the Edicule, and access is rigorously controlled by the officials and monks in charge. The interior is divided into two tiny chapels. The first, the **Chapel of the Angels (23)** (3.4 m by 3 m), is said to contain a part of the rolling stone used to seal Christ's tomb (and subsequently rolled away by the angels). A low doorway leads from the Chapel of the Angels into the tiny **Chapel of the Holy Sepulchre (24)** (2 m by 1.8 m), the **XIVth Station of the Cross**. There's just about room inside for four or five people at at time, who are given 30 seconds or so to have a quick pray. The streaked honey-coloured marble slab covering the burial couch is actually one stone, and dates to at least 1345. Legend suggests that the cut in the slab was deliberately made in order to deter looters from removing it. Marble shelves run around the west, north and east sides of the burial slab. The central part of the shelf is 'owned' by the Greek Orthodox, the left-hand part and left angle by the Latins, and the right-hand part and right angle by the Armenians. The marble icon in the centre (north) belongs to the Greek Orthodox, and is part of the 1809-10 restoration. The silver-coated picture to the left belongs to the Latins, and the painting to the right to the Armenians. The positioning of the candlesticks, vases and pictures is strictly governed by the 'status quo' agreement. On the west wall is a hinged painted icon of the Virgin that opens to reveal a rough masonry wall (possibly part of the 11th-century Byzantine reconstruction).

Leaving the tomb monument, walk round to the far (west) side. It is thought that the miniature and atmospheric **Coptic Chapel (25)** here was built against the west wall between 1809/1810 and 1818. The cupboard under the altar reveals what is generally believed to be the west face of the west wall of the rock-cut Tomb Chamber.

Opposite the Coptic Chapel, in the west exedra of the fourth-century CE Rotunda, is the **Syrian Chapel** (26). Inside the candlelit hole in the wall on the left (south) side it is possible to see part of the first century-BCE to first-century CE rock-cut tomb (27) that was a deciding factor in the argument aimed at establishing the authenticity of the site. The north, west and south exedras of the fourth-century CE Rotunda have all survived, and much of the west rear wall (not visible from the interior) is original up to a height of 11 m.

Return to the entrance to the tomb monument. Facing east you are confronted by the central aisle of the 12th-century Romanesque Crusader Church, now functioning as the **Greek Orthodox Katholikon** (28). It is entered through the incorrectly attributed **Arch of the Emperor Monomachos** (29) that was originally built to support the east apse of the 11th-century restoration programme. The 'eastern' influence in the Crusader Church is not necessarily solely the result of the Greek Orthodox ownership (and subsequent decorative style). Much of the Crusader sculpture, as well as the cupola, displays the conscious decision of the Crusader craftsmen to merge their work with the existing 'eastern' stylistic elements that were already in place in the church. The partition walls (11) that divide the Katholikon from the Crusader side aisles (30) are now redundant following recent renovations. The 'omphalos' (navel) on the floor relates to the tradition of the site of the Crucifixion and Resurrection as being at the centre of the world.

Return to the tomb monument and turn right (north). Beyond the two original 4th- and 11th-century pillars (21), is an **altar** dedicated to **St Mary Magdalene** (31), commemorating Christ's appearance to her on the morning of the Resurrection. The double-doors ahead lead to the **Chapel of the Apparition** (32), sometimes referred to as the **Chapel of St Mary**. The principal Franciscan chapel in the Holy Sepulchre, it honours the ancient tradition of Jesus' appearance to his mother after the Resurrection (though the gospels do not record the event). In the **north aisle** (33), the 12th-century architect went to considerable lengths to preserve the portico of the 11th-century courtyard (built using Byzantine pillars), though what resulted is described as a "remarkable jumble" of decorative pillars and weight-bearing piers that is referred to as the **Seven Arches of the Virgin** (34). At the east end of this aisle is the so-called **Prison of Christ** (35), a small chapel with smoke-blackened walls that honours the eighth-century tradition that Christ was held in a small room with the two thieves whilst their crosses were being prepared. Continuing around the ambulatory (36) of the Crusader church, there are three small chapels set in the three apses. The first (northeast) is the **Greek Chapel of St Longinus** (37), dedicated to the Roman soldier who pierced Jesus' side with a spear whilst on the Cross (John 19:34). A fifth-century CE tradition relates how Longinus (who noted at the time "surely this man is the Son of God") was cured of his blindness in one eye by the blood that spurted out. He subsequently repented and became an early Christian convert. The Armenian chapel in the centre (east) apse is the **Chapel of the Parting of the Raiment** (38), whilst the third (southeast) apse is occupied by the **Greek Chapel of the Derision** or the **Crowning with Thorns** (39).

The 12th-century doorway (40) between the first northeast and east apses led to the Canon's Monastery, built on the ruins of the Constantine basilica. The flight of steps (41) between the east and southeast apses leads down into the **Chapel of St Helena** (42) (known to its Armenian custodians as the Chapel of St Krikor, or Gregory). Note the crosses carved into the walls by early pilgrims. The chapel is generally thought to date to the Crusaders' 12th-century building programme (the vaulted ceiling certainly does), though the north and south walls are almost certainly part of the foundations of Constantine's basilica. The dome above is the one that you meet at floor level when visiting the Ethiopian Monastery (see page 67).

A further 22 steps in the southeast corner of the Chapel of St Helena lead down to the **Chapel of the Invention or Finding of the Cross (43)**. Remarkably, in his account of the discovery of the tomb of Christ (*Life of Constantine*, written c. 337-40) Eusebius neglects to mention how Constantine's mother, the Empress Dowager Helena, discovered the True Cross in a cistern close to the rock of Golgotha. Perhaps it slipped his mind! In fact, the tradition did not appear until 351 CE, 16 years after the completion of Constantine's church. Nevertheless, this spot is revered as the place where Helena found the True Cross. Custody of the chapel is divided between the Greeks and Latins.

Returning up the steps to the ambulatory of the Crusader Church (**36**), continue west along the south aisle, passing the Chapel of Adam (**17**), and ending the tour of the Church of the Holy Sepulchre back at the entrance.

Muristan

The Muristan was developed in the early 11th century by wealthy, but pious, traders from **Amalfi** in Italy. They constructed, or reconstructed, a number of churches and hospices including the Church of St John the Baptist (page 72) and the Church of St Mary of the Latins (the site now being occupied by the Lutheran Church of the Redeemer, see below.

The turning point in the development of the area came with the conquest of the city in 1099 by the **Crusaders**. Many of the knights wounded in the assault were admitted to the small hospital for sick pilgrims that was attached to the Church of St John the Baptist. Some of these knights were to go on to serve the hospital, primarily protecting the sick pilgrims, and with generous endowments from the first two Crusader kings of Jerusalem (Godfrey of Bouillon and Baldwin I) within a short space of time an order known as the **Knights of St John of the Hospital** had been established. This later became the military order known as the **Hospitallers**; subsequently one of the most powerful and wealthy medieval orders whose military role "almost overshadowed its primary charitable purpose". A huge hospice housing 400 knights was built during the mid-12th century, whilst according to one contemporary source, over 2000 patients of both sexes were being treated in the enlarged hospital in the 1170s.

The fall of Jerusalem in 1187 saw the Hospitallers involved in negotiating the terms of surrender with Salah al-Din and, though the Order lost their property, the hospital continued to function until the 16th century. The present name, Muristan, is taken from the Persian word for 'hospital' or 'hospice'. Reports from the 15th century suggest an area in terminal decline, with most of the buildings in a state of dilapidation and decay, and by c. 1524 the whole area appears to have been abandoned. Most of the Crusader structures were plundered for masonry to be used in Sulaiman the Magnificent's 16th-century city walls and as Prag notes (*Blue Guide*, 1989), "It requires considerable imagination to visualize the area as the well-built and busy 12th-century headquarters of a great hospital and military order". The area is now geared towards tourists, with several cafés and restaurants on the fountain square.

Lutheran Church of the Redeemer ① *T02-6276111/6282543, Mon-Sat 0900-1200 and 1300-1500, cloisters 2NIS, tower 5NIS. Prior arrangement is needed to view the medieval excavations below.* Built in 1898 on the lines of the Church of St Mary of the Latins, the 178-step tower of the Lutheran Church of the Redeemer can proudly boast one of Jerusalem's best views. The mosaic in the apse shows Christ the Redeemer, and modern modifications include the striking stained-glass windows.

Greek Orthodox Patriarchate and Museum ⓘ *Tue-Fri 0900-1300 and 1500-1700, Sat 0900-1300, adult 5NIS.* This museum presents an insight into the history of one of Jerusalem's largest Christian groups, and displays some items of archaeological interest including sarcophagi from Herod's family tomb (see page 134). There is also access via the Patriarchate to the roof of the Holy Sepulchre, with spectacular views into the dome above the Rotunda.

Al-Khanqah Mosque Formerly the palace of the Latin Patriarch in Jerusalem, it became a khanqah (convent for Sufi mystics) following the Crusader surrender of the city to Salah al-Din in 1187. The minaret was built c. 1417 (see also 'Mosque of Omar', page 51).

Jewish Quarter

The Jewish Quarter is the smallest of the four divisions of the Old City (c. nine hectares), and the population is exclusively Jewish. The Israeli High Court ruled in 1981 that non-Jews could not buy property there (to preserve the quarter's homogeneity), though similar legislation does not apply to the Old City's other three quarters. The quarter was badly neglected during the period of Jordanian occupation (1948-1967), even systematically looted, and was devastated during its capture by the Israelis in the Six Day War of 1967. One positive consequence of this devastation was the opportunity afforded to archaeologists to excavate here thoroughly before the bulldozers of the rebuilding contractors moved in. The time and effort invested by the archaeologists has been amply rewarded, and there are now a number of important and interesting sites to be seen. However, the heavily-restored buildings and residential nature of the quarter make it the least atmospheric to wander around. A 'combined ticket' is available for entrance into several of the sights, and will save you money.

Ins and outs
Getting there and around Visitors arrive from the 'Western Wall Plaza', from Zion Gate, at the southern tip of the Armenian Quarter; or along the Byzantine cardo maximus, from its north end. **NB** Photography and smoking are frowned upon here on Shabbat, and the bank ATM machine closes.

Background
The ancient city that David established on the southeast ridge (see page 105), and Solomon expanded northwards with the construction of the Temple, gradually developed to occupy the land now comprising the Jewish Quarter during the period of Hezekiah's rule (727-698 BCE). In fact, remains of Hezekiah's fortification of the area can be seen today. The Babylonian sacking of the city in 586 BCE led to the virtual abandonment of this land for the next three centuries or so. Hasmonean and then Herodian rule in Jerusalem saw the rapid expansion of the city, and by the end of the first century BCE the main focus of the Upper City was shifted here. The evidence of this is presented at the Wohl Archaeological Museum in the quarter (see page 86).

The devastation wreaked upon the Upper City by the Romans in 70 CE is also evidenced by the archaeological remains and, following the second rebellion by the Jews (Bar Kokhba Revolt 132-135 CE), much of what is now the Jewish Quarter was occupied by the Roman Tenth Legion (Fretensis). There is little evidence of occupation of this area by Jews in the Byzantine, Early Arab or even Crusader periods (though it should be remembered that the Crusaders massacred most of the Muslim and Jewish population upon their capture of the city in 1099). However, there is considerable weight of evidence to suggest that Jerusalem's only medieval synagogue was built here (see Ramban Synagogue, page 87). It was during the Ottoman period that this south central area of the Old City became known as the Jewish Quarter. The Sephardi community became established here at the beginning of the 16th century, with the Ashkenazi Jews firmly planting roots around 1700. The Karaites sect had been long established by then. All were driven out by the war in 1948.

The reconstruction of the Jewish Quarter following its capture by the Israelis in 1967 has been carefully planned. Although most of the new buildings are modern in design and function, an old bye-law dating to the early years of the British Mandate was invoked, requiring all new buildings to be faced with dressed, natural Jerusalem stone.

Sights

Byzantine cardo maximus Whilst the three parallel streets of the covered bazaar just to the north overlie the Roman-Byzantine cardo maximus of Hadrian's city of Aelia Capitolina, the section of the cardo maximus exposed here is a later southern extension of the main north to south thoroughfare. At the time of the construction of Aelia Capitolina (135 CE), the area in which you are now standing (and indeed most of the present Jewish and Armenian Quarters) was occupied by the camp of the Tenth Legion (Fretensis), and would not have been considered part of Aelia Capitolina itself. Thus, Aelia Capitolina's cardo maximus ran roughly from the present site of Damascus Gate to the junction of Tariq Khan es-Zeit, David Street and Tariq Bab al-Silsila.

The section of restored cardo maximus presented for viewing here represents the **Byzantine** extension of the city, and is usually attributed to **Justinian** (527-565 CE). It is generally believed that the cardo was extended in order to link the two principal churches of the city: the Church of the Holy Sepulchre and Justinian's own Nea Church (page 87). A "magnificent street" some 22.5 m wide, it comprised a broad uncovered roadway (12 m wide) flanked by two rows of 5-m-high columns forming a *stoa* (covered passageway) on either side. The road was paved with large well-dressed stones laid in parallel rows at right angles to the street, with a raised ridge along the centre assisting with drainage. About 180 m of the cardo maximus has been exposed here.

The northern section was laid upon earth fills that covered sections of the **Hasmonean wall** (second to first century BCE) and earlier seventh-century BCE **Israelite wall**. In fact, glass-covered shafts allow visitors to look down upon excavated remains that the Byzantine cardo maximus overlies, thus giving some idea of how the successive levels of construction and destruction of Jerusalem have changed the city's landscape.

'Broad Wall' The section of wall exposed here is part of Hezekiah's expansion of the fortified city (c. 727-698 BCE). The original wall is thought to have run west from the Temple Mount to the present location of the Citadel, though only a 65-m section is exposed here. It takes its popular name from the fact that it is 7 m wide, though what you see here is merely the foundations of partly hewn stones that have been laid without mortar. A line drawn on the adjacent modern building indicates how high the original wall may have been. The function of the wall was to protect the area of the city that had grown up outside the original Solomonic city walls, quite possibly as a result of the Assyrian invasion of Samaria in 722 BCE and the subsequent flow of refugees. The wall was hastily built in advance of Sennacherib's march on Jerusalem in 701 BCE (see *II Kings 18:13*), and required the demolition of a number of eighth-century CE private houses that stood in its way. The archaeological evidence fits perfectly with the written record: "And ye have numbered the houses of Jerusalem, and the houses have ye broken down to fortify the wall" (*Isaiah 22:10*). A map here shows the plan of Jerusalem in the First Temple period. A multi-media tour about Jerusalem during the First Temple period and a scale model can be found in the Ariel Visitor Centre, a little further along **Plugat HaKotel** ① *T02-6286288. Sun-Thu 0900-1600, adult 18NIS, student/child 14NIS*, call ahead (even if it is the same day) for a guided tour in English.

Israelite Tower and Hasmonean defences At the junction of Plugat HaKotel and Shonei HaLakhot is a section of a massive Israelite Tower and Hasmonean defences preserved beneath a modern building (the sign on the door says 'Israelite Tower'). The Israelite Tower is part of a gate dating to the seventh century BCE, and possibly built by Manasseh (698-642 BCE). In fact, a number of arrowheads dating to the Babylonian sack of Jerusalem in 586 BCE were found in the vicinity, scattered amidst signs of the burning that followed the conquest. However, the site is closed for the foreseeable future.

Burnt House (Beit Katros) ① *T02-6287211, Sun-Thu 0900-1700 (last video show at 1620), Fri 0900-1300, adult 25NIS, student 13NIS, child 12NIS*. The archaeological evidence to support Josephus' graphic description of the Roman sacking of Jerusalem following the destruction of the Temple in 70 CE can be seen here at the 'Burnt House'. Josephus relates how the Romans "poured into the streets sword in hand, cut down without mercy all who came within reach, and burnt the houses of any who took refuge indoors, occupants and all" (*Jewish War VI: 403*). Such was the scale of slaughter that the city was deluged with gore "so that many of the fires were quenched by the blood of the slain" (*ibid*). Though the latter is a typical Josephus exaggeration, the debris-filled rooms of this house contained charred wooden beams and fallen stones scorched by fire, thus confirming part of Josephus' account. The date of the fire was further confirmed by the discovery of a coin dated 69 CE amongst the debris, as well as an iron spear leaning against a wall and the bones of a young woman's hand and arm.

The plan of the house is that of a large complex belonging to a fairly wealthy family, though you should bear in mind that what you see today is merely the remains of the basement. The identity of the owner was established following the discovery of a stone weight inscribed "[belonging] to the son of Katros". The Babylonian Talmud refers to such a priestly family who served in the Temple, though the line in question (*Pes. 57a; Tosefta, Men 13:21*) suggests that they were not the most popular people in town. The museum includes a display of household items discovered in situ, the labelled plan of the 'Burnt House', and a video which tells of the destruction of the Temple through a rather lame soap-opera about Katros's family (shown every 40 minutes).

St Mary of the Germans During the medieval period, this area was regarded as the German quarter of Crusader Jerusalem (and Misgav Ladakh was the 'Street of the Germans'). A complex containing a church (St Mary of the Germans), a hospice and hospital was built here around 1128 by the **German Knights of the Hospitallers Order** (from which developed the Order of the Teutonic Knights in the next century) to serve the needs of German-speaking pilgrims. Modifications were made to the building during the Mamluk period, and there is even evidence to suggest that the church was used as a residence for dervishes. The complex was excavated following the Israeli capture of the Old City in 1967, and the crusader-style arches restored.

The steps descending from St Mary of the Germans lead via one of Jerusalem's best **viewpoints** down to the Western Wall Plaza, past a replica of the giant golden menorah from the Second Temple.

Wohl Archaeological Museum ① *T02-6265900 (ext 102), Sun-Thu 0900-1700, Fri 0900-1300, adult 15NIS, student 13NIS, child 7NIS.* This museum contains the well-presented remains of a residential area dating to the first century BCE/first century CE, generally referred to as the **Herodian Quarter**.

The area covers some 2700 sq m of the Upper City of Jerusalem. During the Herodian period (37 BCE-70 CE) Jerusalem experienced great prosperity and rapid growth, with the Upper City becoming the most exclusive residential address. The value of the excavated section that is presented in this museum is that it "provides evidence of an urban plan for a residential neighbourhood, house plans, domestic architecture and art, the living conditions of the city's inhabitants, and various aspects of everyday life in the city in the Second Temple period" (Avigad, New Encyclopedia of Archaeological Excavations in the Holy Land, 1993).

Tour Now located some 3 to 7 m below the present street level, the site here presents the remains of a series of six houses from the Herodian period. Descending the steps, you arrive at an elevated walkway around the **Western Building**. The plan before you here is only the basement of the house, though it superbly illustrates the layout of the water installations and service rooms of a wealthy household. It comprises a number of cisterns, a vestibule, a bathroom, and two mikvehs (ritual baths), of which one is preserved intact. Parts of the mosaic floor from the bathroom remains. The tour continues along the corridor, where finds from the Second Temple period are displayed, including pottery with geometric designs (imagery being forbidden).The '**Middle Complex**' comprises the remains of two separate houses, apparently divided by a common wall. There is a fine mosaic preserved in the large living room, though when first discovered it was covered by a layer of debris directly related to the fire of 70 CE (see 'Burnt House' on page 85). Amongst the artefacts recovered from the house were a number of stone tables: the first pieces of furniture from the Second Temple period ever found. The walkway descends into "the largest and most magnificent of the buildings discovered in the Jewish Quarter" (Avigad, *ibid*) – the '**Mansion**'. The topography of this residential quarter of the Upper City dictated that the floor level here is some distance lower than that of the houses in the Middle Complex (and 7 m below the present street level). This large mansion comprises two storeys, though experts speculate that there may originally have been a third. The number of *mikvehs* found in the complex, including one where the vaulting, double entrance and mosaic-paved corridor were found in a superb state of preservation, has led to speculation that this large villa may have been the residence of members of the family of a high priest at the Temple. Other experts have challenged this assumption, looking to the stylistic Hellenistic influences to dismiss this argument. The 1:25 scale model of the reconstructed mansion allows the visitor to picture the building in its prime.

Batei Mahasseh Square This large square, often filled with Jewish schoolchildren playing, has a number of fragments of columns, capitals and Attic bases scattered about. None was found *in situ* and their exact origins are unclear, though it is certain that they formed part of some monumental structure(s) built nearby during the Hasmonean or Herodian period. The building along the west side of Batei Mahasseh Square, the **Rothschild Building**, dates to 1871, whilst the complex of buildings along the south side, the **Shelter Houses**, were built nine years earlier to house poor immigrant Jews from Holland and Germany. Their basements provided shelter for the quarter's residents during the last weeks of the battle for the Old City in 1948. This area was also badly damaged in the fighting for the city in 1967, though the subsequent archaeological excavations that ensued led to the discovery of remains of the Nea Church beneath the square.

Nea or New Church of Justinian Next to nothing remains of Justinian's Nea Church, dedicated to 'St Mary, Mother of God', though when dedicated in 543 CE it was (and remains) the largest basilica built in Palestine. Its external measurements are something in the region of 116 m by 57 m, which is not so difficult to imagine when you see that the seemingly meagre remains (part of the northeast apse, vaults to the south, external southeast corner) have walls up to 4-m thick.

Though the approximate location of the church just to the east of the south end of the Byzantine cardo maximus was known from the sixth-century **Madaba Map** (see page 54), and sections of it had been exposed during the construction of the Batei Mahasseh complex in 1862, it wasn't until Avigad's excavations (1970-82) that the true identity of the structure was firmly established. It was probably badly damaged in either the Persian invasion of 614 CE or the Arab conquest of 638 CE, and finally destroyed in the ninth century CE.

To view the preserved section of the **northeast apse**, walk down the steps away from the Rothschild Building to the southeast corner of Batei Mahasseh Square. Descend the steps to the right and turn left under the arch on Nachamu Street. Descend a further seven steps, then take the double flight of stairs down. Behind the green metal grille is the entrance to the northeast apse (not always accessible). Sections of the vaulted cistern and external structures can be seen in the archaeological garden to the south (just inside the present Old City walls). The remains can also be seen from above when walking the ramparts.

Four Sephardi Synagogues ① *Sun-Thu 0930-1600, Fri 0930-1230, adult 3NIS.* Construction of synagogues to serve the Sephardi community on this site date to 1610, with the completion of the **Ben Zakkai Synagogue** (named after the first-century CE rabbi and noted sage). A study hall was added on the northwest side in 1625, and converted into the **Prophet Elijiah Synagogue** some 70 years later. Further modification to the complex saw the **Middle Synagogue** added some point later, and the **Stambouli Synagogue** completed by 1857. The entire complex became badly neglected during the period of Jordanian occupation of the Jewish Quarter (1948-67), though subsequent restoration work has been completed using items recovered from Italian synagogues destroyed during World War II.

Ramban and Hurva Synagogues The west side of Hurva Square is occupied by the Hurva and Ramban Synagogues, and the Sidi 'Umar Mosque. Visiting Jerusalem in 1267, the noted Jewish scholar **Rabbi Moses ben Nachman** (known as **Ramban** or **Nachmanides**) discovered that there were only enough Jews in Jerusalem for a game of chess (out of a total population of around 2000). He settled in the city (meaning that the Jewish population were now just one short for a hand of bridge) and founded a synagogue on Mount Zion. Some time in the 14th century CE the **Ramban Synagogue** was moved to the present site, occupying the ruins of a Crusader church (possibly 'St Peter in Chains' or 'Church of St Martin'). The building collapsed in 1474 but was rebuilt in 1523 (possibly as the only synagogue in Jerusalem). Ottoman edicts subsequently banned its use as a Jewish place of worship.

In 1700 a group of Ashkenazi Jews (from Eastern Europe) arrived in Jerusalem and established themselves on a site just to the north of the Ramban Synagogue. Their attempts to build their own synagogue were complicated by internal squabbling following the death of their leader, and the half-built structure was confiscated by the Ottomans to settle the group's debts. Hence the synagogue's name: **Hurva**, or 'the Ruin'. The Hurva was returned to the Ashkenazi community by Ibrahim Pasha in 1836, finally completed in 1856 but destroyed in the fighting of 1948. Recently rebuilt, the Hurva Synagogue reopened in March 2010, triggering unrest among Palestinian groups concerned that it signalled Jewish intent to build a Third Temple on the Temple Mount.

The small **minaret** nearby belongs to the **Sidi 'Umar Mosque** (also known as **Jabi Kabir**), which may well have occupied a former Crusader structure (Church of St Martin?) some time in the 14th century. The minaret shows a number of 15th-century characteristics and is built in the square Syrian style.

Armenian Quarter

Marginally bigger than the Jewish Quarter (c. 10.5 ha), the Armenian Quarter occupies the southwest corner of the Old City. Visitors should note that many of the quarter's would-be attractions are behind high walls and closed doors, and are not open to the casual visitor. The heavy gates are locked at night, as they were in the Middle Ages. It is a 'walled city within a walled city', perhaps explaining why this is the only ethnic/religious quarter of the Old City that occupies the same site as it did in the fifth century CE.

Ins and outs

Getting there and around The two main approaches to the Armenian Quarter are from Jaffa Gate or from Zion Gate. Perhaps the most interesting time to visit the quarter is at the end of April, when the community commemorates the genocide of the Armenian people at the hands of the Turks during World War I. Following a moving service at the atmospheric Cathedral of St James, the Patriarch leads a silent procession along Armenian Patriarchate Street to the Armenian Church of the Holy Saviour on Mount Zion.

Background

Much of this quarter was formerly occupied by Herod the Great's palace, though next to no traces remain. The Armenians were quick to establish a presence in Jerusalem following the adoption of Christianity as the state religion in 301 CE (the first nation to do so), and the period of exile that followed the collapse of the Armenian state in the fourth century CE seemed to strengthen the Armenian community in the Holy Land. Indeed, by the seventh century CE an Armenian visitor to Jerusalem noted 70 Armenian convents/monasteries in the city. Many of these were established by St Gregory (Krikor) the Illuminator, though most were destroyed during the Persian (614 CE) and Arab (638 CE) invasions, and their remains are now scant.

The re-established Armenian kingdom in Cilica (c. 1098-1375) had close links with the Latin kingdom in Jerusalem (with Baldwin I, Jerusalem's second Crusader ruler, also being the Count of Armenian Edessa), and the Armenian revival in the Holy Land was further cemented by the purchase of the Church of St James from the Georgians (some time in the 12th century prior to 1151). Armenian fortunes in Jerusalem fluctuated in subsequent centuries, though not necessarily reflecting fortunes in the home land. However, the genocide committed by the Turks early in the 20th century has galvanized the Armenian community in Jerusalem, who now see themselves not only as the custodians of the religious centre of the Armenian diaspora, but also as the guardians of the Armenian cultural identity.

Sights

Christk Church ℹ *T02-6277727, www.cmj-israel.org. Church daily 0900-1700, services Sat 1000 (except 1st Sat in month) and Sun 0930; museum daily 0900-1700, free.*
Consecrated in 1849, the Anglican Christ Church is the oldest Protestant church in Jerusalem (though the meaning of its claim to be the "first major 'modern' building in Jerusalem" is less clear). After obtaining permission from the Ottoman sultan to build a "prayer hall" for workers next to their consul, the British constructed a church that in fact dwarfed the consul building. Though the initial impression of the church is one of simplicity, closer inspection reveals a number of details that are a clue to the church's unusual history and function. Note the Hebrew writing and Jewish symbols on the stained-glass windows, the Star of David on the table and menorah on the altar.

The church was built by an Anglican missionary society called the **London Society for Promoting Christianity** amongst the Jews (later the **Church's Ministry among the Jews**, or **CMJ**). The society, founded in 1809, drew its inspiration from a line in the *epistle of Paul to the Romans*, which declared: "For I am not ashamed of the gospel of Christ: for it is the power of God unto salvation to every one who believeth; *to the Jew first*, and also to the Greek" (*Romans 1:16*, emphasis added). Like other evangelical groups of the period (and indeed today), the CMJ's founders believed that before the Messiah returned, the Jewish people would be restored to the promised land and that a good many of them would acknowledge Jesus Christ as the Messiah. The CMJ's presence was established in Jerusalem in 1833 both in anticipation, and to precipitate, such events. The organization did much to support the first Aliyah of Russian Jews to the Holy Land in 1882. The founders of Christ Church incorporated Jewish symbols into the church design so that Jews would feel comfortable about entering, and could see how the Christian church acknowledged its Jewish origins. The history of the building and of the CMJ are presented in the small museum on site, along with topographical models of the Old City, worth a quick visit. The church also runs a very attractive guesthouse to the rear and has a nice courtyard café (see page 139).

Ya'qubiyya This small mosque (rarely accessible to visitors) occupies a former 12th-century CE Crusader church dedicated to St James (the Less). The site may originally have been the site of a monastery founded c. 430 CE by Peter the Iberian to house the relics of **St James Intercisus** (or St James the Cut-up), a Persian Christian martyred in 422 CE. Muslim documents of the 14th century CE refer to the building as the Zawiya (tomb) of Shaikh Ya'aqub al-'Ajami (James the Foreigner), and this medieval dedication has been preserved in the name of the mosque today. Parts of 12th-century CE Crusader masonry can be seen in the arch and choir.

Syrian Orthodox Church and Convent of St Mark ℹ *T02-6283304, Mon-Sat 0900-1700, Sun 1200-1700 (if closed, telephone), free, donations accepted.* A remarkable number of traditions are related to this site, occupied intermittently since the 12th century by the Syrian Orthodox (or **Jacobite**) community. A Byzantine tradition links the site to Mary of Jerusalem, mother of (John) Mark (St Mark), and suggests that i) the Last Supper was eaten here (*Matthew 26:17-30; Mark 14:12-36; Luke 22:7-38; John 13-17*); ii) the Descent of the Holy Spirit at Pentecost took place here (*Acts 2:1-47*); iii) the Virgin Mary was baptized in the stone font against the present south wall; and iv) that St Peter came here after his miraculous release from prison by the Angel (*Acts 12:12*)! Little wonder that the site was chosen for a church during the Byzantine period.

The present church was built in the 12th century, with numerous later modifications, though its constructors have not been positively identified. The confusion arises from the fact that the Jacobites fled Jerusalem prior to its capture by the Crusaders in 1099, with much of their property being passed to a Frankish knight. His apparent death in Egypt in 1103 saw the property returned to the Jacobites, though his subsequent reappearance in 1137 (alive and well) further confused the rights to the title deeds. A settlement in favour of the Jacobites was eventually reached.

The entrance portal of the convent is 12th century, and leads to a much more recent courtyard. The key feature is the stone font opposite the door in which the Virgin Mary is said to have been baptized, now adorned with gilt and flowers. The portrait of the Virgin and Child above the font is attributed to St Luke, though it is generally agreed that it dates only to the Byzantine period. Other points of interest include the inscription on the west pillar inside the entrance (said to be sixth-century CE) and the crypt beneath, where the Last Supper possibly took place.

Armenian Convent of St James This large complex, containing the Cathedral of St James, the residence of the Patriarchate, a pilgrim hospice, accommodation for nuns and monks, a seminary, library, museum, printing press, and various other related buildings, is the centre of the Armenian Christian community. On entering, note the impressive complex of locks and bolts on the inside of the main door from Armenian Patriarch Street.

Cathedral of St James ① *T02-6282331, daily during afternoon service, 1500-1530 (the priest will give visitors a short tour afterwards), and morning services 0600-0630. Stand at the rear. Free, donations accepted.* Those who make the effort to visit or worship in the Cathedral of St James are rarely disappointed: it is the finest church in town with an atmosphere during services and festivals that is very moving. Laden with incense, the interior of the cathedral is at its best on fine days, when "sunlight from the high windows and the lights of all the lamps create a dazzling and memorable reflection on the rich vestments, ornaments, tiles and other treasures" (Prag, 1989).

The central part of the present cathedral dates to the 11th century, though it is believed that a friend of the Byzantine empress Eudocia may have endowed some form of Christian establishment near here as early as 444 CE, and installed an Armenian as abbot. It was almost certainly destroyed during the Persian invasion of 614 CE. Between 1072 and 1088 the **Georgian** Christian community established a church and monastery here dedicated to St James the Great. An early Christian martyr, St James (son of Zebedee) was one of the first of the apostles, and was executed c. 44 CE on the orders of Herod Agrippa I. The fortunes of the Georgians took a turn for the worse in the 12th century, and they were forced to sell the church to the **Armenians**. A number of alterations were made to the church, though the Armenians retained the link with St James (in fact the principal relic is said to be his severed head).

During the Ottoman period the Armenian church fell into heavy debt through both mismanagement of its finances and its financial commitments to the Church of the Holy Sepulchre. The arrival of **Gregory the Chainbearer** in 1721 (so called because he wore a chain around his neck for three years whilst begging for restoration donations in the doorway of the Church of the Holy Mother of God in Constantinople) saw the debts repaid and the cathedral lavishly restored. Most of the precious stone and metal ornamentation dates to this period. The appearance of the cathedral was further enhanced by the addition of the decorative blue and white tile work (in the Kütahya style) between 1727 and 1737. **NB** Only the monastic compound and main church (excluding the chapels to the north) are open to visitors.

Armenian Garden The walled compound of the Armenian Garden contains a number of institutions related to the Armenian community, though the area is not open to the public. This area to the south of the Citadel was previously occupied by Herod's palace, though precious little survived the 70 CE sacking.

Armenian Museum Closed for renovation at time of writing, possibly reopening in 2010. Housed in a very attractive former seminary (built 1843), this museum explains the history and culture of Armenia, and also houses some of the gifts that pilgrims have given to the cathedral. The nearby Gulbenkian Library is unfortunately closed to tourists.

Church and Convent of the Holy Archangels (Convent of the Olive Tree) It is sometimes possible (on request) to visit the Church and Convent of the Holy Archangels (also known

Cathedral of St James

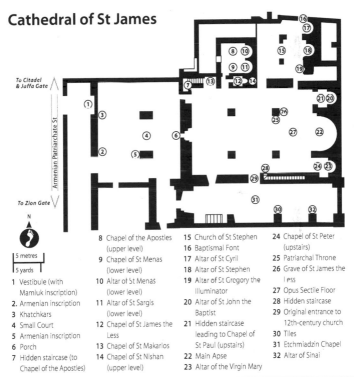

1 Vestibule (with Mamluk inscription)
2. Armenian inscription
3 Khatchkars
4 Small Court
5 Armenian inscription
6 Porch
7 Hidden staircase (to Chapel of the Apostles)
8 Chapel of the Apostles (upper level)
9 Chapel of St Menas (lower level)
10 Altar of St Menas (lower level)
11 Altar of St Sargis (lower level)
12 Chapel of St James the Less
13 Chapel of St Makarios
14 Chapel of St Nishan (upper level)
15 Church of St Stephen
16 Baptismal Font
17 Altar of St Cyril
18 Altar of St Stephen
19 Altar of St Gregory the Illuminator
20 Altar of St John the Baptist
21 Hidden staircase leading to Chapel of St Paul (upstairs)
22 Main Apse
23 Altar of the Virgin Mary
24 Chapel of St Peter (upstairs)
25 Patriarchal Throne
26 Grave of St James the Less
27 Opus Sectile Floor
28 Hidden staircase
29 Original entrance to 12th-century church
30 Tiles
31 Etchmiadzin Chapel
32 Altar of Sinai

as the Convent of the Olive Tree) within the grounds of the Armenian Convent, to the southeast of the Cathedral of St James. With a very beautiful interior, a 14th-century CE tradition places the 'House of Annas' here, where Jesus was taken after his arrest prior to being sent to the House of the High Priest Caiaphas. The olive tree against the north wall of the church is said to mark the site of the scourging. Women still come to eat three olives from the tree, as then they fall pregnant. The outer wall of the church is also said to contain one of the stones that would have cried out aloud had the disciples not praised God (*Luke 19:40*). This may seem risible to some, though as Murphy-O'Connor has pointed out, it is a tradition that "no one can ever prove false"!

Mount Zion

The area now referred to as Mount Zion is a low hill just below the southwest corner of the Old City, outside the current walls. Tradition links it with a number of important Christian events, including the Last Supper, the imprisonment of Jesus in the House of the High Priest Caiaphas, Peter's denial of Jesus (thrice), the Descent of the Holy Spirit at Pentecost, the falling asleep (death) of the Virgin Mary, and the location of the earliest Christian church. Also sited here is the 'Tomb of David', though it is 99.9% certain that he is not buried on this hill, but rather on the 'Ancient City of the Southeast Ridge' – the real Mount Zion.

Mount Zion

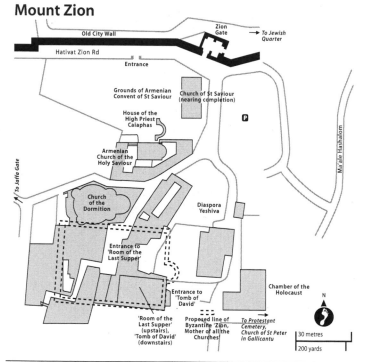

Ins and outs

Getting there and around For those arriving on foot, the principal point of access to Mount Zion is from Zion Gate (a natural continuation of the tour of the Armenian Quarter). There is also parking available at the main entrance to the hill's attractions.

Background

Evidence strongly suggests that the hill now referred to as Mount Zion was enclosed within the city walls as early as the second century BCE, with the walls remaining in place until the Roman sack of Jerusalem in 70 CE, and thus this area was part of the walled city at the time of the crucifixion of Jesus. The hill probably marked the southern limit of the Tenth Legion (Fretensis) camp after the establishment of Aelia Capitolina (135 CE), and remained unwalled until the Byzantine empress **Eudocia** rebuilt the ruined walls around the hill between 444 and 460 CE.

By this time many (though not all) of the Christian traditions associated with this site had been firmly established, and several churches had been built and rebuilt. Though the New Testament does not specify the exact location of many of the key events in the final days of Jesus' life, identifying and locating the sites became a fixation amongst **Byzantine Christians**, who sought to localize every detail of the gospels.

Thus, by the fifth century CE Mount Zion had become associated with the Descent of the Holy Spirit at Pentecost, Jesus' imprisonment in the House of the High Priest Caiaphas on the night before the Crucifixion, Peter's three denials of Jesus before the crowing of the cock (and his subsequent weeping on the rock), and as the site of the seat of the patriarchal throne of James the Less (brother of Jesus) and hence the location of the first church. By the end of the sixth century the tradition surrounding the Upper Room (where the Descent of the Holy Spirit at Pentecost had taken place) had been extended to include the Last Supper in this same room. The tradition surrounding the location of the House of John, where the Virgin Mary fell asleep (and died), was also added to the list. All of these sites were marked by Byzantine churches, and a detailed picture is provided by the sixth-century CE Madaba Map (see page 54). By the end of the 10th-beginning of the 11th century CE, this hill now referred to as Mount Zion had also become associated (incorrectly as it happens) with the burial place of King David.

Having been sacked by the Persians in 614 CE, the various churches on Mount Zion were rebuilt, but stood outside the city walls in a state of ruin when the Crusaders took Jerusalem in 1099. The Crusaders restored and refurbished the venerated New Testament sites, and built the **Monastery and Church of St Mary**. The upper level commemorated the room of the Last Supper (the Cenacle, or Coenaculum), whilst the Tomb of David was located below. Salah al-Din's capture of Jerusalem in 1192 saw Mount Zion once again enclosed within the city walls, though al-Malik al-Mu'azzam's subsequent dismantling of the city's fortifications in 1219 may have also included many of the defensive features that the Crusaders had incorporated into the church.

The Franciscans acquired permission to establish a presence on Mount Zion in 1335, and within 10 years had obtained control of most of the venerated places including the Cenacle. Within 50 years they had built a number of hospices on the hill and a cloister along the south side of the Cenacle. The **Tomb of David**, which had only created minor interest amongst the Crusaders, suddenly became a contested site in the late 14th century CE, with both Muslims and Jews laying claim to it. The reason for this sudden interest, according to Murphy-O'Connor, was the "legend of treasures buried with the king" (*ibid*), and by 1450 the Muslims had gained control of the site and built a mosque into the lower storey of the church. Franciscan (and other Christian, as well as Jewish) rights of access were gradually eroded over the following years, culminating in the 1523-24 decree of **Sulaiman II** ('the Magnificent') that forbade all Jewish and Christian access. In fact, access to the site for non-Muslims remained difficult right up until 1948 when the **Israelis** captured the hill. Between 1948 and 1967, when Jewish access to the Western Wall was impossible, the 'Tomb of David' became the *de facto* main Jewish pilgrimage site in Jerusalem.

Armenian Church of the Holy Saviour The property of the Armenian church has been thoroughly excavated and has revealed a number of interesting finds. In addition to remains of first-century BCE homes and Byzantine-period streets and houses, part of a fifth-century CE apse was also excavated: tentatively linked with the 'Zion, Mother of all the Churches', though most experts believe that this was located slightly further south (see line superimposed on map of Mount Zion). Far more likely is a church associated with the site of the **House of the High Priest Caiaphas**, where Jesus was tried before the High Priest on the night before his Crucifixion, and where Peter thrice denied Jesus before the crowing on the cock, as prophesied. Note that there is an alternative proposed site on Mount Zion for these same scenes (see next page, and another in the Armenian Quarter, page 90).

The 12th-century Crusader church that commemorates these events stands in the southeast corner of the compound. It was acquired by the Armenians in the 14th century CE, repaired and rebuilt in the next century, and is now referred to as the **Armenian Church of the Holy Saviour**. Its key points of interest are the 'Chapel of the Second Prison of Christ' in the southeast corner, and the piece of the 'Stone of Angels' taken from the Church of the Holy Sepulchre in the 13th century CE and placed in the altar here. The church was badly damaged during the 1948 war (and was used by the Israelis as a gun emplacement, 1948-1967), and a new **Church of St Saviour** is laboriously being constructed in the northeast corner of the compound.

Church of the Dormition ① *T02-6719927, Mon-Fri 0830-1200 and 1240-1800, Sat 0830-1730, Sun 1030-1145 and 1240-1730, free, donations accepted. Toilets, souvenir shop, cafeteria.* Built in Romanesque style, with a tall circular tower capped with a grey conical roof and four turrets, the Church of the Dormition is one of Jerusalem's most prominent landmarks. Built between 1901 and 1910 on land presented to the German Catholic Society of the Holy Land by William II of Prussia, the church commemorates the fifth-century CE tradition of the site of the House of John on Mount Zion where the Virgin Mary fell asleep (ie died). Though the church is elaborately decorated, and some careful examination of the detail is highly rewarding, the main draw of the church is the **Chapel of the Dormition** in the circular crypt. A life-sized statue shows a sleeping Mary, with the golden mosaic in the dome above showing Christ receiving her soul, surrounded by six women of the Old Testament (Eve, Miriam, Jael, Judith, Ruth, Esther).

Room of the Last Supper ① *Daily 0900-1700, free.* The whole block of medieval buildings to the south of the Church of the Dormition is part of the 'Monastery and Church of St Mary' that the Crusaders built in the 12th century, though it has undergone significant modification since then. Much of this complex overlies the site of the fifth-century CE **Zion, Mother of all the Churches** (see the superimposed plan on the map of Mount Zion).

The pointed-arched entrance leads to a small courtyard, from where steps in the corner take you up to the groin-vaulted hall. Tradition relates that this is the **Room of the Last Supper** (also known as the **Cenacle** or **Coenaculum**).

Mount Zion has been associated with the site of the Last Supper (*Matthew 26:17-30; Mark 14:12-36; Luke 22:7-38; John 13-17*) since the sixth century CE, though this belief may well have developed from the site's association with the tradition of the Upper Room of the Descent of the Holy Spirit at Pentecost (*Acts 2:1-47*) that developed a century or so earlier. Note that the Syrian Orthodox Church of St Mark in the Armenian Quarter also claims this honour (see page 89). The hall here was probably built in the 12th century, but significantly restored in the 14th century when the Franciscans gained control of the Cenacle. The altar and choir to the east were removed during the later construction of the dome over the 'Tomb of David' in the level below, and a sculptured mihrab (indicating Muslim direction of prayer) was added to the south wall during the early Ottoman period. The coloured-glass windows also date to this period. The pelicans adorning the canopy over the steps in the corner are a medieval Christian symbol of charity. The steps descend to an antechamber of the tomb below, though access is not permitted. Be sure to go up on to the roof for good views of the minaret and steeple close by, as well as a good perspective on the separation barrier and the distant hills.

'Tomb of David' ① *T02-6719767, Sun-Thu 0800-1800, Fri 0800-1400 (closes 1 hr earlier In winter), free. Men must cover heads; cardboard yarmulkes provided for use.* Retracing your steps to the lane outside, turn left and pass beneath a second pointed arch. The cloister that you enter is the one built by the Franciscans c. 1377 after gaining rights to the Cenacle. To the left is the so-called 'Tomb of David'.

As explained in the introduction, King David is not buried here, however, the late 10th-early 11th-century CE tradition has survived, following the revival of interest in the legend in the 14th century CE. A second revival of interest in the site as the Tomb of David stemmed from the Jordanian occupation of the Old City between 1948 and 1967, when Jews denied access to the Western Wall chose this Israeli-held position at which to pray.

The controversy surrounding the site does not end there, though. The relationship between the lines of the 12th-century CE Crusader 'Church of St Mary on Mount Zion' that you see today and the fourth-century CE 'Zion, Mother of all the Churches' has not been definitively established, and thus it is also claimed that the ancient foundations of the present Crusader church are in fact part of a first- or fourth-century CE **synagogue**. A synagogue on Mount Zion is mentioned by both the Bordeaux pilgrim (c. 333 CE) and Epiphanius of Salamis (c. 374-94 CE). A particular point of contention is the **niche** in the wall behind the cloth-draped **cenotaph** itself. It has been suggested that the niche, orientated 'correctly' towards the Temple Mount, would have held the Torah Scrolls of the synagogue. Another view is that the niche is an inscribed arch of the fourth-century CE church. And finally, in order perhaps to allow all competing interests to find an answer that suits their prejudices, it may also be part of an earlier Roman pagan building whose remains were incorporated within the fourth-century CE 'Zion, Mother of all the Churches'. The **Museum of King David** in the cloisters is no longer open but, on exiting the cloister, across the path you can visit the **Chamber of the Holocaust** ① *T02-6715105, Sun-Thu 0900-1545, Fri 0900-1330, suggested fee adult 12NIS, student 6NIS, but any donation acceptable*, a memorial to the six million Jews murdered by the Nazis. This began as a symbolic cemetery in 1949, a place for survivors to come and mourn. Now there are remembrance tablets to over 2000 communities in Europe.

Protestant cemetery A number of prominent Christians are buried here, including three important Middle East/Holy Land archaeologists, **Sir WM Flinders Petrie**, **Leslie Starkey**,

CS. Fisher; and the German industrialist **Oskar Schindler**. The cemetery is on the lower southwest slope of Mount Zion. To find Schindler's Grave (immortalized in the Spielberg film), enter the cemetery gate, then drop down to the second (lower) level. The grave is fairly central (it has no headstone so can be hard to find, though it is usually adorned by small piles of stones). If the cemetery is closed, try calling T052-5388342.

Church of St Peter in Gallicantu ① *T02-6731739, Mon-Sat 0830-1700. Souvenir shop, toilets.* Although now venerated as the site of the **House of the High Priest Caiaphas** (again!), and thus the place where St Peter thrice denied Jesus before the crowing of the cock, it is still not certain when tradition first placed this event at this particular spot. Excavations at the site have revealed a rock-cut crypt (now referred to as the 'First Prison of Christ') above which was built a monastic church some time in the Byzantine period (probably sixth century CE). However, the earliest mention of this as the place where Peter "went outside, and wept bitterly" (*Luke 22:62*) is recorded several centuries later. By the 11th-12th centuries CE the site was firmly on the pilgrim trail, billed (as today) as the 'Church of St Peter in Gallicantu', though this structure had been destroyed by the mid-15th century CE. The present church was built from 1928 to 1932 and has a fine view over the 'City of David (the 'real' Mount Zion; see page 105).

As a further challenge to the identification of this site as the location of the House of the High Priest Caiaphas, the question has been raised as to the positioning of the home of such an important figure on the lower slopes of Mount Zion. Though one can be fairly sure that the city walls enclosed Mount Zion at the time of Jesus' crucifixion, it is less sure that they extended this far down to the edge of the Tyropneon Valley. Thus, would such an important figure as the High Priest have his house outside the city walls? Further, such a wealthy and influential man as Caiaphas would surely have had his property on the very top of the hill, thus making the case of the alternative site to the north of the Church of the Dormition (within the Armenian St Saviour compound) a more compelling one. Either way, the exact position remains pure conjecture.

Mount of Olives

The Mount of Olives stands to the east of Jerusalem, separated from the Old City by the Kidron Valley (see page 103). It is part of a ridge of soft sandstone that has Mount Scopus at its northern end, the Mount of Olives at the centre, and the low rise above the Arab village of Silwan to the south. Much of its west and south slopes are covered by a vast ancient Jewish cemetery, whilst several major events in the life of Jesus in the days leading up to the Crucifixion are commemorated in a number of churches located here. The top of the Mount of Olives marks the beginning of the Last Path, leading on to Via Dolorosa, which many people (both religious and secular) find a spiritual and holistic experience. The various viewpoints high up on the Mount of Olives also offer arguably the best panorama of the whole city.

Ins and outs
Getting there and around The logical place to begin a tour of the Mount of Olives is at the top, thus avoiding a steep upward climb. From East Jerusalem, minibus 75 goes to Al-Tur, the village at the top (4NIS) or spend 25NIS on a taxi. If you are part of a guided tour you will probably be dropped at the summit, though the majority of independent sightseers will reach the Mount of Olives at the bottom: from Lions' Gate in the Old City walls; from the junction of Jericho Road and Sulaiman Street at the northeast corner

of the Old City; or by making their way up from the tombs in the Kidron Valley below. Hence, the description below is from the bottom up.

Warning Lone women should be careful in the high-walled cemeteries and along the east side of the hill from Bethphage; it may be wise not to come here unaccompanied. **NB** Suitably modest clothing must be worn when visiting these sites.

Background

The earliest history of the Mount of Olives relates to a function still undertaken here today: that of a **burial place**. Burial shafts dating to the late third millennium have been found on the east and south slopes of the ridge, whilst by the Late Bronze Age (c. 1550-1200 BCE) the west slope of the Mount of Olives formed part of the main cemetery of Jerusalem. This tradition of burial here on the southwest slopes of the Mount of Olives, and on the other side of the Kidron Valley beneath the east side of the Temple Mount/Haram al-Sharif, stems from the belief that the Kidron is in fact the **Valley of Jehoshaphat** where the whole of humanity will assemble to be judged by God: "I will also gather all nations, and will bring them down into the valley of Jehoshaphat" (*Joel 3:2*), and "Then shall the Lord go forth, and fight against those nations, as when he fought in the day of battle. And his feet shall stand in that day upon the mount of Olives, which is before Jerusalem on the east, and the mount of Olives shall cleave in the midst thereof toward the east and toward the west, and there shall be a very great valley" (*Zechariah 14:3-4*). As well as the Jewish cemeteries here, there are also Muslim and Christian graveyards. Many of the Jewish tombs here were systematically desecrated during the Jordanian occupation of part of Jerusalem (1948-67), when the graves were allegedly broken up for use as paving stones in the latrines. One notable burial in the large Jewish cemetery here is Robert Maxwell (whose grave would make an excellent latrine). For further information on famous Zionists and Jews buried here, see www.mountofolives.co.il which outlines some self-guided tours.

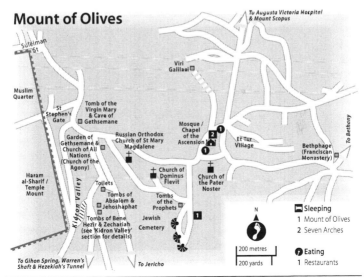

Mount of Olives

There is some evidence to suggest that the Mount of Olives was the site of an Iron-Age Jewish sanctuary, possibly David's 'Nob' (*II Samuel 15:30-32*) or Solomon's temples to foreign gods on the Mount of Corruption (*II Kings 23:13*): the low rise above Silwan. After the construction of the Temple by Solomon, the Mount of Olives became associated with the Ceremony of the Red Heifer (*Numbers 19:1-10*).

The importance of the Mount of Olives to Christians stems from the episodes in the life of **Jesus** that were enacted here, most notably in the days leading up to his arrest and Crucifixion. It is highly probable that on his visits to Jerusalem, particularly during festivals when the costs of accommodation in the city would sky-rocket (as today), Jesus stayed with friends at Bethany (see West Bank chapter, page 228). Thus the road between Bethany and the Temple (pretty much following the route of the tour outlined below) would have been well known to him. It was from Bethphage on the top of the Mount of Olives that Jesus begun his triumphal entry into Jerusalem before the Passover (*Matthew 21:1-11; Mark 11:1-11; Luke 19:28-40; John 12:12-15*); where Jesus foretold the future of the city (*Matthew 24-25; Mark 13:1-4*) and wept over it (*Luke 19:37, 41-44*); and in the garden at the foot of the slope, Gethsemane, that he was betrayed and arrested (*Matthew 26:36-56; Mark 14:32-50; Luke 22:39-54; John 18:1-12*). Luke's gospel also places the Ascension on the Mount of Olives (*Luke 24:50-52*).

The early **Byzantine** period saw numerous churches established on the Mount of Olives to commemorate these events, and by the sixth century CE a Christian visitor (Theodosius, c. 518) noted 24 churches on the hill. Many were destroyed during the Persian invasion of 614 CE, though some were rebuilt immediately afterwards and others later by the Crusaders. However, subsequent years of neglect left the area in a state of ruination and many of the churches that you see today are primarily the result of late 19th-and early 20th-century restoration efforts.

Sights

Tomb of the Virgin Mary ① *Daily 0530-1830 (winter - 1730), free.* The bend in the road outside the Tomb of the Virgin Mary is marked by the reputed **Tomb of Mujir al-Din** (1456-1522), a noted Arab scholar who has provided a valuable commentary on 15th-century Jerusalem and Hebron. A 20th-century dome, supported by four pillars, stands above a simple white stone shrine. The entrance to the Tomb of the Virgin Mary (sometimes referred to as the Church of the Assumption) is located off an open square courtyard below.

Descending into the sunken courtyard (**1**), before you stands the Crusader-built entrance portal (**2**). The church was built by the Benedictines c. 1130 on the ruins of previous Christian shrines. After one has passed through the Crusader entrance, 44 steps descend to the remains of the Byzantine church. Much of the masonry at the upper end of this staircase, including the steps themselves, dates to the 12th century CE. At the 20th step, to the right, is the **tomb of the Crusader Queen Melisande** (died 1161) (**3**). Her body was moved to a new tomb at the foot of the stairs in the 14th century, though this has subsequently become lost. In later years Queen Melisande's tomb became associated with the burial place of the Virgin Mary's parents, **Joachim** and **Anne**. Almost opposite, several steps further down, is another burial niche (**4**), related to the family of the Crusader king Baldwin II. This was later identified with the tomb of the Virgin's husband, Joseph.

As you continue to the bottom of the stairs, the pointed Crusader arches give way to the round vaults of the Byzantine period church. It is not entirely certain when the Valley of Jehoshaphat first became associated as the place of the Virgin Mary's death (it's not mentioned in the gospels), though it is identified as the place of her burial in the anonymous second-third-century CE *Transitus Mariae* (Assumption of Mary). A church may have been built above a rock-cut tomb on this site as early as 455 CE, with a bench *arcosolium* being venerated as the burial place of Mary. Though the seventh century CE saw Mount Zion identified as the site of the Dormition (see page 94), the church here was certainly still functioning in the ninth century CE. It was probably destroyed by the caliph al-Hakim in 1009 before the Benedictines rebuilt the church and added a large monastery. This was largely effaced by Salah al-Din in 1187, with many of the stones from the monastery finding their way into the sultan's new city wall.

The Byzantine **crypt (6)** at the bottom of the steps is 10.6 m below the level of the entrance. The built apse to the left belongs to the Ethiopians, whilst the rock-cut apse to the right (east) is under the custodianship of the Armenians, Greeks, Copts and Syrians. The Eastern Orthodox influence is manifested in the darkness of the church and the incense-thickened atmosphere. At the centre of the east apse (right) is a small square chapel marking the supposed site of the **tomb of the Virgin (7)**. As with the tomb of Christ in the Church of the Holy Sepulchre, this tomb has been cut away from the surrounding rock. To its north, a **niche (8)** stands at the entrance to another tomb of the first-century CE style **(9)**. To the south of the Virgin's tomb a *mihrab* **(10)** marks the direction of Mecca: Muslims revere Mary as the mother of the prophet Jesus.

Tomb of the Virgin Mary

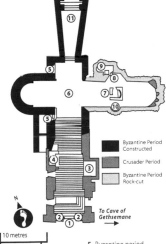

Byzantine Period Constructed
Crusader Period
Byzantine Period Rock-cut

To Cave of Gethsemane →

10 metres
10 yards

1 Sunken Courtyard
2 Crusader entrance portal
3 Tomb of the Crusader Queen Melisande
4 Burial niche of family of Baldwin II
5 Byzantine period entrances
6 Byzantine period crypt
7 Tomb of the Virgin
8 Niche
9 1st century CE style tomb
10 Mihrab
11 Original entrance to Cemetery

Grotto of Gethsemane ① *Daily 0830-1200 and 1430-1700 (on Sun and Thu -1540), free.* Returning to the courtyard, a passageway to the east leads to the Grotto of Gethsemane (or 'Cave of the Oil Press'). Quite possibly a natural cave, it contains a pre-Christian water cistern (below) that seems to have been used later as a Byzantine and then Crusader burial place. At the time of Jesus it appears that an oil press (Hebrew: *Gat Shemen*) was operating here, whilst the cave may have been used as a shelter at other times. During the Byzantine period the cave became associated with a number of traditions surrounding Jesus, including the site where the Disciples rested whilst he prayed "a stone's throw away" (*Luke 22:41*), and where he was betrayed and arrested.

Garden of Gethsemane and Church of All Nations ① *Daily 0800-1200 and 1430-1730 (summer-1800), but go at 1400 as you will probably get in and avoid large crowds, free.* Before entering the Garden of Gethsemane, it is worth continuing a short distance south along the Jericho Road in order to admire the superb west façade of the church. Above the colonnaded portico of Corinthian columns is a glittering gold mosaic depicting Christ as mediator between God and man, and assuming the suffering of the world (hence the alternative name, Church of the Agony). The quote is from the *Epistle of Paul the Apostle to the Hebrews* (*Hebrews 5:7*). The newly landscaped section of the Kidron Valley in front of the church was where Pope Benedict XVI celebrated mass with many thousands of devotees in May 2009.

The garden was identified as early as the fourth century CE as the place where Jesus prayed, was betrayed by Judas and arrested (*Matthew 26:36-56; Mark 14:32-50; Luke 22:39-54; John 18:1-12*), though the tradition may be earlier. The dating of the gnarled olive trees in the garden varies between 300 and 2300 years old, though this upper limit seems unlikely since the Romans are widely believed to have stripped the entire region around Jerusalem bare during their siege of 70 CE.

The present **Church of All Nations** (**Church of the Agony**) was built in 1924 from subscriptions collected worldwide (hence the popular name). It was designed by the Italian architect **Antonio Barluzzi** as a triple-aisled basilica, with the twelve low domes in the ceiling being decorated with the coats of arms of the countries that gave donations towards the church's construction. The purple glass in the windows dims the light entering the church, perhaps representing the "hour when darkness reigns" (*Luke 22:53*) of Jesus' arrest. The focal point of the church, in front of the altar, is the section of bedrock upon which Jesus is said to have prayed prior to his arrest.

The present church largely follows the line of the Byzantine basilica built here between 379 and 384 CE by Theodosius I; in fact the two internal lateral apses include some courses of the Byzantine church, plus sections of the original mosaic floor (under glass) can also be seen. It is generally believed that the church was destroyed in the earthquake of 747/8 CE. The Crusaders rebuilt the church c. 1170, though this time on a slightly different orientation. The church appears to have been abandoned by 1345.

Russian Orthodox Church of St Mary Magdalene ⓘ *Tue and Thu 1000-1200*. This eye-catching church was built by Czar Alexander III in 1888 and is most noted for its seven Kremlin-style gold onion-shaped domes, which are a Jerusalem landmark. Only limited access to the church is possible. Buried within the convent grounds is Princess Alice of Greece, mother of Prince Philip, Duke of Edinburgh.

Church of Dominus Flevit ⓘ *Daily 0800-1145 and 1430-1700, free. Toilets*. This attractive 20th-century church is built on a site that was associated by medieval pilgrims with the tradition of Jesus weeping over the city as he rode towards it (on Palm Sunday). However, the land upon which the church was built shows signs of far earlier usage, the evidence of which can be seen just inside the gate of the grounds, to the right. Excavations in the early 1950s revealed the remains of a **cemetery** first used in the Late Bronze Age (c. 1550-1200 BCE) that later became the **largest necropolis** of the Roman period thus far discovered in Jerusalem. Covering 0.6 hectares, the necropolis contained at least 20 arcosolium burial caves (arched recesses) and 38 pit tombs, most dating to the third-fourth centuries CE, though the site continued in use during the Byzantine period. Seven hard limestone sarcophagi were found, some of which were elaborately decorated. In addition, over 120 ossuaries (secondary burial receptacles into which bones are put after the flesh has decayed) were discovered, about a third of which bear inscriptions (in Aramaic, Hebrew and Greek). The first two tombs on display just inside the gate are thought to date to the period 100 BCE-135 CE, and were generally used for secondary burial in ossuaries. The Late Bronze-Age tombs could not be preserved, though they provided a very rich assemblage of pottery, plus some alabaster and faience vessels and Egyptian scarabs.

Continuing along the path brings you to the **Church of Dominus Flevit** ('the Lord wept'), built in 1955 to a tear-shaped design (discernable from above) by Antonio Barluzzi. The altar points to the west in the direction of the Temple, where Jesus would have faced whilst he prayed. Consequently the church's most notable feature, the chalice window, beautifully frames a view of the Dome of the Rock and Temple Mount. The present church stands on the site of a Byzantine-style chapel, of which mosaics on the floor remain, though experts are quick to point out that it almost certainly dates to the Early Arab period, c. 675 CE. From at least the seventh century CE onwards a liturgical procession began at the top of the Mount of Olives on Maundy Thursday, arriving in Jerusalem on the morning of Good Friday. This may be when the tradition of this site as the place where Jesus wept began. However, the fourth-century CE pilgrim Egeria also mentions such a procession, and excavations have also revealed the remains of a fourth-century CE monastery here. Its dedication has not been established. The small terrace in front of the Church of Dominus Flevit provides an excellent viewpoint for secular visitors, and a quiet place for prayer and meditation for pilgrims.

Tombs of the Prophets ① *Mon-Thu 0900-1500. Admission is free in theory, though you may be expected to pay a tip if you don't have your own torch and have to be shown round.* Despite the claim that these are the tombs of the prophets **Haggai**, **Zechariah** and **Malachi**, who lived c. sixth-fifth centuries BCE, this tomb complex is in fact part of the first-century BCE-135 CE necropolis that you may already have seen within the grounds of the Church of Dominus Flevit. In fact, these style tombs (*kokhim*) did not come into use for Jewish burials until the first century BCE. Its radiating fan-shape is unusual, however. Some of the inscriptions discovered here suggest that the complex was reused for the burial of foreign Christians in the fourth and fifth centuries CE.

Rehav'am Viewpoint One of Jerusalem's best panoramas, the sun is best placed for photography early in the morning. Those who like to pose sitting on a camel in front of a spectacular backdrop will not be disappointed here.

Church of the Pater Noster ① *Mon-Sat 0830-1200 and 1430 1700, 7 NIS.* Early Christian visitors such as Eusebius (c. 260-340 CE) and the Bordeaux Pilgrim (c. 333 CE) record that the Emperor Constantine ordered a church built on the Mount of Olives above a cave that was venerated as a place at which Jesus taught the disciples. The site also became identified with the Ascension (*Luke 24:50-52*), though most early sources refer to it by its popular name, **Eleona** ('Church of the Olive Groves': an Aramaic 'a' added to the Greek 'elaion' creates 'of olives'). Visiting the church in c. 384, the pilgrim Egeria noted that the site was identified with Jesus' teaching on the ultimate conflict between good and evil (*Matthew 24, 25*), and no mention is made of the Ascension, the site of which had supposedly been moved further up the hill.

Following the destruction of the church in 614 CE by the Persians, the fate of the site is not entirely clear. A "Church where Christ Taught his Disciples" is mentioned in a ninth-century CE list, and it is now thought that the site here lay in ruins until the arrival of the Crusaders, when the cave became associated specifically with Jesus' teaching to the Disciples of the **Lord's Prayer**. Early in the 12th century CE a modest oratory was built, followed by a succession of churches destroyed and rebuilt as the fortunes of the Crusaders and Muslims ebbed and flowed.

The property was bought in 1857 by the Princesse de la Tour d'Auvergne, who spent the rest of her life searching for the cave. She is responsible for the cloister here (1868) and the adjacent Carmelite convent (1872). In 1910 the White Fathers discovered the remains of the Byzantine Church of Eleona, and further excavations were made by the Dominicans in 1918. Subsequent appeals were made to raise a basilica above the ancient foundations, though work stopped when funds ran out. The unfinished structure remains as it was left and is now referred to as the **Church of the Pater Noster** ('Our Father').

The site is perhaps most famous today for the 60 plus renditions of the Lord's Prayer inscribed on to ceramic tiles, each in a different language. The collection originally occupied the cloister, though recent additions have expanded into the church, vestibule, and all available walls. More recent translations include Gujarati, Hausa and Igbo. It is also possible to view the cave at the centre of the reconstructed (but unfinished) basilica. The 20th-century basilica was supposed to recreate the fourth-century CE building, though the fact that it was never finished perhaps avoided the controversy over what form the original building actually took. The crypt of the basilica was built around the cave, and it is still possible to descend inside today. It is not thought that the cave itself was originally part of a tomb, though it certainly cuts part of a first-century CE kokhim tomb.

Mosque/Chapel of the Ascension ① *Daily 0800-1430 (summer-1730). 5NIS; if locked call the tel no on the sign and the custodians will come to open up. Small souvenir stall.* Of the four gospels, only Luke mentions the Ascension of Jesus into heaven (*Luke 24:50-52* and *Acts 1:9*). Of course the actual site is not specified, though the Byzantine pilgrims in their zeal to localize every detail of the gospels came to venerate a cave on the Mount of Olives as the scene. The choice of a cave as the place to venerate the Ascension arises probably not from some unusual interpretation of the gospels, but rather from the realities of life in Jerusalem for early Christians: the fear of persecution meant that it was probably safer to congregate in a cave than in the open. As mentioned in the background to the Church of Eleona/Church of the Pater Noster (see previous page), the cave was rapidly forgotten as the place of the Ascension and the venerated site 'moved up the hill'. In c. 384 CE the pilgrim Egeria records that the Ascension was celebrated at the site now occupied by the Mosque/Chapel of the Ascension.

The first church on this site appears to have been built some time before 392 CE by Poimenia, a wealthy and pious Roman woman. It was almost certainly destroyed by the Persians in 614 CE and then restored by Modestus. The round building, open to the sky, is described c. 680 CE by Arculf, including the footprints of Jesus in the dust. Arculf's description is largely confirmed by excavations undertaken in 1960 by the Franciscan Fathers. The present octagonal form dates to the Crusader restoration of 1102, when several other alterations were made. At the end of the 12th century Salah al-Din granted the site to two of his pious followers (Wali al-Din and Abu'l Hasan), and the custodians have been Muslim ever since.

The small mosque and minaret at the entrance to the site date to 1620. The original Crusader shrine featured an outer colonnaded cloister within which stood an octagon of columns and arches, open to the sky. A stone dome on an octagonal drum now covers the octagonal Crusader chapel, and the arches have been blocked. Of particular note are the 12th-century CE Crusader capitals on the columns surrounding the octagon, especially the two featuring bird-headed winged quadrupeds. A sectioned-off area of the floor bears the supposed imprint of Jesus' right foot; the imprint of his left foot was removed to the al-Aqsa Mosque some time around 1200 CE.

Russian Orthodox Convent of the Ascension and Viri Galilaei ① *Tue and Thu 0900-1300, free.* A little to the north of the Mosque/Chapel of the Ascension is the Russian Orthodox Convent of the Ascension, whose tower provides one of the best views from the top of the Mount of Olives. To find it, turn right down the alley just after Royal Taxis. Also to the north is the site of **Viri Galilaei** (see Mount of Olives map), where tradition relates that the disciples were referred to as 'Men of Galilee' immediately after the Ascension (Acts 1:11). The site is marked by a Greek Orthodox Church, though a Byzantine chapel may well have stood here originally.

Bethphage ① *T02-6284352, daily 0700-1145 and 1400-1730, closes one hour earlier in winter, ring the bell for admission. Free, though gatekeeper may expect a small tip.* Bethphage is mentioned in the gospels as the place where Jesus mounted the donkey to make his triumphal entry into Jerusalem, an event that Christians now celebrate as 'Palm Sunday' (*Matthew 21:1-11; Mark 11:1-11; Luke 19:28-40; John 12:12-15*). Though the gospels do not reveal the specific place where the procession began, the Franciscan monastery that now commemorates the event is in all likelihood pretty much 'in the vicinity' of Bethphage.

Within the courtyard of the monastery (ring the bell for admission) is a late 19th-century church (1883) built upon the remains of a medieval chapel. Enshrined within the Crusader chapel is a stone block that is venerated as the mounting-stone that Jesus used to mount the donkey. As Murphy-O'Connor dryly observes (*The Holy Land*, 1993), a mounting-stone may have been necessary to mount a huge battle-charging Crusader steed, but would it really have been necessary for your average Palestinian donkey? Nevertheless, the Franciscans Palm Sunday procession begins from this chapel.

Kidron Valley

The Kidron Valley (Arabic: Wadi Jauz) forms Jerusalem's eastern border, dividing the Old City and East Jerusalem area from Mount Scopus, the Mount of Olives and the Arab village of Silwan. The valley is at its deepest between the Temple Mount/Haram al-Sharif and the Mount of Olives, where it is often referred to by its biblical name, the Valley of Jehoshaphat ('Yahweh judges'). The Kidron owes its importance to this identification as the place where the Last Judgement is due to take place (see for example *Jeremiah 31:40; Joel 3:2; Zechariah 14:3-4*), and this is why so many cemeteries and burial grounds are located on the valley's slopes. There are a number of tombs and monuments of particular note in the Kidron Valley, though a succession of legends, traditions and popular stories have served to obscure many of their original functions.

Ins and outs
Getting around A path leads down opposite the Garden of Gethsemane and Church of All Nations to the tombs; or they can be reached by the modern flight of steps (signed 'Abshalom's Pillar') at the southeast corner of the Old City. For a map showing the position of these tombs, see the 'Mount of Olives' map on page 97.

Tombs of Absalom and Jehoshaphat
The most imposing monument here is the so-called Tomb of Absalom. Resembling a bottle-shape at the top, the upper section is masonry whilst the base below the cornice is cut directly from the rock. It stands 20 m high and is probably the most complete tomb monument in the country. The square, rock-hewn base features an unusual combination of styles, including

Ionic columns at each corner, a Doric frieze above, and an Egyptian-influenced cavetto cornice. The upper masonry section features a concave conical roof resting on a stone pedestal (*tholos*). The entrance to the tomb within is on the south side, high up above the level of the cornice, whilst the other holes hacked in the side were made by grave-robbers. It is generally believed to have been built in the second half of the first century BCE.

The dating of the tomb has negated the popular association with **Absalom**, son of David, who lived almost 1000 years before this tomb was cut. In fact, this association with Absalom was probably first made by Benjamin of Tudela c. 1170 from the reading of a line in the *Second Book of Samuel*: "Now Absalom in his lifetime had taken and reared up for himself a pillar, which is in the king's valley" (*II Samuel 18:18*). In fact, an 18th-century CE commentator relates how passers-by used to throw stones at the tomb because of Absalom's treachery towards his father.

Though the Tomb of Absalom is a tomb in its own right, it also forms part of the **Tomb of Jehoshaphat** that is located behind (cut into the rock). In fact, the Tomb of Absalom may well have acted as a nephesh, or memorial cenotaph, for the burial complex cut in the cliff behind. For whom the eight-chambered catacomb-like burial complex was built is not certain, and it is now popularly known as the Tomb of Jehoshaphat. Its entrance, sealed off by a metal grill, features a finely carved pediment. The style of intricate carvings inside suggests a Herodian period dating (c. 37 BCE-70 CE). The Byzantine period saw these catacombs occupied by hermits.

Tombs of the Bene Hezir and Zechariah

Just to the south is a further burial complex, also featuring a *nephesh* (funerary monument) and a catacomb burial complex. The Tomb of the Bene Hezir is the rock-cut catacomb that you come to first. It has a Doric façade comprising two free-standing and two engaged columns with Doric capitals supporting a Doric frieze. A Hebrew inscription on the architrave (beam resting on the capitals) above the Doric columns identifies individual members of the priestly family of the **Bene Hezir** (see *I Chronicles 24:15*). It almost certainly dates to the late second-early first century BCE, though a 12th-century CE tradition linked it with **St James the Less**, and you still sometimes see it referred to as his tomb.

Just to the south is the nephesh belonging to the Tomb of the Bene Hezir. This freestanding monument was carved directly out of the rock and comprises a cube base supporting a pyramid. All four sides of the cube are decorated with Ionic columns and an Egyptian cavetto cornice. The decorative style strongly suggests that it is contemporary with the Bene Hezir complex, though it is still referred to as the **Tomb of Zechariah**.

Silwan

The village of Silwan (from 'Siloam') occupies the east side of the Kidron Valley, and looks upon the City of David. Sometimes referred to as the 'Tomb of the Pharaoh's Wife/Daughter', the **Monolith of Silwan** is located on the edge of an escarpment as you enter the village. It comprises a large free-standing cube cut from the rock, and previously capped by a pyramid (presumably similar to the 'Tomb of Zechariah'). The pyramid was removed in the Roman period (for an unknown reason) and the Monolith now blends in with the rest of the houses making it difficult to locate without local help. It is a funerary monument probably dating to the ninth-seventh centuries BCE, with a distinct Phoenician-Egyptian influence. The hole cut through the Hebrew inscription was made by the Byzantine hermit who made his home inside.

City of David (Ancient City on the Southeast Ridge)

The low ridge to the south of the Temple Mount/Haram al-Sharif (sandwiched between the Tyropoeon Valley to the west and the Kidron Valley to the east) is the site where David built his capital early in his reign, effectively founding the new city of Jerusalem. Generally referred to as the 'City of David', the site today presents an insight into 4000 years of continuous occupation, of which David's episode was just a small part. Remains from most periods of occupation can be seen in the Royal Quarter, while further down the ridge are a number of interesting sites related to the sophisticated water-supply system that served the city, most notably Warren's Shaft and the extraordinary Hezekiah's Tunnel.

Ins and outs

Getting there and around Exiting the Old City through Dung Gate, turn left (east) along HaOphel Road. Almost immediately on your right, a road (Ma'alot Ir David) leads south down into the Tyropoeon Valley. Take this road downhill, looking out for the entrance to the City of David Archaeological shortly on your left.

Background

Archaeological, epigraphic and biblical evidence of pre-Davidic Jerusalem does not allow a detailed reconstruction of the city's development and history prior to the Israelite conquest, though the exact location of the early city has been irrefutably established – here on the southeast ridge. The exact year of **David**'s conquest is unknown, though it is generally believed to have been fairly early in his reign (997 BCE is often mentioned). The capture of the city is graphically described in biblical sources (*II Samuel 5:6-9*), though some of the key action events are also ascribed to Joab (*I Chronicles 11:4-7*). What is clear, however, is that the resident population, known as the **Jebusites**, were not murdered or expelled but continued to live amongst their Israelite conquerors (*Judges 1:21*).

David subsequently shifted his capital here, and as the city developed to the north and west during the reigns of David's successors (Solomon, then the kings of Judah), the seat of power shifted also. However, this southeast ridge remained settled and within the city walls until the first century CE at least. The subsequent centuries saw the settlement on this ridge alternately enclosed, then excluded from the confines of the city walls, and since about the 11th century CE it has been located outside. It remained an important part of Jerusalem, however, not least because of the complex water-supply system built here that drew water from the Gihon Spring in the Kidron Valley and supplied it to the city. Extensive excavations were begun by Warren in 1867, and have continued intermittently until the present day. Opposite the main entrance to the City of David (over the road in the Giv'ati parking lot) recent digs have uncovered what archaeologists believe to be the palace of Queen Helena of Adiabene (in northern Mesopotamia, now in northeast Iraq). Helena settled here and built herself a palace in the Lower City (Josephus, *Jewish War, V, 253*). She died in Adiabene in 65 CE, though her body was sent to Jerusalem for burial (in the Tombs of the Kings in East Jerusalem, see page 116). Also at this site a large hoard of gold coins (267 pieces) has been unearthed, dating from the early years of the reign of Heraclius (610-641 CE). It is hoped the site will open to the public around 2012.

The site

ⓘ *T*6033, www.cityofdavid.org.il (see www.ticketnet.co.il for booking tours). Adult 25NIS, student 21NIS, child 13NIS, additional 10NIS for 15-min 3D movie. Open Sun-Thu 0800-*

1900 (in Aug -2100, winter -1700), Fri-1500. Last entrance to Hezekiah's Tunnel 2 hrs before closing. Two excellent guided tours available, adult 60NIS, child 45NIS, book in advance. First Temple Period tour includes Hezekiah's Tunnel and lasts 3 hrs (summer 1000 & 1600, winter 1000 & 1400); Second Temple Period tour includes underground streets and lasts 2 hrs, at 1400. If entering the tunnel, be prepared to get wet and bring a torch (or rent one for 4NIS).

'Large stone structure' (remains of David's palace?)   The foundations of this monumental building, discovered in 2005, are believed by some archaeologists to be the palace of David/the Israelite kings. There is still dispute, however, over whether the fieldstones that you see here which supported the structure (nothing of the upper levels has survived) are 9th or 10th century BCE. Certainly the huge buttress found lower down the slope is hefty enough to support a monumental building of particular importance. In the vicinity, two bullae (clay seals bearing impressions) were found, both measuring 1 cm in diameter and lettered in ancient Hebrew with the names of two court ministers from the time of Jeremiah who are mentioned in the same verse of the Old Testament (*Jeremiah 38:1*). It is also worth noting that, as yet, no epigraphic evidence has been uncovered from the reigns of either David or Solomon in the City of David).

Royal Quarter   The so-called Royal Quarter (also known as Area G) represents a century's worth of archaeological excavation of some 14 centuries of settlement (see map below). Archaeologists believe that the houses built on the ridge c. 1800 BCE were constructed on the natural slopes and terraces. Some time in the 13th-12th centuries BCE a 'stepped stone structure' was built to flatten the ridge and to make construction easier. This was done by building stone compartments, filling them with rubble, then building above them. It is thought the podium was extensively modified and repaired by David, then Solomon (10th-9th centuries BCE), and strengthened by means of the massive stone ramp or glacis that you can clearly see here today.

During the seventh century BCE terraces were cut into this ramp and a number of houses were constructed. One such house, the four-roomed 'House of Ahiel', has been partially preserved including the monoliths that supported the roof, an outer stairway and a small room over a cesspit to the north that is presumably a toilet. Part of a separate house to the north has also been identified, taking is name, the 'Burnt Room', from the destruction debris found here that resulted from the Babylonian sacking of the city in 586 BCE (*II Kings 25:9*). A good description of the destruction inflicted here by the Babylonians is provided by Nehemiah (Nehemiah 2:13-16).

The high defensive wall along the crest of the ridge was built by Nehemiah in the fifth century BCE, and later was rebuilt in the second century BCE by the Hasmoneans.

Warren's Shaft   'Warren's Shaft' takes its name from one of the men who 'discovered' it in 1867, Sir Charles Warren (who later went on to become Commissioner of the Metropolitan Police in London at the time of the 'Jack the Ripper' murders). Entrance is via an Ottoman-period building, from where 80 iron steps descend to a tunnel which gradually widens to a platform before dropping down to a large cave. From here, a natural vertical fissure, 'Warren's Shaft', descends about 13 m to a horizontal tunnel (which later evolved into 'Hezekiah's Tunnel', see below). For many years the shaft was believed to be part of the Canaanite defensive system designed to protect Jerusalem's water source, and it was thought that water would have been drawn up in buckets through the entrance to the

Ancient City on the southeast ridge, Kidron Valley & Tyropoean Valley

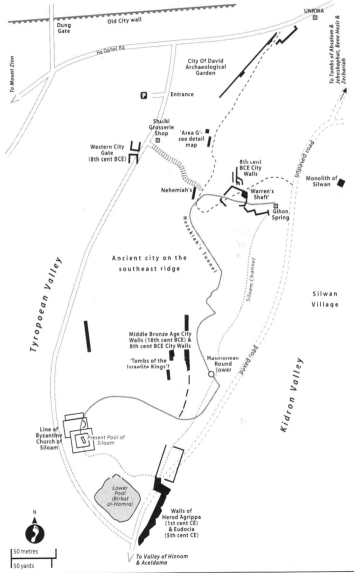

shaft. However, more recent excavations have ascertained that in fact the fissure served no function to the Canaanites and was merely revealed when the Israelites lowered the level of the tunnel in the eighth century BCE.

Gihon Spring and Hezekiah's Tunnel From Warren's Shaft, the 'Secret Tunnel' continues to the Canaanite Pool which, being outside of the city walls, was surrounded by massive fortifications that continue to be excavated (hence the concrete and metal supports much in evidence). The pool was fed by the Gihon Spring, the first written reference to which is the biblical account of Solomon's anointment as king by Zadok the priest and Nathan the prophet (*I Kings 1:33, 38, 45*). It takes its name from the Hebrew 'to gush forth', which describes the way in which the siphon worked (though this effect is no longer active). As discussed earlier, the ancient city's water source was vulnerable to attack during sieges, so with the prospect of the Assyrian king Sennacherib's advance on the city, **Hezekiah** (727-698 BCE) began work on constructing defensive measures. After all, "why should the kings of Assyria come and find so much water?" (*II Chronicles 32:4*). The Siloam Channel that led from the Gihon Spring to the Siloam Pool (also known as the 'Birkat al-Hamra') was blocked, and the source disguised. Hezekiah's water engineers then embarked upon an ambition construction project to divert the waters from the Gihon Spring to the Siloam Pool via a new channel cut in the rock, but within the city walls: **Hezekiah's Tunnel**.

The gradient between the spring and the end of the tunnel is very slight, around 30 cm, and thus the tunnel required considerable planning. Running for 533 m, it follows a particularly winding course, which is attributable to the necessity of avoiding bands of hard rock whilst exploiting natural fissures, the inadequacies of surveying techniques and the need to avoid the burial places on the south end of the ridge (see 'the Weill Excavations' on page 109). Hezekiah's engineers worked towards each other from either end; a process described in the so-called **Siloam Inscription** found mounted on the wall at the south end of the tunnel. This contemporary account, written in Hebrew, is now in the Istanbul Museum, though the Israel Museum in Jerusalem has a copy.

It's possible to walk along the entire length of the pitch-black tunnel, emerging at the 'Byzantine Pool of Siloam' after about half an hour. For the most part the water is about 50 cm deep, though it is deeper (about 70 cm) for a short while at the beginning of the tunnel. You will be walking in this water so some form of flip-flop is recommended, as well as light-weight trousers/skirt that will dry easily. Bringing a torch is essential, especially if you are entering independently rather than with a guided tour. It is impossible to get lost, though women should probably not attempt this walk unaccompanied. Do not attempt the tunnel walk if you are any way claustrophobic, and bear in mind that it is a very cold walk in winter.

Two flights of steps, probably medieval, lead down to the tunnel. About 20 m into the tunnel it takes a sharp turn to the left. The chest-high wall here blocks a channel that leads to Warren's Shaft. The point where the two groups of miners met is clearly visible, though the group working from the south had to lower the level of the floor because they had started too high. The tunnel eventually emerges into the Byzantine Pool of Siloam, which was until very recently believed to be 'the' Shiloah/Siloam Pool (see below) at which Jesus performed the miracle of curing the bind man (*John 9:1-12*; one of only two miracles he performed in Jerusalem, the other being at the Bethesda Pools). By the mid-fifth century CE this pool had become firmly linked with Jesus' miracle, and the Empress Eudocia had the pool rebuilt with the Church of Siloam constructed above it. Sections of pillars from the Byzantine building can be seen submerged in the water. The church stood to the north, with an aisle that overhung the end of the pool, with the Piacenza pilgrim (c. 570 CE) describing the church as a "hanging basilica". All that remains to be seen today is a narrow stone-lined pit (c. 18 m by 5 m) occupying a fraction of the Byzantine pool, with Hezekiah's Tunnel entering from the north. The church was destroyed by the Persians in 614 CE, the whole area being left in a state of desolation and villagers from Silwan occasionally shifting the accumulated debris so that they could draw water. The mosque was built in the late 19th century CE.

From the Byzantine Pool of Siloam, the route passes a Second Temple Period 'stepped street' (and the main sewer running beneath it) which leads up to the Temple Mount. Note that every two steps are followed by a platform area, giving some breathing space for the people climbing up to the Temple.

Only discovered in 2004, the true **Shiloah (Siloam) Pool** now contains an orchard owned by the village of Silwan and is fenced off. What you see here is the eastern edge of the pool where large stone steps lead down to the square area of the pool itself. Long before its association with Jesus' miracle, the Shiloah pool was used by Jews for ritual purification ceremonies, particularly around the Feast of Tabernacles when water from the pool was carried up to the Temple in a gold ewer. It is hoped that eventually the pool will be excavated in its entirety.

From the Siloam Pool, there is a choice from three routes back to the top of the slope. You can take a seat in one of the minibuses waiting on the road for 5NIS. Alternatively, on exiting the pool area, turn left to walk up the fairly steep path through the Arab village of Silwan, passing a couple of sites of minor interest on the way (detailed below). Or you can walk through the underground stepped street to emerge on Ma'alot Ir David street (from where an escort will accompany you back to the site entrance).

If you continue south from here you would eventually come to the Monastery of St Onuphrius (Aceldama) in the Valley of Hinnom (see below).

The Weill Excavations (Tombs of the House of David) On the lower slopes of the Southeast Ridge is a large area that has been substantially, but inconclusively, excavated. The area has undoubtedly been worked as a quarry, probably some time between the second century BCE and second century CE (though experts can't agree), but there are also some far older shafts cut into the bedrock that are suggested as the Tombs of the Israelite kings.

As discussed in the description of the so-called Tomb of David on the Mount Zion tour, all the written evidence suggests that David and his sons and successors were buried within the walls of his city (I Kings 2:10). Weill, who excavated this area in 1913-14, proposed that the two 'tombs' located here belonged to David and his family members. The most impressive one is entered by a deep shaft leading to a vaulted tunnel 16.5 m long and 4 m high. A stone bench with a niche may have been intended for a coffin. In addition to the area being used as a quarry, the 'tombs' had been looted in antiquity, which fits in neatly with Josephus' observation that Hyrcanus took 3000 talents from the Tomb of David to finance his mercenary army and pay off Antiochus VII Sidetes in the early second century BCE (The Jewish War, I, 61). The jury is still out on this one.

Ancient walls Sections of the **Middle Bronze Age city wall** (18th century BCE) can be seen on the above-ground route back to the site entrance. The ancient wall is distinguishable by the massive blocks of roughly cut masonry, overlain by sections of the **eighth century BCE city walls**, preserved in places to a height of 3m.

Beyond here is the Tyropoeon Valley, which defines the western limits of the ridge upon which the City of David stood. In antiquity it was a considerably deeper ravine, extending as far north as the present location of Damascus Gate, though centuries of building, destruction and rebuilding have filled it in somewhat. The name translates as

Cheesemakers' Valley, though the origins are unclear. It may have been the inspiration for the "Blessed are the Cheesemakers" line in Monty Python's Life of Brian, though as the Samaritan observes, "it's not supposed to be taken literally, and obviously refers to any manufacturer of dairy products".

Valley of Hinnom

The Valley of Hinnom begins to the northwest of the Old City, in the vicinity of the Mamilla Pool in Independence Park. It sweeps down in a gently curving northwest to southeast arc, defining the western boundary of the Old City, before turning east to join up with the Tyropneon and Kidron Valleys at a point to the south of the Old City (see topographical map of Jerusalem, page 60).

Much of the west side of the Valley of Hinnom is now occupied by the New City, so the various places there are included within the description of the 'New City, Southwestern suburbs' (see page 132). Described below are the points of interest on the east side of the valley, notably the Sultan's Pool and the Monastery of St Onuphrius (Aceldama).

Ins and outs
Getting there and around To reach the sights described here on the east side of the Valley of Hinnom, exit Jaffa Gate and head south along the busy Hativat Yerushalayim. Just before the junction where Hativat Yerushalayim swings east (left) in a loop around Mount Zion, and the Hebron Road heads southwest (right), to the right of the road is the Sultan's Pool. Take the smaller road straight ahead to reach the Greek monastery on the site of Aceldama (600 m).

Background
The Valley of Hinnom has traditionally marked the boundary between the tribes of Benjamin and Judah (*Joshua 15:8, 18:16*), and was often the site of cultic places for the worship of non-Israelite gods (*II Kings 23:10; Jeremiah 32:35*). This is probably the reason why the valley became associated with the 'Valley of Slaughter' on the 'Day of Vengeance' that Jeremiah describes so vividly: "And the carcases of this people shall be meat for the fowls of the heaven, and for the beasts of the earth; and none shall fray them away" (*Jeremiah 7:32-33*). This tradition evolved into the Jewish concept of the 'hell of fire', or Gehenna (the latter word being the Greek and Latin form of 'Hinnom Valley'). The valley was used as a burial place in Roman and Byzantine times, notably at the southern end, and from this developed the tradition of Aceldama (see below). The 20th century CE has seen the construction of much of the 'New City' of Jerusalem on the west side of the valley.

Sights
Sultan's Pool The 'Sultan's Pool' (Arabic: *Birkat al-Sultan*) takes its name from Sulaiman II ('the Magnificent') who restored much of Jerusalem in the 16th century CE, including the present city walls and this pool. However, the origins of the pool here are much older, perhaps being part of the Herodian low-level aqueduct system that brought water to the city from 'Solomon's Pools' close to Bethlehem. The pool here was known to the Crusaders as the 'Germain's Pool', and was also restored by al-Nasir Mohammad in the 13th century CE. Despite Sulaiman II's restoration work, it soon fell into disrepair and by the 19th century it was generally referred to as just a muddy pool. It has now been filled in, and contains the Merrill Hasenfield Amphitheatre as the centrepiece to a large public park. This is one of Jerusalem's most atmospheric venues for live music, and tends to be the place where

major international acts perform. Check listings in the *Jerusalem Post* and *Hello Israel*, which can be found in Ramparts Walk ticket office.

Monastery of St Onuphrius (Aceldama) ① *Flexible hours. Free, though donations expected.* St Onuphrius was a Byzantine-period Egyptian hermit whose claim to fame was the length of his beard, worn long to hide his nakedness! This site became associated with a number of traditions in the Byzantine period (and revived by the Crusaders), most notably as the Aceldama or 'Field of Blood' that the high priests bought as a burial place for foreigners with the 30 pieces of silver with which Judas betrayed Jesus. 'Field of Sleeping' is a more accurate translation of the Aramaic, and thus the site is also claimed as the traditional place where Judas hung himself. The monastery features a small cave (now used as a chapel) that a 16th-century CE tradition claimed as the place where eight of the apostles hid during the Crucifixion. The cave is part of a series of first-century BCE to first-century CE rock-cut Jewish tombs that are to be found in the vicinity. Two distinct burial complexes close to the monastery are associated with Aceldama, one belonging to the Western Church and one belonging to the Eastern Church. Also nearby is the medieval charnel house built by the Order of the Knights of the Hospital of St John for the burial of pilgrims.

East Jerusalem

To Palestinians, the term 'East Jerusalem' refers to the whole of the walled Old City, the districts just to the north such as Sheikh Jarrah, and those to the east and southeast including the Mount of Olives, Kidron Valley, Silwan, Tyropneon Valley and Mount Zion. These various districts would be the desired capital of a Palestinian state. For most tourists and visitors to Jerusalem (and for the purposes of this book), 'East Jerusalem' is considered to be the area of the city just to the north of Damascus Gate.

Ins and outs
Getting there and around Buses 6 and 1 from the Central Bus Station go to Damascus Gate at the heart of East Jerusalem, whilst minibuses for Ramallah, Bethlehem and destinations in East Jerusalem go from/to the two bus stations near Damascus Gate. Most visitors to the various sites in East Jerusalem arrive from the Old City via Damascus Gate.

Sights
Pontifical Institute Notre Dame of Jerusalem Centre ① *102-6279111, notredamecenter.org, daily 0930–1230 and 1430–1830.* Founded as a centre for pilgrims by the Augustinian Fathers of the Assumption in 1887, this imposing building is very much a statement about 19th-century Catholic France. It was built with subscriptions raised in every parish in France so that the French presence in the Holy City "would no longer be a nomad camped under a tent ... but ensconced in her own palace, equal to her rivals" (quoted in Collins and Lapierre, *O Jerusalem*, 1972).

The building's solid granite walls and defensive capabilities meant that it was immediately pressed into service during the battle for Jerusalem in 1948; in fact it was to play a pivotal role. As former President of Israel Chaim Herzog observes, "a few hundred yards from the centre of the Jewish city in Jerusalem, the Arab Legion was halted. The Jewish city had been saved by the stubborn struggle of the defenders of Notre Dame" (*The Arab-Israeli Wars*, 1982).

The considerable damage inflicted in 1948 was eventually repaired and Notre Dame now functions again as a very pleasant pilgrim hostel, despite having had to shut for 6 months during the second intifada. Since 2006, it has housed a permanent exhibition on the Holy

East Jerusalem & northern suburbs

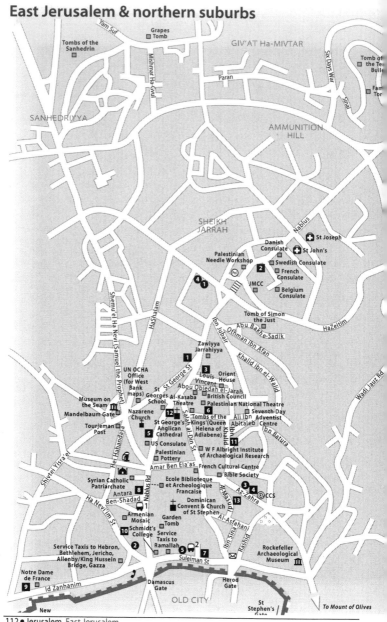

Tombs of the Sanhedrin

Yam Suf

Mishmar Ha-Gvul

Grapes Tomb

GIV'AT Ha-MIVTAR

Paran

Six Days War

Tomb of the Ten Buil

Fam Tor

Sinai

SANHEDRIYYA

AMMUNITION HILL

SHEIKH JARRAH

Nablus

St Joseph

Danish Consulate

St John's

Palestinian Needle Workshop

Swedish Consulate

French Consulate

JMCC

Belgium Consulate

Ha Zeitim

Tomb of Simon the Just

Abu Bakhe Sadik

Othman Ibn Afan

Khalid Ibn el-Walid

Shemu'el Ha Nevi (Samuel the Prophet)

Ha Shalom

Zawiyya Jarrahiyya

Ibn Jubair

St George St

Louis Vincent

Abou Obiedah el-Jarah

Orient House

British Council

UN OCHA Office (for West Bank maps)

Georges School

Al-Kasaba Theatre

Palestinian National Theatre

Museum on the Seam

Mandelbaum Gate

Nazarene Church

St George's Anglican Cathedral

Tombs of the Kings'(Queen Helena of Adiabene)

Seventh Day Adventist Centre

Ali Ibn Abitaleb

Ibn Batura

Wadi Jauz Rd

Tourjeman Post

US Consulate

Palestinian Pottery

W F Albright Institute of Archaeological Research

Salah al-Din St

Amar Ben Ela'as

French Cultural Centre

Bible Society

Shvtei Yisra'el

Syrian Catholic Patriarchate

Antara

Ben-Shadad

Ecole Biblioteque et Archeologique Francaise

Az Zahra

CCS

Al Masud

Dominican Convent & Church of St Stephen

Armenian Mosaic

Garden Tomb

Schmidt's College

Al-Asfahani

Ha Nevi'im St

Nablus Rd

Service Taxis to Hebron, Bethlehem, Jericho, Allenby/King Hussein Bridge, Gazza

Service Taxis to Ramallah

Suleiman St

Rashid

Ibn Sina

Rockefeller Archaeological Museum

Notre Dame de France

Id Zanhaim

Damascus Gate

Herod Gate

New

OLD CITY

St Stephen's Gate

To Mount of Olives

Shroud of Turin. The 5-m-high statue of the Virgin Mary presenting her child to Jerusalem remains the building's crowning glory.

Schmidt's College This large building opposite Damascus Gate (on the corner of Nablus Road) was built as the German Catholic Hospice and College in 1886, though it later served as the temporary headquarters of the British administration following General Allenby's capture of the city in 1917, and later as the HQ of the Royal Air Force.

Rockefeller Museum ① *Sultan Suleiman, T02-6282251, www.imj.org.il. Sun, Mon, Wed and Thu 1000-1500, Sat 1000-1400. Free. Toilets; small bookshop. Guided tours on Mon and Wed, shuttle bus leaves from Israel Museum at 1100 (as part of entrance fee to Israel Museum, call to ask about English). No photos.* This magnificent limestone building (constructed 1927-1929) was built using funds from J.D. Rockefeller to house the antiquities of Palestine that had been gathered together by the Department of Antiquities of the Mandate Government. Built in neo-Gothic style, the architect incorporated aspects of local Byzantine and Islamic design, most notably the peaceful garden courtyard at the heart of the building. The exhibits are superb, though the presentation has changed little since the museum opened, and there is no sense of the dynamism that is a feature of most museums in Israel – consequently it is often mercifully peaceful. The exhibits are presented in chronological order, starting in the south octagon and following a clockwise route. Notable features include the eighth-century CE wooden panels from al-Aqsa Mosque; stucco work and other decorative fragments from Hisham's Palace in Jericho; and the 12th-century CE marble lintels from the Church of the Holy Sepulchre.

Garden Tomb ① *T02-6272745, Mon-Sat 0900-1200 and 1400-1730 (busiest on Sat). Admission and guided tours free (mainly*

N

| 200 metres |
| 200 yards |

■ **Sleeping**
2 Ambassador
3 American Colony
4 Az-Zahra
6 Christmas
7 Golden Walls
8 Jerusalem
5 Legacy (YMCA East) & Cardo Restaurant
9 Notre Dame de France Guesthouse & La Rotisserie Restaurant
1 Olive Tree & Arabesque Restaurant
10 Palm
14 Regency Jerusalem
11 Ritz
12 St George's Cathedral Pilgrim's Guesthouse
13 Victoria

🍴 **Eating & drinking**
1 Askadinya
5 Eiffel Sweets
2 Hummus & fuul places
4 Pasha's & Borderline
3 Philadelphia & Hong Kong House

🚌 **Buses**
1 Nablus Rd Bus Station
2 Suleiman St Arab Bus Station

English, but also in Arabic, Dutch, French, German, Hebrew). Toilets; souvenir shop. The Garden Tomb is proposed as an alternative site for the crucifixion and resurrection of Jesus Christ, and many visitors prefer its landscaped and ordered efficiency to the mayhem of the Holy Sepulchre. There is indeed a very pleasant garden (*John 19:41*), and a tomb cut in the rock-face (*Matthew 27:60*; *Mark 14:46*; *Luke 23:53*; *John 19:41*), complete with what appears to be a groove for a rolling stone (*Matthew 27:60*; *Mark 15:46*; *Luke 24:2*), and from the vantage point overlooking the Sulaiman Street Arab bus station, the cliff-face does appear to resemble a skull (*Matthew 27:33*; *Mark 15:22*; *John 19:16*). Yet this is where imagination must be tempered with the hard facts of reality. Notwithstanding the convincing evidence that suggests that the Church of the Holy Sepulchre does in fact stand upon the site of Christ's crucifixion, the archaeological evidence supporting the claim of the Garden Tomb is conspicuous by its absence. The tomb chamber features none of the characteristics of a first-century CE burial place, such as *arcosolia* (rock-cut troughs or burial benches beneath an arched opening), with the configuration of the tombs that you see today characteristic of the ninth-sixth centuries BCE. Thus, it cannot have been the "new" or "unfinished" tomb that the gospels describe. There is also evidence to suggest that the body benches here were cut back significantly in the Byzantine period, and this would have been highly unlikely if the early Christians had considered this to be the tomb of Jesus. Further modifications were also made by the Crusaders, when the site was used as a stable!

Though the rock-face above the Sulaiman Street Arab bus station had already been identified as a possible Golgotha (Thenius 1842; Fisher Howe 1871; Conder 1878), it was the "feverish mind" of **General Charles George Gordon** ('of Khartoum') who popularized the Garden Tomb as Christ's sepulchre. As Amos Elon points out, it was not the form of the cliff face that so convinced Gordon this was the 'place of the skull', but rather the 1864 British Military Ordnance Map of Jerusalem! Apparently, the contour line marking 2549 feet makes a perfect "death's-head, complete with eye-sockets, crushed nose and gaping mouth" (Amos Elon, *Jerusalem: City of Mirrors*, 1989)!

Cynics would argue that the speed with which the Anglican Church rushed to endorse Gordon's identification had more to do with the absence of any Protestant-owned 'holy sites' within the city than with actual belief in his claims. The Garden Tomb is now administered by the (British) Garden Tomb Association, and not only provides a pleasant place for prayer or contemplation, it also acts as a valuable visual aid in recreating an image of the Crucifixion.

Dominican Convent and Church of St Stephen ① *T02-6264468. The Ecole has an excellent research library (Mon-Sat 0900-1145), and organizes a programme of lectures.*

The present Church of St Stephen (1900) is part of a complex founded some 10 years earlier as the first graduate school in the Holy Land dedicated to the study of the Bible and biblical archaeology: **Ecole Biblique et Archéologique Française de St Etienne.** The school, run by Dominican monks and financed in part by the French government, has been instrumental in deciphering the Dead Sea Scrolls.

The first church on this site was built c. 455-460 by the Empress Eudocia to house the shrine for the bones of St Stephen, the first Christian martyr (*Acts 6:5* to *8:1*), whilst the empress herself was later buried here. The sixth-century CE monastery built here was destroyed by the Persians in 614 CE and, though a small chapel was built here soon after, it was the Crusaders who substantially redeveloped the site. The Knights Hospitallers restored the chapel in the 12th century CE, though the whole complex, including large stables, was pulled down in 1187 so as not to provide the advancing Salah al-Din with a strategically placed stronghold. The stables were redeveloped in 1192 as a hospice to house pilgrims, since the Ayyubids forbade Christians from lodging within the city walls. It was at this time that the name 'St Stephen's Gate' (more commonly called Lions' Gate) was shifted from its original position (the present 'Damascus Gate') to its present one at the northeast gate in the walls. Excavations within the walls of the Dominicans' property have revealed the plan of the **Byzantine church** (upon which the present church is built, and incorporating some of the original mosaics), some of the **Hospitallers' stables**, the **Byzantine and medieval chapel**, and a **Byzantine tomb complex**. It is suggested that the presence of the many reused columns found here is the reason why Sulaiman II chose the title *Bab al-'Amud* ('Gate of the Column') for the entrance now referred to as Damascus Gate. He notes that Ottoman-period gates invariably took their name from something outside them, and thus the association with the column of Hadrian's Roman paved square *inside* Damascus Gate may be erroneous.

Armenian Mosaic ⓘ *The mosaic is not easy to find, and the building is rarely open (officially daily 0700-1700, but don't rely on this). On HaNevi'im Street, just south of the (closed) Ramsis Hostel, is a small cul-de-sac behind rusted iron gates. The entrance is behind the grill on the left.* Of outstanding workmanship, the mosaic (measuring 6.3 m by 3.9 m) was discovered in 1894 during the digging of the foundations of a new house. Its decorative style has led to a sixth-century CE dating, though the exact year that it was laid is not certain. An Armenian inscription reading "To the memory and for the salvation of all the Armenians the names of whom the Lord knoweth", together with the discovery of several burial caves in the vicinity, have led to the assumption that this was a Byzantine mortuary chapel (though it has been identified by some as the Church of St Polyeucht). The multi-coloured tesserae feature a number of birds, including peacocks (drinking the elixir of life, and thus symbolizing life after death), ducks, storks, pigeons, fowl, an eagle (symbolizing evil), and a caged bird representing an interpretation of the relationship between the body and the soul.

Mandelbaum Gate and Tourjeman Post The huge swathe of 'empty' land on either side of Shivtei Isra'el Street and Shemu'el HaNevi Street was the no-man's land between the Israelis and Jordanians in the years that control of the city was divided (1948-1967). The only crossing point between the two spheres of influence was the UN-supervised spot that became known as the Mandelbaum Gate: the crossroads were marked not by a gate, but by a house belonging to a wealthy businessman – Mandelbaum. The house (marked by a plaque) is located at the meeting point of the following roads: Shivtei Israel, Samuel the Prophet (Shmuel HaNevi), Hel Hahandasa (Engineer Corps) and St George.

Just across the road is the Tourjeman Post. Formerly a small museum offering a Zionist perspective on the years 1948-1967, it is now the **Museum on the Seam** ⓘ *4 Chel Hahandasa, T02-6281278, www.mots.org.il, Sun-Thu 1000-1700, Tue 1000-2100, Fri 1000-1400, adult 25NIS, student 15NIS*, a "socio-political contemporary art museum" which has excellent changing exhibitions by international and local artists. The bullet-holed and battle-scarred building has been left as it is.

St George's Anglican Cathedral ⓘ *No set opening hours, free.* Built in 1898, this beautifully maintained church now acts as the cathedral of the Anglican Episcopal Diocese of Jerusalem and the Middle East. There are many British links to the past, including a font donated by Queen Victoria and a tower dedicated to the memory of Edward VII, though the years 1910-17 saw the complex occupied by the Ottoman army's High Command. Following General Allenby's capture of the city on 9 December 1917, the instrument of Turkish surrender was signed in the bishop's study here. Within the complex is a highly recommended guesthouse, see page 139.

'Tombs of the Kings' ⓘ *Closed at the time of writing, with no date set to reopen*. The so-called 'Tombs of the Kings', the most magnificent Roman period tomb in Jerusalem, has been labouring under a misnomer for over a century now. Although mentioned in several ancient sources including Josephus (*Jewish War V, 147; Antiquities XX: 17-96*), and well known to travellers from the 16th century CE onwards, the tomb was excavated in 1863 by de Saulcy, who was so struck by the magnificence of the monument that he identified it as the Tombs of the Kings of Judah, hence the popular name. The tomb was in fact cut c. 50 CE and belongs to **Queen Helena**, the dowager queen of Adiabene in northern Mesopotamia (now in northeast Iraq), a town with a sizeable Jewish merchant community who had converted the royal family to Judaism. Some time between 44 and 48 CE the dowager came on a pilgrimage to Jerusalem, her visit coinciding with the great famine that struck the city. Helena immediately threw herself into a one-woman famine relief programme, procuring food from such far-away places as Egypt and Cyprus. She died in Adiabene c. 65 CE, but her body (along with that of her sone Izates) was sent to Jerusalem for burial. The tomb is closed to the public at present, but bring a flashlight in case this situation has changed.

American Colony Hotel The 'American Colony' was one of several new suburbs of Jerusalem established outside the old walled city at the end of the 19th century. Its founding members were the American lawyer and church leader Horatio Spafford and his Norwegian wife Anna, whose religious consciousness had been raised in a tragic shipwreck in 1874 in which their four young children were drowned. In 1881, with a group of friends, the Spaffords settled in the Holy Land, occupying a large house in the Old City between Damascus Gate and Herod Gate and devoting their lives to charitable work amongst Jerusalem's poor.

Fifteen years later they were joined by a large group from the Swedish Evangelical Church, the story of their journey being fictionalized and told in Selma Lagerlof's Nobel-prize-winning *Jerusalem*. The large influx of new settlers required more space, and so the group rented (and later bought) a large mansion built outside the walled city by a rich Arab landowner, Rabbah Daoud Amin Effendi el Husseini. The community soon expanded further, requiring adjacent properties also to be rented, and in a very short space of time the whole area was being referred to as the American Colony.

In the opening years of the 20th century, the foundations of the subsequent American Colony Hotel were laid when Baron Ustinov (grandfather of Peter Ustinov) made an arrangement to lodge visiting pilgrims there. The main function of the building, however, continued to be charitable, with hospital and clinic facilities being run through the Turkish occupation, World Wars I and II, the Israeli-Arab war of 1948 and subsequent Jordanian occupation, and the Six Day War of 1967. It was not until the Colony became a de facto part of Israel that the hospital facilities were deemed no longer necessary, and the building became upgraded to form the *American Colony Hotel*. This remains one of Jerusalem's most prestigious addresses, having played host over the years to (in alphabetical order): General Allenby, Lauren Bacall, Joan Baez, Gertrude Bell, Saul Bellow, Carl Bernstein, John Betjeman, John Le Carré, Marc Chagall, Graham Greene, Alec Guinness, Gayle Hunnicutt, T.E. Lawrence, Malcolm Muggeridge, Peter O'Toole, Dominique LaPierre, Donald Pleasance, John Simpson, Leon Uris, Peter Ustinov and Richard Widmark. The hotel is a favourite haunt of journalists and Palestinian officials.

Nearby, along Abu Obiedah ibn el-Jarrah Street, is **Orient House**, which used to be the *de facto* headquarters in Jerusalem of the PLO. It was forcibly closed by the Israeli authorities in August 2001 during the second intifada, but has recently been put to use again by the World Health Organization Office for the Palestinian Territories. Just to the north of the American Colony Hotel, on Nablus Road, is the **Zawiyya Jarrahiyya**, or tomb of

Amir Husam al-Din al-Jarrahi (died c. 1201, an early 13th-century CE holy man). The shrine is meant to bring good fortune to those who pray here (with special good luck available to those involved in raising chickens and egg production!). The mosque was added in 1895.

Tomb of Simon the Just Jewish tradition relates that this is the tomb of Simon the Just (Hebrew: *Shimon Hatsadik*), a High Priest at the Temple in the fourth century BCE who was renowned for his piety. The rock-cut tomb undoubtedly dates to the Middle to Late Roman period, with a Roman inscription mentioning a Roman woman by the name of Julia Sabina, and is certainly not that of Simon. Nevertheless, the tomb remains a place of Jewish pilgrimage, particularly popular amongst Sephardi (Oriental) Jews. To reach the tomb head north along the Nablus Road past the American Colony Hotel. Where the road dips before the hill up to Sheikh Jarrah, take the road to the right (east). Take the left fork and then the next left fork, and the tomb is on the left. Head coverings must be worn. There is little to see here, however, apart from the surprising sight of Orthodox Judaism in the midst of a Palestinian neighbourhood.

Northern suburbs

There are several points of interest in the Northern suburbs of Jerusalem, to the immediate north of the area covered in the 'East Jerusalem' section. The location of the various places of interest here can be found on the 'East Jerusalem and northern suburbs' map (see page 112).

Sights
Ammunition Hill To the north of the American Colony Hotel is the suburb of Sheikh Jarrah. Taking its name from the small Arab village established here at the end of the 19th century CE, the district is now home to a number of administrative buildings and foreign embassies. It is Sheikh Jarrah where demolitions (and the threat of demolition) of Palestinian houses are proving a consistent obstacle to peace (for more information see Israeli Committee Against House Demolitions, www.icahd.org). The low hill to the north, between Sheikh Jarrah and the newer Jewish suburbs of Sanhedriyya and Giv'at Ha-Mivtar, is Ammunition Hill.

During the period 1948-1967, when most of East Jerusalem (including the Old City) was controlled by Jordan, this low hill not only controlled the road leading to the Israeli enclave on Mount Scopus, but also the road between Ramallah and the Old City. The Jordanians, recognizing the strategic importance of the hill as well as remembering the fierce battles that had taken place in 1948, had heavily fortified what had come to be known as 'Ammunition Hill'. The night of 5/6 June 1967, saw Israeli paratroopers take the hill in a particularly bloody and hard-fought battle. The hill is now a war memorial to the 183 Israeli dead, and features an **underground museum** ① T02-5828442. *Sun-Thu 0900-1800 (winter -1700), Fri 0900-1300, entrance free, buses 4, 8 or 28 to bottom of hill. Wheelchair access.* This is basically the Jordanian command bunker, with an auditorium (screening a number of films that explain the Israeli version of history), an outdoor museum (tanks, pillboxes, trenches) that explains the battle for Ammunition Hill, plus picnic gardens.

Giv'at Ha-Mivtar To the north of Ammunition Hill is the Jewish suburb of Giv'at Ha-Mivtar. A couple of minor tombs – **Tomb of Simon the Temple Builder** and **The Family Tomb** – are hidden within this residential district. This suburb has also revealed the world's only archaeological evidence of crucifixion. Despite the fact that thousands were crucified by the Romans, archaeological evidence for this form of execution was completely lacking until

Yehohanan ben Hagkol ('The Crucified Man from Giv'at Ha-Mivtar') was excavated here in 1968. Nothing is known about him except his name and the fact that he died some time between 7 and 70 CE, with the iron nail driven through his heel bone confirming how he died. A replica is displayed in the Israel Museum (the real bones having been given a Jewish burial).

Tombs of the Sanhedrin (The Judges) A small park in Jerusalem's northern suburb of Sanhedriyya contains a number of tombs characteristic in style and workmanship of Jewish tombs from the first century CE. Because the number of burials is approximate to the 70 judges of the Sanhedrin who met in the Temple and monitored and maintained Jewish religious law, the site became known as the Tombs of the Sanhedrin. There are in fact 55 kokhim (roughly oven-shaped rock-cut burial places), four arcosolia (rock-cut bench burials beneath arched openings) and two cave/ossuaries (secondary burial containers), though there is nothing to suggest that the tombs have any connection with the Sanhedrin; in fact, they appear to be standard family burial places.

The most notable of the tombs in this quiet fir-strewn park are tomb 14 towards the northwest corner and tomb 8 to the east. The former has an intricately carved pediment.

The so-called 'Grapes Tomb' is part of the same tombs complex, though located outside the park some 200 m to the east. At a point along Red Sea (Yam Suf) Road, opposite Mishmar Ha-Guvl Street, take the steps down between apartment blocks 8 and 10 (sign-posted 'Doris Weiler Garden'). At the bottom of the steps is another first-century CE Jewish burial cave, comprising a porch, central chamber, three rooms with *loculi* and one chamber with arcosolia. The pediment above the entrance is decorated with vine tendrils and bunches of grapes (hence the name). An interest in first-century CE Jewish tombs would have to be your reason for coming here (bus 39 from the city).

Mount Scopus

Mount Scopus is a low hill (903 m) to the northeast of the Old City, part of the soft sandstone ridge of which the Mount of Olives is also a part. It is a strategic highpoint overlooking the city (the name deriving from the Greek skopus, meaning 'look out'), and the list of generals and armies that have camped out on this high ground is long and impressive. The Roman general Cestius camped here in 66 CE during the early stages of the Jewish Revolt (Josephus, *Jewish War II*, 528), though he was subsequently forced to beat a hasty and costly retreat. Titus was more successful four years later, launching his attack on the city from this vantage point (*Jewish War*, V, 67). The Crusaders also camped here in 1099, whilst more recent conquerors have included the British in 1917 and Moshe Dayan's Israeli forces in 1967. The 20th century saw a number of institutions established on Mount Scopus.

Ins and outs
Getting there and away Egged Buses 23 and 28 run to Mount Scopus, plus Bus 82 from the Nablus Road Bus Station.

Sights
Hebrew University Though proposals for a modern Jewish university in Jerusalem had existed since the end of the 19th century, and land for this purpose had been bought on Mount Scopus in 1913, it was not until 1925 that the university was formerly opened. Though the Hebrew University set itself the task of resurrecting Hebrew culture, it was also charged with, in the words of its first president, Dr Judah Magnes, "reconciling Arab and

Jew, East and West". Its success as a centre of learning is unquestioned, though whether it has fulfilled the latter requirement is a point of contention. In the late 2000s, around 10% of its students were Arab, with virtually all of these being 'Israeli Arabs' drawn from Galilee.

From 1948, the university spent 20 years isolated from the rest of Jerusalem: a pocket under Israeli control at the centre of the Jordanian-held West Bank. The new campus was subsequently established in the suburb of Giv'at Ram, on Jerusalem's western side. Following the Israeli victory in the Six Day War of 1967, the campus on Mount Scopus not only reopened, but also expanded significantly, with many new faculties being added.

Tombs on Mount Scopus Excavations on Mount Scopus have revealed a number of tomb complexes, several of which can be found within the recently 'renovated' Botanical Gardens of the Hebrew University.

The **Five Tombs complex** dates to the first century CE, and forms part of the vast Jewish necropolis that spread across this hill. The tombs are in fact separate entities, though overcrowding on the necropolis meant that they were so close together, the *kokhim* actually interconnected.

Dating to the same period is the **Tomb of Nicanor**, located approximately 50 m to the southeast. A Greek inscription on one of several decorated ossuaries that were found when the cave was excavated in 1902 mentions "the sons of Nicanor of Alexandria" (who is said to have donated one of the gates of the Temple). The burial cave is one of the largest of the period in Jerusalem, and features a 17-m-long façade entered through a pillared porch. The burial catacomb is complex, featuring four burial chambers containing loculi on several levels.

The **Tomb of a Nazirite Family** was discovered in 1967 during the extension of the university, and was subsequently dismantled and moved to its present position on the southeast side of the Botanical Gardens. The tomb comprises a central chamber roofed with a barrel vault, with three side chambers branching off. No burial installations are cut in the tomb, though two sarcophagi and fourteen ossuaries were found. An inscription in Hebrew on one names "Hananiah son of Jehonathan the Nazirite", whilst another mentions "Salome wife of Hanahiah son of the Nazirite". Both are thought to date to the second half of the first century CE. Comparisons are often made between this tomb and the Tomb of Herod's Family near the King David Hotel in the New City (see page 143).

Brigham Young University ① *T02-6265666, http://ce.byu.edu/jc/. Buses 23 and 28*. Also know as the Jerusalem Centre of Near Eastern Studies, this Mormon university (whose establishment religious Jews opposed) is architecturally acclaimed, with gardens, terraces, alleyways and courtyards that can be explored on a tour (one hour, free, phone to book). The views are spectacular, and free concerts are held every Sunday at 2000 (recommended, book as far in advance as possible).

British World War I cemetery On the northwest slope of Mount Scopus is the British World War I cemetery, superbly maintained by the Commonwealth War Graves Commission.

Augusta Victoria Hospital On the south side of Mount Scopus, on the road to the Mount of Olives, is the **Augusta Victoria Hospital** ① *T02-6279911, daily 1200-1600*. Built in 1898 by Emperor Wilhelm II of Germany, and dedicated to his wife, the Empress Augusta Victoria, the most striking feature of the hospital and hospice complex is the 60-m-high tower. When open, it provides excellent views of the city and surrounding area.

New City

The area to the northwest, west and southwest of the walled Old City is variously described as the New City, or West Jerusalem. There are numerous places of interest within the New City; some very ancient and others post-dating the establishment of the State of Israel. The sites are fairly spread out, the information below attempts to broadly group the various places of interest by location.

City centre and area north of the Jaffa Road

Russian Compound

Though now containing the City Hall, police district headquarters, and law courts, the large area to the northwest of the Old City was previously owned by Imperial Russia, and is still referred to as the Russian Compound. The four-ha plot was bought with a grant from the Imperial Treasury following a visit to the Holy Land by the Grand Duke Constantine Nicholaevitch in 1859. Growing numbers of visiting Russian pilgrims through the course of the 19th century meant that the traditional hospices and monasteries within the Old City could no longer cope with the demand, and the Grand Duke's assessment was that new facilities needed to be provided. Of course, the construction of grand edifices such as the Cathedral of the Holy Trinity (consecrated in 1864) would also reflect Russia's sense of its standing in the world, and thus the building here was on a grand scale. Within 20 years the high-walled enclosure of the Russian Compound housed a cathedral, consulate, monastery, hospital and hospice capable of accommodating 2000 Russian pilgrims annually.

The mass flow of Russian pilgrims, generally poor peasants, continued, and in 1881 additional accommodation was provided by the 'Alexandrovsky Hospice' (see page 67). By the beginning of the 20th century, each Easter saw the arrival of up to 9000 Russian pilgrims, though events soon took a dramatic turn. The Russian Revolution saw the number of pilgrims slow to a trickle, and the buildings of the Russian Compound were taken over by the British Mandate administration who used them as a police headquarters and prison. This is the complex that became known to Jews fighting for an independent state as 'Bevingrad', after the British Foreign Secretary Ernest Bevin. The Israeli government purchased the estate in 1955, though its British function remains largely unchanged. Recent renovation has produced an 'open-plaza' feel to the public space (Safra Square), which has been planted with palm trees. To the north of the Russian Compound (on the north side of HaMalka Street and east side of Monbaz Street) are some of Jerusalem's trendiest bars.

The **Cathedral of the Holy Trinity** still stands at the heart of the Russian Compound, and is open to visitors. The grand Kremlin-style onion-shaped domes are executed far better on the Russian Orthodox Church of St Mary Magdalene (on the Mount of Olives).

An interesting feature near the church (by the police station) is the large **monolithic column** still lying in its quarry bed. Its size (12.15 m long, approximately 1.75 m in diameter) is comparable with the description of the columns in the Royal Portico of Herod the Great's Temple, and it is suggested that this is what it was intended for until the fault at one end was discovered.

The former British prison nearby now houses the **Underground Prisoners Museum** ① *T02-6233166, Sun-Thu 0900-1700, adult 15NIS student/child 10NIS*, dedicated to the memory of Jewish freedom-fighters (or terrorists, according to your viewpoint) from the British Mandate period.

New City: centre & area north of Jaffa Road

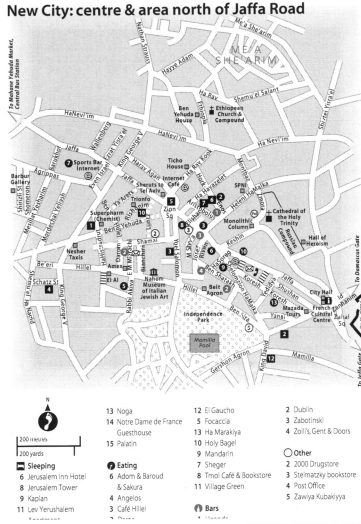

13 Noga	12 El Gaucho	2 Dublin
14 Notre Dame de France	5 Focaccia	3 Zabotinski
Guesthouse	13 Ha Marakiya	4 Zolli's, Gent & Doors
15 Palatin	10 Holy Bagel	
	9 Mandarin	○ **Other**
■ **Sleeping**	7 Sheger	2 2000 Drugstore
6 Jerusalem Inn Hotel	8 Tmol Café & Bookstore	3 Steimatzky bookstore
8 Jerusalem Tower	11 Village Green	4 Post Office
9 Kaplan		5 Zawiya Kubakiyya
11 Lev Yerushalem	● **Bars**	
~~Apartment~~	1 ~~Uganda~~	

🍴 Eating
6 Adom & Baroud
& Sakura
4 Angelos
3 Café Hillel

Me'a She'arim Quarter

To the north of the Russian Compound is the Me'a She'arim Quarter: Jerusalem's principal ultra-Orthodox Jewish neighbourhood. The name literally means 'hundred gates': a reference to the defensive architectural style of the quarter that sees the outer walls of the houses providing a continuous protective façade, with the '100 gates' leading to the main, and then private courts. These design practices provide not only privacy, but also defensive measures, considered essential when the quarter was built away from the walled Old City in 1874. The name is also a pun; an invocation of fruitfulness and plenty drawn from a line in the First Book of Moses, *Genesis*: "Then Isaac sowed in that land, and received in the same year an hundredfold: and the Lord blessed him" (*Genesis 26:12*).

Yet it is not just the architectural features that conjure to mind the *shtetl* (Jewish ghettoes) of pre-Holocaust Eastern Europe: it is the quarter's residents. The most visible attachment to the past is the appearance of the ultra-Orthodox men (in their black frock-coats, wide fur-brimmed hats, stockinged feet, and speaking Yiddish), who would appear to be more at home in a ghetto of 18th-century Poland or Lithuania than a 21st-century Mediterranean/Middle Eastern nation. Many of the more confrontational ultra-Orthodox groups who oppose the modern State of Israel, such as the radical Neturei Karta ('Guardians of the City', www.nkusa.org), have a popular base in Me'a She'arim and conduct their campaigns through the inflammatory posters that are present throughout the quarter. In fact, more than one observer has suggested were it not for the posters that hold the old stone blocks of the houses together, the whole quarter would have fallen down years ago!

Ticho House and Ethiopia Street

ⓘ *9 HaRav Kook Sreet, T02-6245068, imj.org.il, Sun, Mon, Wed and Thu 1000-1700, Tue 1000-2200, Fri 1000-1400, free.*

Most visitors now know Ticho House (Beit Ticho) for its superb restaurant, though this former home of prominent ophthalmologist Dr Abraham Ticho and his artist wife features a gallery showing some of Anna's beautiful work as well as high-quality temporary exhibitions. It is an excellent place for sitting and relaxing, especially on one of the nights when there are concerts accompanying dinner or brunch. After lunch, head to charming Ethiopia Street and visit the **Ethiopian Church** ⓘ *daily 0600-1300 and 1400-1700, free, leaves shoes by the door*, built between 1896 and 1904. Be aware that the inner sanctum is only for the priests.

Zion Square

The focus of the New City is Zion Square (Kikar Zion), although the construction of the Jerusalem light rail system and the seven-storey department store being built do tend to kill the atmosphere somewhat. However, the pedestrianized streets that radiate from Zion Square (Ben Yehuda, Yoel Salomon, Josef Rivlin, Dorot Rishonim and Mordechai Ben Hillel) are all lined with shops, cafés, restaurants, bars and nightclubs where young Jerusalemites and foreigners gather to shop, eat, drink and be seen. On Friday and Saturday afternoons, when the weather is fine, there's barely enough elbow space to hold your knife and fork, though early Friday and Saturday evenings see the whole area eerily deserted.

Mahane Yehuda and Nahalot

ⓘ *Sun-Wed and Thu -2000, Fri -1500.*

In the heart of the predominantly Sephardi Orthodox neighbourhood of Mahane Yehuda (about 1 km northwest of Zion Square) is a market that provides a fitting contrast to the 'civilized' shopping experience of Ben Yehuda Street: this is a true Middle Eastern market.

Visiting Me'a She'arim

There are a number of important things to bear in mind if you decide to visit Me'a She'arim. Quite naturally, the people who live in this quarter do not consider themselves to be a 'tourist attraction', and find nothing unusual in the way that they dress and conduct themselves; in fact, they consider themselves to be the norm.

Thus, visitors to Me'a She'arim should conduct themselves, and dress, in a modest manner. Men should wear long trousers, and preferably a long-sleeved shirt. Women must wear a long, loose-fitting skirt (even long trousers are unacceptable), a long-sleeved, loose-fitting shirt, and it may also be wise to cover hair (though shaving it off and wearing a wig is not necessary). Public shows of affection should be avoided.

Both male and female residents of the quarter dislike being photographed, so discretion, or better still abstinence, is recommended. Photography should be avoided on Shabbat (Sabbath) at all costs (and it's probably best not to visit on Shabbat either). Thursday evenings are, however, an interesting time to visit when the streets are packed and the restaurants pumping out traditional food.

The reaction to those who do not act or dress in an appropriate manner is unpredictable. Immodestly dressed women may find men crossing the road to avoid them, or being hissed at and called a 'whore', though spitting and stone-throwing are not unknown. Those who sneak photographs with long lenses risk expensive repair bills.

It is particularly exhilarating and crowded in the pre-Shabbat rush. Mahane Yehuda is on the edge of the attractive old streets and alleys of Nahalot, which are well worth a wander. You will find a few interesting little shops, pretty courtyards and squares, and the **Barbur Gallery** ① T077-7500619, www.barbur.org, Sun-Thu 1400-2000, Fri 1000-1400, also see page 150, which has some thought-provoking exhibitions. Information plaques on many of the buildings will inform you about the area's history as one of the first neighbourhoods built outside the Old City walls in the 19th century.

Museum of Italian Jewish Art
① 27 Hillel, T02-6241610, Sun-Thu 1000-1300, Wed 1600-1900, adult 5NIS.
The Museum of Italian Jewish Art is a collection of religious art and artefacts from Italy housed in the former 18th-century synagogue from Conegliano Veneto near Venice. At the end of World War II Conegliano Veneto no longer had a Jewish population, so in 1952 the interior of the town's synagogue was carefully dismantled and shipped to Israel. The polished wood benches, brass chandeliers and gold altar decorated with foliate designs are unusually ornate. A Shabbat service in Italian is still held here.

Artists House
① 12 Schmcul Hanagid, T02 6253653, www.art.org.il/www.schatz.co.il, Sun-Thu 1000-1300 and 1600-1900, Fri 1000-1300, Sat 1100-1400, free.
This beautiful period house, built in the Islamic style, was the home of the Bezalel school of art until 1990 (ask them to put on the short film showing the history of the building and its founders), and now hosts quality rotating exhibitions. There is also an appealing **restaurant** ① T02-6222283, Sun-Thu 1700-0200, Fri and Sat 1200-0200, which is quite a social hub, and excellent gallery/shop (closed Wednesday).

Western suburbs

The western suburbs of the New City, particularly Giv'at Ram, are home to most of Israel's public institutions, most notably the Parliament building (Knesset), Supreme Court, Prime Minister's Office and the newer campus of the Hebrew University. This large, green, open space also contains a number of places of interest, such as the Israel Museum, Bible Lands Museum, Monastery of the Holy Cross, and some of the city's more upmarket hotels. Allow a full day to explore all these sites (though the Israel Museum alone could probably justify a day in itself).

Ins and outs
Getting there and around There are buses direct to most of the buildings and museums, though many visitors with spare time on their hands choose to take a bus to the Central Bus Station, cross the road, then work their way north to south through the landscaped park. For orientation, refer to the 'New City (including Western suburbs, Western outskirts and Southwestern suburbs)' map on page 126.

Supreme Court
ⓘ *Qiryat Ben-Gurion, T02-6759612/3, marcia@supreme.court.gov.il, Sun-Thu 0830-1440, free guided tours in English at 1200, also guided tours for the blind (call to book). NB you must bring your passport.*
The **Israeli Supreme Court** opened within a new architectural masterpiece in 1992, after operating from a rented building in the Russian Compound for 44 years. Contrasting elements of light and dark, circles and planes, old and new materials all represent themes related to the city of Jerusalem or the system of justice. These are explained during the tour. Between the Supreme Court building and the Knesset to the south is the pleasant **Wohl Rose Park**, featuring many species of roses.

Knesset (Israel Parliament)
ⓘ *Off Ruppin, T02-6753538, www.knesset.gov.il. Guided tours in variety of languages Sun and Thu 0830-1430. Public gallery Mon-Tue 1600-2100, Wed 1100-1300. Enter from north side. NB you must bring your passport and be prepared for a thorough body/bag search. Buses 31 and 32a from Central Bus Station, Buses 9, 24 and 28 from Jaffa Road.*
The Israeli Parliament, or Knesset, stands at the centre of Sacher Park, to the south of the Israeli Supreme Court building. A modern, futuristic building (inaugurated in 1966), the rather austere exterior belies the lavishly decorated interior. Of particular interest are the tapestries and mosaics designed by Marc Chagall. The public gallery is open to visitors when the Knesset is in session and, though the debate is in Hebrew, the body language and decibel level translates into any tongue. Guided tours of the building are also available. The large bronze menorah opposite the entrance (to the north) was a gift from the British Parliament.

Israel Museum
ⓘ *Rehov Rupin, PO Box 71117, T02-6708811, www.imj.org.il. Sun, Mon, Wed and Thu 1000-1700, Tue 1600-2100; the Shrine of the Book Sun-Thu 1000-2200, Fri 1000-1400, Sat 1000-1700. Adult 36NIS, student 26NIS, child 18NIS, repeat visit within 3 months 18NIS, family 100NIS. Audio guides available. Shuttle bus on Mon and Wed at 1100 from Israel Museum to Rockefeller Museum for guided tour – must be reserved in advance. Buses 9, 17, 24, 31, 31 and 99 run from the city centre to the museum.*

The Israel Museum in Jerusalem has the country's foremost collection of antiquities and art, with the historical, archaeological and monetary value of many of the exhibits too vast to contemplate. At the time of writing, the museum complex was undergoing a 'campus renewal program' due to finish in summer 2010. Until then, all the permanent exhibitions are closed except for the Second Temple Model and the Shrine of the Book. Check the website for the latest situation, and to view the programme of lectures, films, concerts and temporary exhibits. When it reopens, visitors to Israel who intend exploring the country's major archaeological sites should either begin or end their journey here.

Model of Second Temple ① *Tours in English Sun, Mon, Wed and Thu at 1100. Audio guides available (also in Arabic, French, Russian, Spanish).* This 1:50 scale model re-creates Jerusalem at the end of the Second Temple period, as the First Jewish Revolt was beginning in 66 CE. It is an extremely useful tool for helping to visualize how the city would have appeared at this time, when it was twice as large as the present Old City.

Shrine of the Book ① *Free tours of the Shrine of the Book in English take place on Sun, Mon, Wed and Thu at 1300, Tue 1630, Fri and Sat 1100. Audio guides available (languages as above). No photography allowed inside.* A highlight of the Israel Museum complex, the Shrine of the Book houses part of the collection of manuscripts known as the **Dead Sea Scrolls**. The distinctive white-tiled roof of the building is designed to resemble the lid of one of the jars in which the scrolls were stored. A film detailing the story of the scrolls shows every hour in the complex adjacent to the shrine, and is recommended. For further details of the scrolls, see page 274.

The Shrine of the Book building is divided into three sections: the corridor, the main hall and the lower exhibition area. Displayed in the dark corridor are a number of remarkably well-preserved artefacts dating to the time of the Bar Kokhba Revolt (132-135 CE) that were retrieved from a cave in the Nahal Hever near Qumran. The centrepiece of the main hall is a huge facsimile of the Isaiah scroll, whilst in the wall cases are fragments from the **Habbakuk Commentary, War of the Sons of the Light and the Sons of Darkness**, and the **Community Rule**, amongst others. Some are originals whilst others are accurate copies. The lower exhibition hall currently contains the Aleppo Codex exhibition, the 10th-century manuscript that travelled to Egypt and Syria before returning to Israel in the 1950s.

Bible Lands Museum

① *25 Granot, opp Israel Museum, T02-5611066, www.blmj.org. Sun, Mon, Tue and Thu 0930-1730, Wed 0930-2130, Fri 0930-1400. Adult 32NIS, student 20NIS. English tours at 1030, additional on Wed 1730. Buses 9, 24 and 28.*
The Bible Lands Museum features one of the largest (and most valuable) private collections of antiquities from the Middle East. Presentation is excellent, with artefacts arranged chronologically from the time of hunter-gatherers until the Byzantine Era, encompassing wonderful ancient Egyptian, Iranian and Persian period pieces on the way. The museum also hosts a wide range of events, from cheese and wine evenings to workshops, courses and concerts. The changing exhibitions are of a similarly high standard, as is the gift shop (but the café is average). Look out for the events programme in hotels/tourist information centres.

Hebrew University To the west of the Israel Museum is the Giv'at Ram campus of the Hebrew University. When studies were suspended at the original Hebrew University on

New City: western suburbs, western outskirts, southwestern suburbs

Related maps

A Jerusalem Old City, page 32.
B East Jerusalem and northern suburbs, page 112.
C New City: centre and area north of Jaffa Road, page 121.

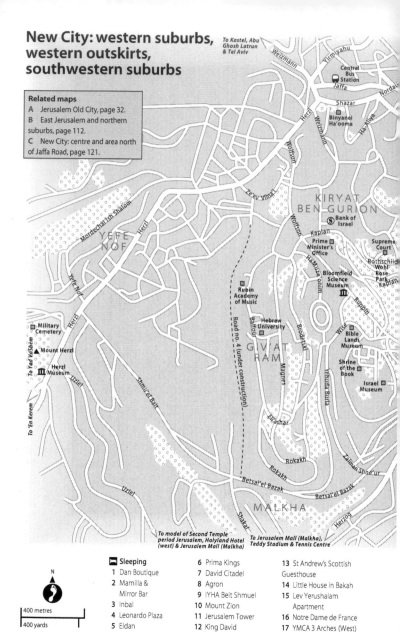

Sleeping
1 Dan Boutique
2 Mamilla & Mirror Bar
3 Inbal
4 Leonardo Plaza
5 Eldan
6 Prima Kings
7 David Citadel
8 Agron
9 IYHA Beit Shmuel
10 Mount Zion
11 Jerusalem Tower
12 King David
13 St Andrew's Scottish Guesthouse
14 Little House in Bakah
15 Lev Yerushalam Apartment
16 Notre Dame de France
17 YMCA 3 Arches (West)

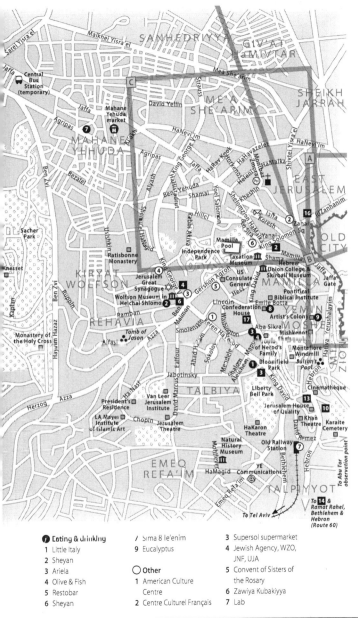

Eating & drinking
1 Little Italy
2 Sheyan
3 Ariela
4 Olive & Fish
5 Restobar
6 Sheyan

7 Sima 8 le'enim
9 Eucalyptus

○ **Other**
1 American Culture
  Centre
2 Centre Culturel Français
7 Lab

3 Supersol supermarket
4 Jewish Agency, WZO,
  JNF, UJA
5 Convent of Sisters of
  the Rosary
6 Zawiya Kubakiyya

Mount Scopus (see page 118) between 1948 and 1967, this new campus was established here. After 1967 some of the faculties returned to Mount Scopus, though the campus here still houses the Faculty of Science, the Science Library, the Institute for Life Sciences, the Institute for Advanced Studies, as well as the Jewish National Library (T02-6585027), and halls for 3000 students. Of particular interest in the National Library is the superb **Ardon Window**, a huge stained-glass window featuring Kabbalistic symbols.

Also part of the Hebrew University is the **Bloomfield Science Museum** ① *Ruppin Street, T02-5618128, www.mada.org.il, Mon-Thu 1000-1800, Fri 1000-1400, Sat 1000-1600, adult 30NIS, student/child 25NIS, buses 9 and 28, featuring interactive "science is fun" displays that are particularly appealing to children.*

Monastery of the Holy Cross

① *Hayyim Hazaz, daily 1000-1500, entry 15NIS, shop, cold drinks, toilets.*

Though the monastery complex is incongruously set next to a major road on the edge of the upmarket suburb of Rehavia, it is still sufficiently isolated to give some impression of how it may have appeared some 950 years ago. When the monastery was founded (1039-1056) it was quite remote from the defensive walls of the Old City, and hence its thick buttressed walls, fortress-like appearance and tiny entrance way. Though dating from the 11th century, the monastery that was founded here by King Bagrat of Georgia actually stands upon the site of a fifth-century CE Byzantine church (also founded by a Georgian, the confusingly named Peter the Iberian). The original church marked the traditional Byzantine site of the tree from which the cross used in Jesus' crucifixion was made. The Byzantine church was destroyed by the Persians in 614 CE, though a section of the original mosaic floor to the right of the altar can still be seen.

Much of the church that you see today dates to the 11th century, though alterations have been made throughout the years. The Georgians fell upon hard times during the 16th century and the church was subsequently sold to the Greek Orthodox in the latter half of the century (though it is still an extremely sacred place for Georgians). The unusual frescoes were added in the 17th century ('unusual' since they feature the heady mix of Christian saints, pagan gods and Greek philosophers!), whilst the clock-tower dates to the 19th century. There is a little museum displaying millstones, immense metalwares and wooden effigies. Go upstairs to where the refectory, with a marble table that can seat 66, is being restored.

Tomb of Jason

① *Alfasi, between Ramban and Azza, Rehavia. Mon-Thu 1000-1300. Nearest buses 9, 17 and 22.*

About 500 m northeast of the Monastery of the Holy Cross, in the suburb of Rehavia, is the Tomb of Jason. Excavated in 1956, the tomb takes its name from an Aramaic inscription that is a three-line lament to Jason. Though robbed in antiquity, it is suggested that the tomb was actually used by several generations (about 25 burials in all), with the mixture of Hasmonean and Herodian pottery suggesting that it was in use from the early first century BCE to the early first century CE. Beyond the forecourt and the outer and inner courts is one of the tomb's more interesting features: the entrance porch is marked by a single Doric column (made of stone drums) between two pilasters, a unique feature on any tomb of this period thus far excavated in Israel. The plastered walls within the porch feature a charcoal drawing of three ships, plus the reference to Jason. Several further charcoal drawings of ships were found in the irregularly shaped burial chamber.

Western outskirts of the New City

There are a number of notable places of interest in the western outskirts of the New City that visitors to Jerusalem should make every effort to see. In particular, the Holocaust Memorial at Yad Vashem should be on everybody's 'must visit' list.

Ins and outs
Getting there and around Public transport access to the various sights in the western outskirts is extremely straightforward, all being on the route of Bus 27. For orientation, refer to the 'New City (including Western suburbs, Western outskirts and Southwestern suburbs)' map on page 126.

Sights
Biblical Zoo ① *T02-6750111, www.jerusalemzoo.org.il, Sun-Thu 0900-1700/1800/1900 winter/spring/summer, Fri 0900-1630, Sat 1000-1700/1800 winter/summer, last tickets an hr before closing, adults 45NIS, students/children 35NIS. Souvenir shop, toilets, snack bar. Buses 26, 33 and 99.* Recently expanded and re-vamped, the zoo features animals now rare in Israel that are mentioned in the Bible, as well as other species in danger of extinction. It's a good family excursion, being both educational and well-run. The zoo is located just to the southwest of Jerusalem (Malkha) Mall, not far from the train station.

Mt Herzl ① *Cemetery Sun-Thu 0800-1645, Fri 0800-1300, Sat 0900-1645, free, map provided. Toilets, small café. Buses 13, 17, 18, 20, 23 and 27 stop outside.* The hill on the western outskirts of Jerusalem, Mt Herzl (Har Herzl), is home to the **Military Cemetery** as well as the tombs of Israel's past prime ministers and presidents, including Levi Eshkol, Golda Meir and Yitzhak Rabin. One 'Great Leader of the Nation' who is not buried here is Menachem Begin who requested to be buried on the Mount of Olives, where he lies near his wife and to fellow members of the Etzel and Lehi resistance movements. The centrepiece of the cemetery is the grave of **Theodore Herzl**, whose body was moved here in 1949, a stark black tomb in the Ceremonial Plaza with a handful of rocks placed on top (as per the custom). His life and works, including a reconstruction of his Vienna study, are presented through an audio-visual tour in the **Herzl Museum** ① *T02-6321515, museum@wzo.org.il Sun-Thu 0845-1515, Fri 0845-1215, adult 25NIS, student/child 20NIS,* call ahead to book a place on a 80-min tour (English/French/German/Spanish/Russian available) just inside the gates. This takes the form of a mini-movie (as too many Israeli audio-visuals in museums are wont to do). Visitors move through 'sets' whilst Herzl's immense contribution towards the creation of a Jewish state is lightly sketched out, followed by a 10-minute propaganda film that makes 'modern' Israeli society look decidedly unattractive. The western slopes of Mt Herzl are occupied by the extensive **Jerusalem Forest** (good picnic spots) and the memorial to the Holocaust, **Yad Vashem** (see below). A pathway connects Mt Herzl cemetery to Yad Vashem.

Yad Vashem (Holocaust Memorial) ① *T02-6443802, www.yadvashem.org, Sun-Wed 0900-1700, Thu 0900-2000, Fri 0900-1400 (last entrance an hr before closing times), free. Take buses 13, 17, 18, 20 or 27 to Mt Herzl, from where it is signed; 99 is the only bus to go right to the museum entrance. It's a 5-10-min walk from the main road, or there's a free shuttle bus every 15 mins. Allow at least 2 hrs for the main museum, plus an hour for other outlying buildings and memorials. NB Respectful dress should be worn. There are guided tours in English at 1100 for 30NIS, or an audio tour is available for 20NIS. Cafeteria has pleasant terrace with views.*

The most moving experience for many visitors to Israel, Yad Vashem ("a memorial and a name", from Isaiah 56:5) pays homage to the six million Jews who died in the Holocaust. Entering from the east, you pass along the **Avenue of Righteous Gentiles** – a memorial garden to non-Jews who risked their lives protecting Jews – to the **Holocaust History Museum**. This museum features harrowing photographs and testimony documenting the Holocaust in Europe, and the factors that created it, though some of the presentation is controversial. Children under 10 years old are not permitted to enter. To the west of the museum is the **Hall of Names**, where 'Pages of Testimony' by Holocaust survivors and their families fill over three million pages.

The same building also features an **art museum** of work produced in the concentration camps and Jewish ghettoes. To the west of here is a **railway boxcar** that was used to transport Jews to the camps, and now serves as a memorial monument. Below is the **Valley of the Destroyed Communities** that commemorates the Jewish communities in Europe that were eliminated during World War II. North of the Historical Museum is the **Hall of Remembrance**, where an eternal flame (*ner tamid*) is a memorial to the six million Jewish victims of the Holocaust, with the names of the 21 major concentration and death camps engraved on the floor.

Ein Karem

Though Jerusalem continues its relentless expansion westwards, the former Arab village of Ein Karem retains a rural feel, with cyprus and olive trees filling its stony hillside terraces. The village is traditionally associated with the home of Zechariah and Elizabeth, the parents of John the Baptist, and consequently as the birthplace and early home of John. The Virgin Mary's visit to her cousin Elizabeth is also commemorated here. Now something of an artists' colony, the village is dotted with glassmakers/jewellery/ceramic workshops as well as souvenir stalls (pay a visit to Yitzhak Greenfield's gallery, signed, whose paintings and prints have Jerusalem themes).There are also a number of attractive restaurants and cafés; in fact, Ein Karem is a good place to visit on Friday evenings/Saturday lunch when most of West Jerusalem is deadly quiet (though you'll need to take a taxi).

Getting there and away Bus 17 runs through the village from Jerusalem Central Bus Station. Alternatively, it is possible to follow the signed track down from the Jerusalem Forest by Yad Vashem/Mt Herzl (see page 129). In the centre of the village, where the restaurants are clustered, signs point down alleys on either side of the road to the places of tourist interest.

Sights
Franciscan Church of John the Baptist ① *T02-6413636, daily 0700-1145 and 1430-1745, closes 1 hr earlier in winter, Sun mornings only, free. Souvenir shop, toilets.* Most of the present church dates to the late 17th century, though it stands on far older foundations. Its somewhat fortress-like appearance reflects its remote location away from Jerusalem and its eventful past. Parts of a fifth- to sixth-century CE church underlie the present structure, hinting at the Byzantine tradition linking the village with John the Baptist, though the remains of a Roman marble statue of Venus/Aphrodite found here suggest that an earlier pagan temple may well have once stood on this spot. The original Byzantine church was damaged and rebuilt a number of times until the Crusader Knights Hospitallers, and then the Templars, took it over. Following the Crusader defeat in 1187 it was occupied

by the Muslims, not returning to Christian hands until the Franciscans acquired it in 1621. However, they were unable to establish a presence and restore the church until 1674: the year to which much of the present structure belongs. It was expanded in 1860, the main doorway to the west added in 1885, and a new bell-tower constructed in 1895. The main feature of the church is the **Grotto of St John**, reputedly built over the house of Zechariah and Elizabeth, and thus the Baptist's birthplace (*Luke 1:5-25, 57-66*).

Two fifth- to sixth-century CE chapels are also built against the southwest wall of the present church. The most interesting of these is the **Chapel of the Martyrs**, to the north. Discovered in 1885 during the construction of the west doorway, the chapel contains a mosaic with a Greek inscription offering "Greetings, Martyrs of God". It is still unclear as to whom this dedication refers.

Notre Dame de Sion ① *Mon-Fri 1000-1200 and 1400-1700 (summer -1730), Sat 0900-1700 (summer -1730), Sun closed, 2NIS. Music in the church every Sat at 1200 (around 45NIS).* Beautiful gardens with views across the wadi to the Russian Monastery and the Church of the Visitation – the classic image of Ein Karem – and a peaceful enclave that is a joy to wander around. The Congregation of Our Lady of Sion was founded in France in the mid-19th century by one Theodore Ratisbonne, who was born a Jew but became a Catholic priest after a religious experience. His brother Alphonse came to Jerusalem in 1855 where he built the Ecce Homo Convent on the Via Dolorosa (see page 57). The house in Ein Karem dates from 1861, and here Christian orphans from Lebanon and the local Arab community were looked after by the sisters. After the Arab villagers were ousted in 1948, the house became a guesthouse and remains so to this day (see Sleeping, page 140). The Sion Community now, as then, seeks to "witness God's faithful love for the Jewish people and remember that the roots of Christianity are in the Jewish tradition" – note the Hebrew script utilised in the church and cemetery.

Virgin's Spring About 400 m to the south of the Church of John the Baptist (follow the sign) is a small abandoned mosque built over a spring. A 14th-century CE tradition notes this as the place where the Virgin Mary drew water during her three-month stay with her cousin Elizabeth.

Church of the Visitation ① *T02-6417291, daily 0800-1145 and 1430-1800, closes one hour earlier in winter, free. Toilets.* Climbing the hill to the right past the Rosary Sisters Orphanage, steps lead to the Church of the Visitatio Mariae, or Church of the Visitation. The 'upper' church was built in 1955 over 'lower' Crusader and Byzantine remains. The west façade of the church features a mosaic depicting the Virgin Mary mounted on a donkey meeting with her cousin Elizabeth (the 'Visitation', *Luke 1:39-56*). The modern 'upper' church features a number of paintings depicting events in the life of Mary, plus the glorification of the Virgin throughout the centuries. The artist must have been proud of them, as he even included himself in one of the pictures (when facing the altar, look at the painting on the right wall, second along from the altar, to spot him). However, it is the older 'lower' church that is of the greatest interest. The Crusader church is built above the Byzantine remains around a cave that pious legend links with the story of Elizabeth hiding the baby John from Herod's soldiers. The shape of a baby is vaguely visible in the rock.

Hadassah Medical Centre ① *Chagall Windows T02-6776271. English-language tours Sun-Thur 0830-1230, Fri 0930-1130; synagogue Sun-Thu 0800-1315 and 1400-1545, Fri 0800-1245,* *adults 10NIS, students 5NIS. Buses 19 and 27.* The Hadassah Medical Centre was built here in 1963 when the original hospital of the same name on Mount Scopus was inaccessible (1948-1967). It is one of the world's foremost teaching hospitals, with a reputation for also providing treatment to Israel's Arab neighbours. Those without medical insurance who intend using the facilities should bear in mind that a night here can cost more than a night at the King David Hotel!

The hospital is worth visiting to see the magnificent **stained-glass windows** by **Marc Chagall** in the synagogue. Depicting the 12 tribes of Israel (based on *Genesis 49* and *Deuteronomy 33*), four of the windows were badly damaged in the 1967 war, requiring delicate repair work by the artist himself. Chagall decided to remember the war by leaving some of the bullet holes in place.

Southwestern suburbs

The Southwestern section of the New City largely comprises the suburbs Yemin Moshe, Talbiyeh, 'Emeq Refa'im and Rehavia. These suburbs are divided from the walled Old City by the Valley of Hinnom. The background to the Valley of Hinnom, and the sites on the east and southeast side of the valley, are included in the section that begins on page 110. The places described below are largely associated with the expansion of Jerusalem beyond the confines of the Old City at the end of the 19th century CE.

Ins and outs
Getting there and around   Most of the sites detailed below can be reached by heading to the east end of Independence Park, then heading down King David Street (all pretty much within walking distance of the Old City and New City centre).

Sights
Independence Park   At the centre of Independence Park is the **Mamilla Pool** (89 m by 59 m by 5.8 m deep), probably once part of the Herodian aqueduct system that brought water to the head of the Valley of Hinnom from Solomon's Pools near Bethlehem. A number of traditions surround this location, invariably involving massacres of innocents by various groups. The Mamilla Pool became part of the Mamluk water system sometime in the 15th century CE, with a channel linking it to the Pool of the Patriarch's Bath in the Christian Quarter. At the time of writing the Pool was fenced off.

In the 13th century CE the main Muslim graveyard was established here, continuing in use until the 20th century. In a grove to the east of the park, about 100 m from the Mamilla Pool, is the **Zawiya Kubakiyya** – the burial place of Amir Aidughidi al-Kubaki (d. 1289). A former slave in Syria, al-Kubaki rose to become Governor of Safed under the Mamluk sultan Baibars, though in later years he fell from grace and was banished to Jerusalem. The cube-shaped tomb, supporting a low dome on a drum, uses much secondary Crusader material, and it has been suggested that it was originally the mortuary chapel used to bury the Canons of the Church of the Holy Sepulchre. In fact, in the centre of the mausoleum stands a Romanesque Crusader sarcophagus. **NB** Independence Park has something of a reputation as a meeting place after dark for gay men.

Opposite the park is the **Jerusalem Great Synagogue** ① *58 HaMelekh George Street, T02-6230628, tours Sun-Thu 0900-1300, Fri 0900-1200*, seat of the Chief Rabbinate and with wonderful windows by Marc Chagall. Next door is the **Wolfson Museum** (Hechal Shlomo), ① *4th floor, T02-6247908/6247112, adult 15NIS, student/child 10NIS, Sun-Fri 0900-1300,* which features a small but interesting collection of Jewish liturgical art and folklore, plus a Torah library. Slightly further up the road is the **Jewish Agency** ① *48 HaMelekh George, T02-6202222*, the headquarters of the World Zionist Organization (and its archives), the Jewish National Fund (JNF) and United Jewish Agencies.

Mamilla Avenue The Alrov Mamilla Avenue opened in 2007, a huge renovation project and seemingly a great success for an historic street that was very decrepit. Designed by Israeli architect Moshe Safdie to incorporate the existing 19th-century structures, the whole length of Mamilla Avenue was narrowed and each brick moved to its new location (you can still see the numberings on many of them). The result is a busy shopping mall that has several designer shops, cafés and restaurants. Look out for the Stern House (slated for demolition, but saved) where Theodore Herzl stayed for a short while during his one visit to the Holy Land in 1945. It's now a Steimatzsky's Bookshop with a small basement museum about Herzl, and was left in its original position, thus demonstrating the original width of the street.

Hebrew Union College ① *13 King David, T02-6203333.* The Skirball Museum at the Hebrew Union College (at the north end of King David Street) has a small collection of items excavated by the Biblical Archaeology School here, however, it was closed at the time of writing (indefinitely). The College, part of the Reform Movement within Judaism, runs regular Ulpan courses.

Jerusalem International YMCA Three Arches Not your run-of-the-mill YMCA, this Jerusalem landmark (nick-named 'Yimka' in Hebrew) was built in 1933 to a design produced by the firm of architects responsible for the Empire State Building, and with funds provided by the New Jersey millionaire James Jarvie. Considering the synthesis of styles, the building is remarkably attractive, as well as being a nice place to stay (see Sleeping on page 143). The three aspects of the YMCA philosophy – mind, body, spirit – are represented by the three different buildings: the right (when facing the front) is the theatre/concert hall, the left is the pool/gym, and In the centre is the soaring **Jesus Tower** ① *Sun-Thu 0800-2000, Fri 0800-1300, 10NIS, minimum of 2 persons required*, which, at 90 m high, provides good views of the city. Note the sculptures by the doorway of the Samaritan woman and the pascal lamb, as well as the exquisitely carved column capitals depicting native flora and fauna along the aisles.

King David Hotel The King David Hotel was long considered the most prestigious residence in Jerusalem, though these days there are new pretenders to the throne. However, in a head-to-head contest, its celebrity guest list of former residents easily matches the American Colony Hotel in East Jerusalem (see page 141).

The King David Hotel is less famous for its celebrity roll-call (such as the scene in the film version of Leon Uris' *Exodus* in which Paul Newman and Eva-Marie Saint share a drink on the terrace), than for the events of 22 July 1946. Around lunchtime on that day over 300 kg of explosives placed in a milk-crate detonated, demolishing one wing of the hotel. The bomb had been placed by the Irgun – the Jewish resistance (or 'terrorist', according to your viewpoint) movement headed by the future Prime Minister of Israel, Menachem Begin. Its target was the British Mandate administration, whose offices occupied most of the building. The victims included 28 Britons, 41 Arabs, 17 Jews and five 'others' dead, with hundreds injured; most were civilians. The controversy over the bombing, including details of the sequence of events, continues to this day. Begin publicly mourned the

Jewish victims alone, blaming the British for failing to act on the telephone warning in time (which was phoned through by a 16-year-old girl). Other sources suggest that the bomb detonated six minutes early, but, even so, insufficient time had been given to evacuate the building. The Jewish establishment condemned the outrage, and the British called it the "ninth worst terrorist act this century", yet it achieved its objective: the cost of a continued British presence in Palestine was too much to bear, and the decision on the future of Palestine was handed over to the United Nations.

'Tomb of Herod's Family' Just to the south of the King David Hotel, Aba Sikra Street leads to the north end of Bloomfield Park and the so-called '**Tomb of Herod's Family**'. Though Herod himself was buried at the Herodium (see page 215), Josephus mentions a family tomb belonging to Herod to the west of the city (*Jewish War I, 228; I, 581; V, 108; V, 507*). However, the evidence that this is indeed the burial place of Herod's family is purely circumstantial, based on Josephus' vague description and the fact that the tomb lies directly across the Valley of Hinnom from Herod's former palace. The tomb was robbed in antiquity, which has not helped in its identification.

However, the tomb itself is well constructed and contained sarcophagi rather than mere niches for the bodies, suggesting that it was indeed the burial place of someone rich or important. Although the catacomb itself is closed, the tomb is interesting for the large rolling stone which seals the entrance – currently the only place in Jerusalem where this feature can be be seen (as the King's Tombs are closed, see page 116). There is some uncertainty concerning the dating of the tomb. Some of the features could be of the second half of the first century BCE, thus making it reasonable that Herod's father Antipater (d. 43 BCE) was buried here, as suggested by Josephus. However, some of the features are certainly later, though this could simply mean that the tomb was intended for later descendants.

Yemin Moshe and the Montefiore Windmill Yemin Moshe is a small neighbourhood of some 130 houses, the first quarter to be established outside the walls of the Old City in 1891. It was virtually abandoned and became a slum during the period of Jordanian occupation (1948-1967), but has subsequently been redeveloped. Running to the south of the Yemin Moshe Quarter, at the bottom of the hill, are two rows of terraced houses known as Mishkenot Sha'ananim ('tranquil settlement'). These were amongst the first houses to be built outside the city walls (c. 1860), and formed part of an attempt to provide affordable, comfortable accommodation for poor Jewish immigrants in the 19th century. Their benefactor was the Anglo-Jewish philanthropist, Sir Moses Montefiore. The houses were restored in 1973 and now function as a conference centre and guesthouse (but only for the accommodation of artists, writers and scholars), and indeed the whole area has something of the 'artists' colony' about it.

The incongruous **Montefiore Windmill** ① *Sun-Thu 0900-1600, Fri 0900-1300, free*, was built to enable the community to produce their own flour, though the scheme never really came to fruition. It is now a museum detailing the campaigns and achievements of Montefiore.

Sunset from this point (or anywhere in Bloomfield Park) is particularly scenic, as the walls of the Old City gradually change colour as the sun goes down.

Liberty Bell Park and the 'German Colony' Popular with strollers and picnicking families, this park was laid out to commemorate the bicentennial of Israel's patron and ally, the United States of America. It contains a replica of the Liberty Bell in Philadelphia.

The suburb to the southwest of Liberty Bell Park, '**Emeq Refa'im**, was the main German Colony of 19th-century Jerusalem, with many of the houses displaying a northern European influence. The colony was founded by the same 'Templars' German Protestant Christian group who established the German Colony in Haifa some three years earlier. Most of the community were expelled during World War II.

There are several notable museums located in this district, including the highly recommended **L A Mayer Institute of Islamic Art** ① *2 HaPalmach, T02-5661291/2, www.islamicart.co.il, Sun, Mon and Wed 1000-1500, Tue and Thu 1000-1900, Fri and hol eves 1000-1400, Sat 1000-1600, adult 40NIS, student 30NIS, child 20NIS, bus 15*. Known for the extraordinary story of the theft of the museum's world-famous watches and clocks collection, which were stolen over 25 years ago but now returned almost intact: the unique Marie Antoinette watch, valued at many millions of dollars, proved too hard for the thief to sell on. The museum is a good place to be on a Saturday afternoon when virtually nothing else is open and it's almost empty.

Natural History Museum ① *6 Mohilever, T02-5631116, Sun, Tue and Thu 0900-1330, Mon and Wed 0900-1800, Sat 1000-1600, adult 15NIS, student/child 12NIS. Buses 4, 14 and 18.*
This museum displays indigenous (stuffed) animals of Israel, as well as information on life sciences, the environment and the human body.

St Andrew's Church St Andrew's Church of Scotland, was built in 1930 to commemorate the Allied victory in World War I, and the Scots who died during the capture of the Holy Land. The church was designed by Clifford Holliday and is said to reflect his interest in the Armenian style of monastic architecture. The church operates a highly recommended pilgrim guesthouse (see Sleeping, page 144) and a handicraft shop from which profits go to a number of Palestinian self-help groups.

Khan Theatre The road that heads south, passing on the west side of St Andrew's Church, leads to the old railway station (opened in 1892 when the line to Jaffa was completed). The station has been derelict for a number of years, but is now slated to become a new café/theatre/shopping complex. Just before the station, housed in a former Ottoman period caravanserai, is the **Khan Theatre** ① *2 David Remez Square, T02-6718281, www.khan.co.il*, shows are in Hebrew but some have English subtitles or these can be arranged by prior request – see website for program; the pleasant café-bar is only open on performance night; buses 4, 6, 8, 10, 14, 18 and 21.

Cinémathèque ① *T02-656433, www.jer-cin.org.il; full listings on website, or consult newspapers*. Just below the Hebron Road is the Jerusalem Cinémathèque, which features nightly screenings, annual film festivals, theme nights, and 'movie marathons'. The café here is a good vantage point over the Himmon Valley to Mount Zion.

Abu Tor Observation Point Further southeast along Hebron Road is the cable car monument, a site that was previously occupied by the St John's Ophthalmic Hospital (built 1882), part of which now forms the old wing of the Mount Zion Hotel. It is possible to arrange a visit in advance (T02-6277550, daily 0900-1600). Continuing south along Hebron Road, just before the Dan Boutique Hotel, a road leads left (east) to the Abu Tor Observation Point. In Crusader times this hill was known as the 'Hill of Evil Counsel', from the tradition that this was the site of the House of the High Priest Caiaphas (yes, another one!) where Jesus was taken the night before his crucifixion. The present name is taken from the tradition that one of Salah al-Din's warriors, to whom the hill was given, used to ride into battle on the back of a bull. His tomb on the hill became a place of Muslim pilgrimage, though most visitors nowadays come to admire the view across to the Old City.

Southern section of the New City

There is a scenic viewpoint and an archaeological site in this southern section of the New City (directly south of the Abu Tor Observation Point, see above). The Talpiyyot industrial estate here is home to some of Jerusalem's trendiest nightclubs.

Haas Promenade
Another fine view of the Old City, Valley of Hinnom and Mount Zion can be had from the south of the city, on the Haas Promenade. This is a particularly popular spot in the early evening or night-time. It is reached by heading south towards the suburb of Talpiyyot on the Hebron Road, and turning left (east) just beyond the 'Peace Forest'.

Ramat Rahel
Running parallel to the Hebron Road as it runs south through the suburb of Talpiyyot is the Betar Road. This road leads to **Kibbutz Ramat Rahel**, an independent collective within the municipal borders of Jerusalem. In addition to its agricultural activities, the kibbutz also has a rather luxurious **guesthouse ($$$$)** ① *T02-6702555, www.ramatrachel.com*, and leisure/recreation centre, plus some interesting archaeological remains. The kibbutz was also the scene of heavy fighting in the 1948 war, with control of the hill fluctuating between the Jews and the Arabs.

The modern kibbutz occupies a prominent hill (818 m above sea level) at a point roughly equidistant from the Old City and Bethlehem. Not a great deal is known about the ancient site, though many scholars now support an identification with the biblical **Beth-Haccherem** *(Jeremiah 6:1, 22:13-19; Nehemiah 3:14)*. The earliest settlement suggests a stronghold dating to the ninth or eighth century BCE, though the most prominent ancient remains are from a magnificent **citadel-palace** built by one of the later kings of Judah, probably **Jehoiakim** (608-597 BCE). Sections can still be seen here, though the best-preserved decorative remains (three complete proto-Aeolic capitals and several incomplete fragments) have been removed to the Israel Museum. The citadel-palace complex was almost certainly destroyed during the Babylonian invasion of 586 BCE.

Though remains have been found from the Babylonian-Hellenistic periods (586-37 BCE), and the Herodian period (37 BCE-70 CE), the next significant finds date to the third century CE. These comprise a **Roman bathhouse** and **villa** built by the Tenth Roman Legion c. 250 CE. Both were renovated and used during the Byzantine period. Also in the Byzantine period, c. 455 CE, a large **church** and **monastery** were built on the hill by Lady Ikelia, possibly to mark the traditional site where Mary rested on her way to Bethlehem. The plan of the church is readily identifiable, though only a small section of the mosaic floor was preserved. The site appears to have been abandoned since the seventh to eighth century CE.

Abu Ghosh

An interesting Crusader church, a more rural setting and excellent Middle Eastern restaurants make Abu Ghosh good for a half-day out from Jerusalem. The present name of the village (13 km northwest of Jerusalem), preserves the name of a 19th-century CE sheikh who used to levy tolls on pilgrims using this route to Jerusalem. The former Arabic name for the village, Qaryet el-Enab, in turn preserves the biblical name, Kirjath-jearim, a small village on the border of the tribes of Judah and Benjamin. It was at Kirjath-jearim that the Ark of the Covenant was kept during the 20-year period between its restoration by the Philistines (*I Samuel 6:21-7:2*) and its removal to Jerusalem by David (*II Samuel 6; I Chronicles 13:5-14*). The village from this period occupied the hill-top area (Deir el-Azhar) and is now marked by a large statue of the Virgin Mary and the infant Jesus in the grounds of the Notre Dame de l'Arche d'Alliance. This **modern church** ① *daily 0800-1130 and 1330-1800; free, donations accepted; ring the bell if locked*, (1924) stands on the site of a Byzantine chapel that was built to mark the traditional site of the house of Abinadab, where the Ark was kept (*I Samuel 7:1*). Parts of the chapel's fifth-century CE mosaic floor can still be seen.

In the second century CE, the settlement moved to a new site on the valley floor when the Romans built a reservoir over the spring here. The reservoir was entered via two stepped passages hewn from the rock (and now incorporated into the Crusader church, see below). In the mid-ninth century CE, a caravanserai was built east of the Roman reservoir, water from which supplied a pool beneath a pavilion at the centre of the caravanserai's courtyard, whilst a large reservoir was built on the east side. The caravanserai continued in use up until the Crusader period, and was later restored by the Mamluks some time between 1350 and 1400.

During the Crusader period, the village became associated with the gospel story of the resurrected Christ's appearance to two disciples on the road to Emmaus (*Luke 24:13-35*). The reason for the Crusaders locating the biblical Emmaus here was based largely on circumstantial evidence; they simply selected the nearest village that was located the necessary 60 stadia (11.5 km) from Jerusalem, believing that the spring and reservoir would have been a suitable place for Jesus and the disciples to stop for their meal. In 1142, the village and all its land were granted to the Order of the Hospitallers, and a large Crusader church was built above the reservoir. The eastern reservoir built in the ninth century CE was turned into a great vaulted hall, whilst the Early Arab period caravanserai was considered to be the place where the meal took place. In latter years the Crusaders located Emmaus at el Qubeibeh (see below). The **Crusader church** ① *T02-6342798, Mon-Wed, Fri and Sun 0830-1100 and 1430-1700; free, donations accepted; the church is marked by the sign 'Eglise de Croisse – Crusaders Church'; Superbus 185 runs to Abu Ghosh from Shazar in Jerusalem (one street south of the Central Bus Station, parallel to Jaffa,* is very well preserved, particularly the crypt over the Roman reservoir, thanks in part to extensive renovations carried out at the end of the 19th century CE. The church was presented to Napoleon III at the conclusion of the Crimean War, and subsequently entrusted to the French Benedictine Lazarus Fathers. To find the church in the village head for the tall minaret of the adjacent mosque.

El-Qubeibeh

The **church** ① *T02-952495 extn 4; daily 0800-1145 and 1400-1700; free, donations accepted*, (to the northwest of Abu Ghosh) is the venue of a popular pilgrimage on Easter Monday. Though el-Qubeibeh lies the necessary distance from Jerusalem to qualify as Emmaus, the association with the gospel tradition is rather nebulous. Located on the Roman road to Jerusalem (parts of which can still be seen), in the eighth or ninth century CE a number of houses (still visible) were built here by Arab settlers, who thus founded a village. Some time in the first half of the 12th century CE the Canons of the Holy Sepulchre in Jerusalem acquired the land, ostensibly for tax farming purposes. The village probably took its name, Parva Mahomeria, from the small Muslim shrine that stood in the village (el-Qubeibeh means 'little cupola'). A small fortress and hospice were built to service the needs of Christian pilgrims using this route to Jerusalem. It is now widely believed that later Christians became confused as to why a church had been established here; the only tradition that seemed to fit the location was the gospel story of Christ's resurrection appearance at Emmaus and, given that the distance matched certain versions of Luke's gospel, the tradition stuck. The present Franciscan church here was consecrated in 1902, though the foundations of the Crusader-period church are still visible. Visitors are shown a wood panel in the floor to the left of the nave, which is claimed to be part of the house of Cleopas (though this is highly unlikely).

Jerusalem listings

For Sleeping and Eating price codes and other relevant information, see pages 9-13.

😴 Sleeping

The majority of upmarket accommodation is found in the New City, whereas budget hotels, hospices and hostels tend to be in the Old City and East Jerusalem. The Old City/East Jerusalem area is more atmospheric, but starts shutting down after dusk. The New City is blander but has better shopping, dining out and nightlife options. You pays your money and takes your choice (though in reality the two areas are little more than a 30-min walk apart). Advance booking is highly recommended during holidays (all denominations, all price categories), and essential at hospices and places orientated to pilgrimage-tours. Even budget places will require reservations backed up by credit card during peak Christmas/Easter seasons. Note that tour groups get significant discounts on the 'spot rates' used here. The Old City backpacker hostels offer the cheapest accommodation in Israel (around 50-70NIS per night for a dorm bed). The rates quoted are regular season, and presume breakfast is included unless otherwise stated.

Old City *p31, map p32*
$$$ Austrian Hospice, 37 Via Dolorosa, T02-6265800, www.austrianhospice.com. This busy, well-maintained hospice has been a landmark since 1863. Single/double/triple rooms are expensive but there are also high-standard large dorms (**$$**). Plum walls with golden framed paintings in the hallways, black-and-white tiled floors. Curfew (but key available); half-board option. Some of the best Old City views from the roof; popular garden café. Reservations essential.
$$$ Christ Church Guesthouse, Omar ibn al-Khattab Sq, Jaffa Gate, T02-6277727, www.cmj-israel.org. Sedate but welcoming atmosphere, lovely lounge areas and corridors hung with rugs and artefacts conjure up imperial times. Rooms in the older wing more characterful and colonial but new wing has a/c. Flowery courtyard and café where breakfast is served; some family rooms (**$$$$**); meals available (Shabbat dinner); 2300 curfew; check-out 1000; church on your doorstep; unmarried couples cannot share.
$$$ Gloria, 33 Latin Patriarchate, Jaffa Gate, T02-6282431/2, www.gloria-hotel.com. Great location and fine views from restaurant and rooftop. Unexciting rooms with sizable bathrooms, but plasticky fittings and endless off-putting dark corridors upstairs. Arabesque decor in public areas is much nicer. Good value; no religious vibes.
$$$ Lutheran Guest House, 7 St Mark's, T02-6266888, www.guesthouse-jerusalem.com. Very well-run guesthouse, with spotless 1-4 person rooms set around a peaceful courtyard; new rooms just built at roof level; lovely stone walls throughout. Meals available. Mainly German guests. Booking essential.
$$$-$ Armenian Guest House, 36 Via Dolorosa, T02-6260880, armenianguesthouse@hotmail.com. Doubles/triples can be a great deal, apartment-style with kitchen, washing machine, dining room. Decor is fairly spartan but inoffensive. Single EURO55, double EURO74, dorms EURO20. Courtyard restaurant is OK; no curfew.
$$$ East New Imperial, Jaffa Gate, T02-6282261, imperial@palnet.com. Historic building (previous guests include Kaiser Wilhelm II in 1898), with hallways so packed with memorabilia and antique furniture it's like a museum. Cheapish doubles, all with bath (though these tend to be recent additions 'into' the room); 5 have 'the' front balcony views on to the Citadel and Jaffa

Gate. Some suites (**$$$**) can fit families. Very friendly, free internet, breakfast $5. Recommended (but not for those who want high-spec fixtures and fittings).

$$$ Notre Dame de Sion Ecce Homo Convent, 41 Via Dolorosa, Lion Gate, T02-6277292, www.eccehomoconvent.org. Romantically located above the Lithostrata, next to a basilica and by the Ecce Homo arch. Spotless rooms (doubles $80), some with marvellous views; huge public terraces; single-sex dorm $24 (partitions separate the beds). Austere atmosphere, not for backpackers. B&B; half-board available. Advance bookings only. Ask about their curfew.

$$$-$ Hashimi, 73 Souq Khan es-Zeit, near Damascus Gate, T02-6284410, hashimihotel. com. Better backpacker choice for those after some peace and quiet. Single-sex dorms (100NIS with breakfast) are newly kitted out in dubious taste, public areas marbled, awesome views of the Al Aqsa from the roof terrace and indoor dining area, Private rooms (**$$$**) are overpriced, strictly no unmarried couples, and alcohol forbidden. 1030 checkout, curfew 0230-0600. Internet 15NIS per hr or free Wi-Fi, use of kitchen.

$$$-$ Citadel Youth Hostel, 20 St Mark, T02-6284494, citadelhostel@mail.com. A rocky rustic cave on the lower 2 levels, the rooms become more modern and less enticing as you ascend. Single/double/triples, with/out bath, and a couple of cramped 10-bed dorms (60NIS). Shared shower/toilets truly are cubby holes. But decor is appealing - Bedouin style - and so is the atmosphere and rooftop views, Beds changed daily but only private rooms get towels. Free Wi-Fi (or 10 mins use of pc). No breakfast, but use of kitchen (hot drinks 4NIS) and no curfew (quiet requested after 2330). Recommended to book ahead, only 11 rooms. Day trips on offer to the usual places for $50.

$$$-$ Petra Hostel, 1 David St, T/F6286618, www.newpetrahostel.com. Excellent location just inside Jaffa Gate with fabulous views from the roof (if you look beyond the wasteland of Hezekiah's Pool). The rambling historic building has basic rooms (all en suite) – nothing special, minimal tasteless furnishings, fans. Pay more for balcony views (200-300NIS). Better for backpackers: dorms are pleasant, old-style, with balconies (6-8 beds, 70NIS); June-Oct sleep on the roof (40NIS). Clean linen, free use of kitchen, fridges on each floor; internet access (10NIS per hr); 24-hr reception; no curfew; 1000 check-out; baggage storage. 'Interesting' clientele (lots of 'Jerusalem Syndrome' types); takes credit cards.

$$-$ Golden Gate, 10 Souq Khan al-Zeit, T/F02-6284317, goldengate442000@yahoo. com. Single sex dorms sleep 6-9 (some with single beds rather than bunks), private rooms all en-suite, new and tiled throughout (blankly decorated), small outdoor terrace (no views), not on the main backpacker circuit. Breakfast and free tea/coffee. No alcohol and 2400 curfew.

$$-$ Hebron Hostel, 8 Aqabat Etkia, off Souk Khan El Zeit, T02-6281101, ashraftabasco@hotmail.com. One of the Old City's nicest hostels and one of Jerusalem's most popular backpacker options, with variety of rooms and dorms. 18 per room in mixed/female dorms (40NIS) but feels spacious enough and rock walls/arches add appeal. Very hot showers and clean toilets. Some private rooms (doubles 180/150 NIS with/out baths), but check a few as they vary. Roof terrace; tearoom below has cheap meals, drinks and internet (10NIS per hr). Competitively priced tours. Check-out 1100, curfew 0100, friendly staff. Recommended.

$ Al-Arab, Tariq Khan es-Zeit, near Damascus Gate, T02-6283537. Long-established backpacker favourite and cheapest in town. Rather run down: grubby toilets and showers (irregular hot water and peep-holes), variously sized dorms (including one with 46 beds on the roof!), private rooms (**$$**). Kitchen not terribly hygienic; no curfew. Popular despite its shortcomings.

$ New Swedish, 29 David, T02-6277855, www.geocities.com/swedishhostel. Cramped 14-bed mixed dorm, and 6 pokey rooms (**$$**, but much cheaper low season and decent discount for long stays). All share clean showers and very cosy kitchen; free tea/coffee; TV room. Friendlier than competitors, but not a place for anyone who values privacy. In peak season, backpackers find themselves on a mattress behind reception. No alcohol. Internet 6NIS per hr.

East Jerusalem *p111, map p112*

$$$$ American Colony, 1 Louis Vincent, off Nablus, T02-6279777, www.americancolony. com. Historical building now houses East Jerusalem's (many would say, Jerusalem's) classiest hotel. There's a certain simplicity to the interior decor, while antiques and wall-hangings dotted about the public places add classic Arabian style. Small heated pool (in summer) and gym; palm- and flower-filled garden, attractive courtyard (for a great Sat brunch). To appreciate your stay fully, go for the more luxurious Pasha Deluxe rooms ($510) with sleek tiled bathrooms, although smaller standard rooms will be refurbished in 2010. An intimate feel throughout and excellent restaurant. Recommended.

$$$$ Olive Tree, 23 St George, T02-5410410, www.olivetreehotel.com. Rooms are just big enough, with modern-retro decor (but beginning to get scuffed), stone-tiled bathrooms, flat-screen TVs. No pool; charge for internet. Book online for 10% discount.

$$$$ Ambassador, Nabus, Sheikh Jarrah, T02-5412222, www.jerusalemambassador. com. Favoured by tour groups, but don't let that put you off because rooms here are spacious, decorated in a modern style with classic furniture, a/c, TV, free Wi-Fi, wide beds and big bathrooms. Those with balconies facing the Old City are best. Welcoming restaurant serves Middle Eastern/French/ Italian food and has outdoor seating in summer. Bedouin tent in the garden, fitness centre and sauna. A bustling social place.

$$$$ Legacy (formerly YMCA East), 29 Nablus, T02-6270800, jerusalemlegacy.com. A halls-of-residence exterior belies a beautifully refurbished interior – all cream and white, contemporary sofas, subtle lighting and clean wooden lines. Rooms vary in size (some have fabulously large balcony), fridges, flat-screens, safes, fluffy dressing gowns and smellies. Indoor pool, squash, basketball and gym. Nice outdoor coffee shop in summer, and Cardo restaurant on the top floor is a great spot (see Eating page 146).

$$$$ Jerusalem, 4 Antara Ben-Shadad, off Nablus, T6271356, F6283282. Attractive old building, with well-furnished rooms (some with excellent balcony views) in the Arab style which are quaint but with modern amenities. Busy patio restaurant attracts interesting folk; friendly management. Recommended and advance booking is essential, especially as there aren't many rooms.

$$$$-$$$ Christmas, 1 Ali Ibn Abitaleb, T02-6282588, christmas-hotel.com. Modest hotel catering largely for pilgrims but without a stuffy atmosphere and always bustling with activity. Rooms are cosy and pleasantly furnished and there's a good garden restaurant/bar. No seasonal price increases.

$$$ AzZahra, 13 Az-Zahra, T02-6282447, azzahrahotel.com. It's not luxurious but a/c rooms in a romantic old building have Arabesque lamps, high ceilings, old doors and atmosphere (some with good balcony). 15 rooms, mostly twin bed, with kettle, fridge, TV. Large bathrooms, but a down point is "shower" attachment on the tubs. Courtyard/restaurant is a good place for a beer and has decent menu.

$$$ Golden Walls, Sultan Suleiman, T02-6272416, www.goldenwalls.com. Excellent though noisy location between Damascus and Herod gates: pleasant lobby lounge, good views from rooftop café (breakfast and BBQs up there when weather's hot). Many rooms recently refurbed in modern Arabic style, bright and airy with sparkling bathrooms – request one of these, they're priced the same (db $130-150 depending on season).

$$$ Ritz, corner of Ibn Khaldun/Ibn Batura, T02-6269900, jerusalemritz.com. 104 functional a/c rooms are newly decorated and very clean, though with no sense of style. Other options with this price tag are more interesting and atmospheric, but staff here are nice and efficient. Free Wi-Fi.

$$$ St George's Cathedral Pilgrims Guesthouse, 20 Nablus Rd, T02-6283302, stgeorges.gh@j-diocese.org. Tranquil setting around cloistered courtyard; most rooms were part of the choir school and are simple yet very spacious with attractive stone walls. Sensibly run, mostly pilgrim groups but independent travellers welcome, reservations recommended (no choice as to which room you are allocated, some upstairs ones lack the Jerusalem stone walls). Reasonable value by Jerusalem standards with no seasonal price hikes. Alcohol available, a/c, tv, and cathedral and lovely gardens on the doorstep. Good choice.

$$$ Victoria, 8 al-Masoudi, T02-6274466, www.4victoria-hotel.com. Modest rooms (some triples), with TV/fan, newish furniture and clean bathrooms, but hand-held shower fittings. Some have balcony. Pleasant staff, breakfast hall a bit dingy; alcohol available. Scope for negotiation on price.

$$-$ Palm Hostel, 4-6 HaNevi'im, T/F02-6273189, newpalmhostel@yahoo.com. A real travellers hang-out, this is where to come for political chat, a friendly hectic atmosphere, crowded dorms (some with attached bath) and grotty but cheap rooms. Recently the Palm has overtaken premises next door (previously the Faisal), where the atmosphere is more staid but rooms are freshly renovated and tiled (though tiny) with a/c-cum-heater. Flexible midnight curfew; free internet; breakfast and hot drinks included.

Northern Suburbs *p117, map p112*
$$$$ Regency Jerusalem, 32 Lehi, Mount Scopus, T02-5331234, www.regency.co.il.

Bold, modern design featuring hanging gardens and waterfalls in the lobby, palm-fringed pool area, plus true 5-star facilities (including Jerusalem Spa complex, with indoor pool). Amazing views of the city from Mount Scopus. Recommended.

$$$-$$ Mount of Olives, 53 Mount of Olives Rd, Al-Tur, Mount of Olives, T02-6284877, www.mtolives.com. Friendly family-run place; mainly pilgrims but without the pious atmosphere. A few of the 55 basic rooms have awesome views, 7 have been revamped with new furnishings and bathrooms, TVs, and are more spacious – all are competitively priced. It has appeal for its Arab village location and proximity to some of the city's holiest sites. B&B, alcohol available. Minibus 75/sheruts go to Damascus Gate till 1700, otherwise it's a taxi or a real schlep uphill. **NB** Lone women are not advised to roam the area at night.

New City *p120, map p126*
$$$$ Dan Boutique, 31 Hebron, T02-5689999, www.danhotels.com. Formerly the Ariel, some distance south of city centre, this hotel has undergone a recent refurb and become part of the Dan group (though is less pricy than others in the chain). Boutique here means mod cons meet retro, it's trying to be hip and almost hits the mark. Black, cream, silver and gold trimmings, flock wallpaper, TVs in the public spaces showcasing animation, 'funky' bar, fitness centre, cartoon art in the bedrooms, decent sized bathrooms with nice toiletries - and everything new. Jewish vibes. Try the central reservations T03-5202552 for seasonal discounts.

$$$$ David Citadel, 7 King David, T02-6211111, www.TheDavidCitadel.com. Bustling with Bar Mitzvahs, this high-end hotel in a premier location meets professional standards. Restaurants (nice terrace) are slick without a hint of stuffiness, plush rooms, big pool with plenty of loungers – in fact, everything's on a giant scale and light reflects off every marble surface. All the services and facilities that you would expect, for the money. Recommended.

$$$$ Inbal Jerusalem, 3 Jabotinsky, T02-6756666, inbalhotel.com. The full facilities you would expect for the price, with a fresh contemporary feel and sociable airy public spaces. Good shops, very professional staff. Recommended.

$$$$ King David, 23 King David, T02-6208888, www.danhotels.com. Flagship of the Dan chain with a famous history, this place used to ooze style but it's starting to look dated in comparison to the swanky new upstarts. The quiet grassy grounds have an inviting pool, the veined marble tables, parquet floors and dark furnishings are classic. To appreciate the experience fully you really need to stay in one of the 'deluxe' or 'executive' rooms facing the Old City ($700+). Tennis, fitness centre.

$$$$ Leonardo Plaza, 47 King George, T02-6298666, www.leonardo-hotels.com. Ex-Sheraton, excellent service and facilities that you would expect. Regular rooms are spacious and better than many others at the same price; expect to pay more for an Old City view or extra $70 for balcony or 'smart room'. Good restaurants and sushi bar, seasonal swimming pool, popular with Jewish families.

$$$$ Mamilla Hotel, mamillahotel.com. Luxurious new hotel in keeping with the upmarket shopping street of the same name that it adjoins. The stylishly lit lobby sets the tone for the spacious rooms, with glass-walled (liquid gel) bathrooms, soft-pile carpets and minimalist sophisticated decor. The basic studio costs US$360 but can go up to $480 on Jewish holidays. Holistic spa (due to open Sep 2010) and sublime pool; dairy restaurant and brasserie on roof both excellent; and the Mirror Bar is one of 'the' places for the Jerusalem elite to be seen (or there's the Winery for a less dressy drink). However, some staff don't yet seem to be quite at the same level as the top-class facilities.

$$$$ Eldan, 24 King David, T02-5679777, www.eldanhotel.com. Beginning to get shabby and scratched around the edges. Rooms have picture windows and all the amenities, comfy beds, but bathrooms a bit disappointing. Bustling coffee shop; sloppy staff. Worth considering if there's a cheap online deal (which there frequently is).

$$$$ Harmony, Yoel Moshe Salomon, Nachalat Shiva, T02-6219999, www.atlas.co.il. Typical Atlas hotel styling and features, which comes as a pleasant change in Jerusalem. Grey and white decor splashed with bright colours, contemporary furnishings, art installations and books to browse. Rooms with a/c, fridge, tea/coffee, safe, hairdryer, free Wi-Fi. Entrance is via the Salomon Centre, a weirdly empty mall, but otherwise an excellent location next to hippest restaurants of the new city, easy walk to the Old City and East Jerusalem. Price includes afternoon refreshments (exc Shabbat), which can be taken in the trendy lounge/foyer.

$$$$ Prima Kings, 60 King George, T02-6201201,www.inisrael.com/primahotels/kings. The best flower-filled balconies in the city; fair-sized rooms, attractive restaurant and lively lobby coffee shop. Half-board available. Good central location for both old and new city.

$$$$ YMCA 3 Arches, 26 King David, T02-5692692, www.YMCA3arch.co.il. Famous Jerusalem landmark, in very appealing building with ornamental public areas (the foyer-salon is especially glorious). Though renovated, the 56 rooms are rather sombre, but there's use of the indoor pool, fitness room, squash and tennis. Nice restaurant/terrace.

$$$ Jerusalem Tower, 23 Hillel, T02-6209209, www.jthotels.com. Perfect location if you want the city-centre vibe, with great views from the 12th floor of the concrete tower. Rooms rather small but recently refurbed in an almost-art-deco way, though bathrooms disappoint. Public areas cheap and dated.

$$$ La Perle, 6 Hahistadrut St, T77-5525251, laperle-hotel.com. Intimate new hotel (6 doubles, 6 singles) with a central location and subtly decorated rooms. 15% discount for stays over 3 nights, includes continental breakfast at the café next door. Management are accommodating about check-in/out times – and in all other matters. Good choice, book ahead.

$$$ Lev Yerushalayim All Suite Hotel, 18 King George, T2530-0333, levyerushalayim.co.il. Part of the Royal Plaza chain, this apartment hotel has 1-2-bed suites with kitchenette (dishes for rent), lounge/dining area (20% discount for monthly stays with no breakfast). Good value for money, suitable for families and excellent location – but rooms are a bit gloomy. Expensive internet.

$$$ Little House in Bakah, 1 Yehuda, T02-6737944, littlehouse@o-niv.com. Quite a unique little place, in a renovated Ottoman mansion. Smaller than most with just 35 rooms; large garden with pine trees. Polly restaurant is homely and comes recommended; breakfast is good; free Wi-Fi and tea/coffee. Bakah is nice old neighbourhood, not far from the nightlife of the German Colony, and a short drive to Bethlehem. An interesting choice.

$$$ Montefiore, 7 Schatz, T02-622111, www.montefiorehotel.com. On a pedestrianized street (near cool Bezalel Street), this welcoming and modern hotel has shiny new furniture, big, comfy beds, nice bathrooms, cool-ish restaurant; safe/fridge/etc. Just squeezes into this price bracket at $149 per double. A good choice.

$$$ Notre Dame de Sion Ein Karem, 23 HaOren, Ein Karem, T02-6430887, www.sion-ein-karem.org. Idyllic setting in the walled gardens of a convent. Rooms to accommodate 1-5 persons, pricier in the Hermitage. Communal fridges; half/full board available. By reservation only; complicated rules about check-ins/outs.

$$$ Palatin, 4 Agripas (entrance on Even Israel), T02-6231141, palatinhotel.com.

Popular and cosy; most rooms recently renovated with attractive stone-tiled floors, muted furnishings, plenty of mirrors, small shower rooms. Older cheaper rooms with carpets are scruffier. Check-out 1200; nice management (book ahead, will negotiate on price).

$$$ St Andrew's Scottish Guest House, 1 David Ramez, T02-6732401, www.scotsguesthouse.com. Quiet rooms ($140-150, $10 more for room with Old City view; other rooms look over the garden), furnishings are tasteful though simple, excellent bathrooms, no TVs, heater-a/c, kettle. A grand 1930s building where Ottoman tiles mix with colonial charm; feels remote, yet both old and new city are walkable, as are restaurants on Emek Refaim. Dinner available; free Wi-Fi; relaxing Allenby lounge for sunset drinks; rooftop; charming library/tv room; church adjacent. No curfew, mixed clientele, lovely staff. 1 suite ($180), 1 bland apartment ($240/300 for 4/6 people); pre-booking essential. Can pay to use the pool at the Mount Zion hotel, nearby (100NIS).

$$$ Jerusalem Inn Hotel, 7 Horkanos, T02-6252757, jerusalem-inn.com. Close to city centre but mercifully on a quiet backstreet, recently remodelled rooms are spotless and tastefully and modestly furnished, plus older cheaper rooms are popular ($95 double); a/c/heaters, fridge, TV, generous breakfast. Best to book through website.

$$$ Habira, 2nd Fl, 4 HaVatzelet, (crn Frumkin), T02-6255754, hotelhabira@gmail.com. Set back from noisy Jaffa Street, but still surrounded by cheap eats and cool nightlife. A homely little place, with TV, a/c, fridge, big beds, plenty of furniture; no curfew. S/D/T/Q 250/350/450/600NIS. Considered an historical site by fans of Menachem Begin.

$$$ Kaplan, 1 HaHavazelet, T02-6254591, natrade@netvision.net.il. Small rooms in an old-school guesthouse (jigsaw art, primrose and blue paint, hard beds), but it's cheaper than most for a private room (doubles

$70); TV, a/c, 4-bed room for 300NIS; some rooms with balcony; clean, central location. Free internet and tea/coffee, use of kitchen; extremely pleasant management.

$$$ Mount Zion, 17 Hebron, T02-5689555, www.mountzion.co.il. Excellent views (especially at sunset) from most rooms; best in the 19th-century Ottoman-period 'citadel' wing; some balconies. Deceptively large hotel, but still feels friendly. Unique oriental furnishings can border on bad taste in some suites. Ask for a renovated room, as older ones are tired and shabby. Outdoor pool (closed in winter), Turkish bath, health centre, average breakfast. Possible to walk to both old/new city. Despite minor faults, the vast majority of people enjoy their stay here.

$$$ Zion, 10 Dorot Rishonim, T02-6232367, F6257585. Hard to find a more central location. Lovely period building but disappointing interior; a/c, fridge, tiny balconies; management lackadaisical; no breakfast.

$$$-$ Jerusalem Hostel & Guesthouse, nr Zion Sq, 44 Jaffa, T02-6236102, jerusalem-hostel.com. The only 'hostel' in West Jerusalem has an excellent central location (though extremely noisy at time of research due to the tram-line construction outside). Shame the old building retains few features: stone floors are covered by carpets and decor is 80s-style. All rooms have en suite showers; cheaper plastic 'bungalows' on roof are tiny (need to stoop, shared bath, NIS180), cramped but clean 16-bed dorms (NIS70) are popular. Kitchen facilities, sociable dining room; centrally controlled a/c, TV, towels, free internet; long-stay discounts possible; no curfew.

$$$-$$ Noga, 4 Bezalel, T02-6254590/5661888. More apartment than hotel, with self-contained rooms (sleep 2-4) with kitchenette, heating; minimum 2-night stay; advance booking essential. It's a good deal, and a cool street to 'live' on. Call Kristal to book a room.

$$$-$$ Agron Guest House, junction Keren Ha-Yesod/Agron, T02-6558400, www.iyha.org.il. Don't be put off by the large lettering stating "Conservative Judaism" on the front of the building - the hostel is not affiliated and are keen to point out all races and creeds are welcome. Spacious modern dorms (114NIS, essential to book ahead) or private rooms (doubles 340NIS, each extra adult 100NIS) are functional but spotless. Those on the 4th floor have balconies (some with Old City view). Heating, a/c, fridge, kettle, TV, free internet; check-out 1000; nice and informative staff. Buses 7, 8, 9, 31 and 32.

$$$-$$ Beit Shmuel Hotel and IYHA Hostel, 6 Shamma, behind Hebrew Union College, T02-6203455/6, www.beitshmuel.com. Part of World Union for Progressive Judaism but welcomes all-comers. 6-bed 'dorms' ($219) in the 'hostel' section which feels quite studenty but is very clean. Private rooms (**$$$**) in the 'hotel' half are Scandinavian-styled and spacious, with cool colours, sofa, fridge etc; some have Old City views. Check-out 1100; no curfew; luggage storage. Young friendly staff are a big plus; check for discounts online.

Ein Karem p130

$$$ Notre Dame of Jerusalem Center, 3 HaZanhanim, T02-6279111, notredamecenter.org. Historic castle-like building opposite New Gate, aimed primarily at Roman Catholic pilgrims (though others welcome). Fine views, grand public areas, well kept rooms, free Wi-Fi. Recommended high-class restaurant (La Rôtisserie, see Eating page 146). Reservations recommended – despite there being 150 rooms (doubles $150, or rather magnificent suites).

$ IYHA Ein Karem Youth Hostel, off Ma'ayan, Ein Karem, T02-6416282. A wonderful rural setting with valley views, peeling and dusty exteriors, very much for long-stayers – rooms are booked out months in advance or ask to pitch a tent. Bus 17.

❷ Eating

Restaurants are listed in Jerusalem's Menus (free from the tourist office; bear in mind that the places mentioned have paid to appear in these brochures, but the discount coupons are attractive). As a general rule, restaurants in the New City and Jewish Quarter of the Old City are kosher and close on Shabbat (whilst those in East Jerusalem and the rest of the Old City aren't and don't!). Most places in the New City take credit cards, whilst those in the Old City tend not to.

Old City and East Jerusalem
p31 and 111, maps p32 and 112
The cheapest places to eat are probably the 'hummus and fuul' places on HaNevi'im, just outside Damascus Gate. There are plenty of 'falafel and shwarma' places in East Jerusalem and in the Muslim Quarter. Across the road from Damascus Gate are plenty of fruit and veg stands.

$$$ Arabesque, American Colony Hotel, 1 Louis Vincent, off Nablus, T02-6279778. Good food, in pleasant surroundings. Sat brunch in the courtyard is wonderful if you're feeling flash (1200-1530, around 140NIS).

$$$ La Rôtisserie, Notre Dame of Jerusalem Centre, 3 HaZanhanim (opposite New Gate), T02-6279114. Recently renovated, this elegant restaurant in a beautiful old space attracts Jerusalem's elite. Soft greys and white linens sit well against stone walls and decadent lighting. Up-lit pillars split the room to give an intimate feel. Pleasant pre-dinner drinks area and bar to prop up. The Spanish-inspired menu is interesting, dominated by fish and seafood, also pork; well reviewed and expensive. Daily 1230-1530 and 1900-2200.

$$$-$$ The Cardo, 5th Floor at Legacy Hotel, 29 Nablus Rd, T02-6270827. Pretty good value Mediterranean cuisine (eg salads 35NIS, mains 55NIS and up) and worth it for the surroundings: simple appealing decor, sweeping views to the Mount of Olives from the huge windows or terrace, long bar to tempt drinkers. Promise to replace your meal should you be dissatisfied. Daily 1200-2400.

$$ Armenian Tavern, 79 Armenian Patriarchate, Armenian Quarter, T02-6273854. Atmospheric setting in part of Crusader-period church: vast pieces of metalware, mother-of-pearl, mirrors, icons, etc adorn ceilings. Try the stuffed vine leaves; salads 15-35NIS, main dishes 50-60NIS, pasta 35-45NIS. Recommended. No credit cards. Mon-Sat 1200-2200. Mainly meat, gets mixed reviews.

$$ Askadinya, 11 Shimon Hatzadik, T02-5324590. An East Jerusalemite favourite for a mix of Italian/Western cuisine but using traditional local ingredients. Cobbled courtyard with cosy rooms off it, live (loud) music on Thu nights, daily 1200-2400 (bar stays open longer if there are still drinkers).

$$ Azzahra Hotel and Restaurant, 13 Az-Zahra, East Jerusalem, T02-6282447, azzahrahotel.com. Surprisingly pleasant and relaxed venue; indoor or courtyard nicely lit at night. Good place to unwind with relatively cheap booze. Everything from pizza to Palestinian food you can peruse the menu online). Tue-Thu 1200-2300.

$$ Borderline/Pasha's Restaurant, 13 Sheikh Jarrah, East Jerusalem, T02-5825162, borderlineofjerusalem.com. Reliable oriental food (mezze 10NIS, mains 45-90NIS) and relaxed atmosphere (beer 20NIS). Shady yard with drifts of nargilla smoke, good mix of people (popular spot with NGO types). Food served 1200-2300, but stays open later for drinking (-0100).

$$ Papa Andreas, 64 Souq Aftimos, Muristan, T02-6284433. Pleasant rooftop restaurant, with nice atmosphere even if it is strictly for the tourists. St Peter's Fish, spinach pie and salad, shishlik, mezze with salad and hot pitta. Good lunchtime specials, or just smoke a nargilla.

$$ Philadelphia, 9 Az-Zahra, East Jerusalem, T02-6289770. Well-reputed restaurant that has been here since the time of Jordanian control, and is a great place to eat authentic

Palestinian food. Long and famous clientele list (newspaper clippings adorn the walls), decor is Christmas colours and plastic plants. A bit of a den (seedy staff at times: lone women beware); also good for cheap beer and mezze. Daily 1200-2400.

$$-$ Hong Kong House, 9 Az-Zahra, East Jerusalem, T02-6263465. Chinese lanterns mixed with office furniture and pictures of Al Aqsa, but good cheap fix of hot'n'sour soup or egg rolls. Also take-away. No alcohol. Sat-Thu 1200-2100.

$ Abu Shukri, 63 Tariq al-Wad, Muslim Quarter, T02-6271538. One of the Old City's best-known hummus places. Daily 0730-1730.

$ Abu Shuky, Tariq al-Khanqah. Almost the same, but even better. Possibly the best hummus in Jerusalem? Stuff yourself for 15NIS. No English sign: ask around. Closes early (0900-1530 except Sun), but if you are late there is always Lina just up the street (blue sign) which stays open till at least 1630 – though the hummus ain't a patch.

Abu Sair Sweets and Jaffar Sweets on Tariq Khan es-Zeit are two good places to get your daily sugar fix. However, for kanafeh (mild cheese, baked in strands of honey syrup mixed with pistachios) save yourself for **Eiffel Sweets**, Sultan Sulieman St, T02-6263614, where it is dangerously good and very authentic.

$ Gate Café, just inside Damascus Gate. Good little spot for watching the world go by (without being spotted yourself), run by the right-on Hytham, fair prices, and free wireless connection. All are welcome.

New City p120, map p126

The New City's shwarma and falafel places are located on and around Ben Yehuda, though they're slightly pricier than those found in the Old City. Cheapest fruit and veg is found in Mahane Yehuda Market.

$$$-$$ Adom, Feingold Courtyard, 31 Jaffa, T03-6246242. Veteran Jerusalem restaurant. Menu is French-Italian: risotto is excellent, as is the fish; specials menu changes daily. Unfussy and unpretentious.

$$$-$$ The Colony, 3 Beit Lehem (Bethlehem) Street, German Colony. Secluded location with balcony. Delicious food and superb service.

$$$-$$ Darna, 3 Horkanos, T02-6245406, www.darna.co.il. Kosher Moroccan cuisine (tagines, cous-cous and plenty of lamb), but not for vegetarians. Beautiful interiors in this rambling 200-yr-old building with tiled floors, a tented area, trees, lamps and candles. Business lunch is a good deal at 70NIS. Sun-Thu 1200-1500 and 1830-2400, Sat after Shabbat.

$$$-$$ El Gaucho, 22 Rivlin, Nahalat Shiva, T1800-422000. Big steaks and kebabs in this reliable Argentinean chain. Not cheap but the meat is excellent.

$$$-$$ Eucalyptus, Hutzot Hayotzer (Artists' Colony), Yemin Moshe, T6244331. New location (its 7th) but continued rave reviews. Moshe Basson is one of Israel's most renowned chefs and never fails with his innovative Middle Eastern menu. The upper level (Sabras café) serves dairy and vegetarian dishes. Recommended.

$$$-$$ Olive & Fish, 2 Jabotinsky, T02-5665020. A faithful grill restaurant, with plenty of out-of-towners, the setting is warmly comfortable and familiar and the food commendable. They also run 'Olive' restaurant in the German Colony, on Emek Rafa'im, which is equally attractive.

$$$-$$ Restobar, 1 Ben Maimon (corner with Azza St), T02-5665126, www.restobar.co.il. One of few places open on Shabbat – when consequently it's heaving (best book a table on Fri night). Mood changes depending on time of day: laidback café for brunch-time, morphing into a bar at night (though you wouldn't say it's 'hip'). Either way, the atmosphere is relaxed and buzzy, and the food fresh and good quality. Outdoor decking or a welcoming oval bar to eat, drink and chat over. Wi-Fi. Daily 0830-0200, or later.

$$ Angelo, 9 Horkenos, T02-6236095. Possibly the best homemade pasta in town and good pizza. Kosher so good for veggies, main dishes around 50NIS. Daily 1600-2400.

$$ Cafe Hillel, 36 Jaffa. There are many in the Hillel chain, but this corner location is always buzzing and very convenient.

$$ Focaccia Bar, 4 Rabi Akiva, T02-6256428. Busy Mediterranean/Italian café/restaurant; good patio scene. Worth knowing, as it's open every day 0900-0200.

$$ Lavan Café Restaurant, T02-6737393, 11 Hebron Road (in the Cinematheque). Perfect spot with a view of the Old City (especially lovely at sunset) through huge windows. Italian staples 45-60NIS (all veg/fish), great risotto, salads around 45NIS, bread made in-house. Breakfasts served till 1700 (1300 on weekends). Or just sip (very good) wine on the outdoor bar stools facing the view. The service is decent. Daily 1000-2400.

$$ Little Italy, 38 Keren Ha-Yesod, T02-5617638. Excellent Italian vegetarian food, plus some fish; main dishes 50NIS+. Sun-Thu 1200-2300, Fri 1200-1400.

$$ Mandarin, 2 Shlomzion HaMalka, T02-6252890. One of Israel's oldest Chinese restaurants, with Hong Kong/Chinese chefs. Main dishes are reasonably priced.

$$ Sheyan, 8 Ramban, T02-5612007, www.sheyan.co.il. Black and red softly lit Chinese decor, and outdoor seating below the Rahavia windmill, all make for a pleasant dining environment. Mixture of loosely Asian dishes, lots of sweet'n'sour, sushi, veg options (tofu), spring chicken skewers. Around 100NIS per person. Sun-Thu 1230-1500 and 1800-2300, Sat after Shabbat.

$$ Te'enim, Confederate House, 12 Emil Bota, Yemin Moshe, T02-6251967. A worthy long-timer of the Jerusalem veggie scene, Te'enim ("figs") has a café-feel and a menu with vegan options too. Tofu is used creatively in oriental offerings, in addition to the more commonplace soups and salads. Bit hard to find, tucked away on the edge of historic Yemin Moshe (approach from Emile Bota Street, next to King David Hotel). Sun-Thu 0900- 2300, Fri 0900-1430.

$$ Ticho House, 9 HaRav Kook, T02-6244186. Innovative salads (with bread) are a meal in themselves; also exciting range of fish/veg dishes; or just stop in for coffee and cake. Currently a delightfully tranquil setting with garden terrace, but threatened by the luxury apartment block being constructed next door. Sun-Thu 1000-2300, Fri 1000-1500, Sat dusk-2400. Also live music (reservations necessary), Tue Jazz 2030, Fri chamber music 1100 and Sat dinner to Jewish tunes.

$$ Tmol Café and Bookstore, 5 Salomon, T02-6232758, www.tmol-shilshom.co.il. Set on a quiet courtyard, this mainly vegetarian café is a delight. Lovely 1st-floor terrace or cosy cluttered interiors; nice staff; attracts the intelligensia. Pasta/salads 40-50NIS, fish 80NIS, Fri buffet is expansive, 55NIS, 0900-1230. Sun-Thu 0900-2400 or later, Fri 0900–late afternoon, Sat eve.

$$-$ Holy Bagel, Jaffa, www.holybagel.com. With several branches around the city, this chain has become a phenomenon (but who knows for how long). Their bagels are delicious and come in every form and filling. A cheap eat (just).

$$-$ Sheger, on alley between Jaffa/Agrippas. Delicious Ethiopian meals in this white-washed cubby hole with tiny tables; veg (30-35NIS), meat (35-40NIS), beers 10-12NIS. Flags painted on the walls, simple and authentic. At 10 Agrippas, look for the Arcadia sign and go down the alley.

$$-$ Sima, 82 Agrippas, T02-6233002. Handily on the edge of Mahane Yehuda market, this popular place has reasonably priced salads and hummus (8-20NIS), and a line up of steaks, kebabs, shishlik and liver which come with rice/veg/salad on a plate (44NIS) or in a pitta (35NIS). Half-way between a café and a restaurant, it's a proper Jewish experience.

$$-$ Village Green, 33 Jaffa, T02-6253065, www.village-green.co.il. Excellent and wholesome veggie dishes, pies, quiches, great soups; self-service canteen style, outdoor/indoor. Pay by weight so don't pile your plate too high; about 40NIS for a huge feed. Excellent salads, lots of seeds, dressings, hot and cold mixes to choose from. Can take-away. Check website for coupon giving 10% discount. Sun-Thu 0900-2200, Fri 0900-1430.

$ HaMarakiya, 4 Koresh, T02-6257797. Devoted solely to soup, this little place rotates the flavours: six different vegetarian varieties per night (28NIS). It's very groovy, full of hand-me-down furniture, communal tables, red walls, trendy clientele and the local city's LGBT community. Alcohol is served; the basement is a den; prices very reasonable. Sun-Fri 1800-last customer.

Sakura, Feingold Courtyard, off 31 Jaffa, T6235464. Israel's best Tokyo-style sushi bar; main dishes around 60NIS. Recommended.

Ein Karem p130

There's are several excellent restaurants clustered together in the village, which are open during Shabbat – and hence very busy (though of course, you will have to get there by car/taxi). Best are:

$$ Karma, 74 Ein Karem, T02-6436643, www.karma-rest.co.il. The standard menu of pasta/pizza/salads (38-48NIS) is given an interesting twist, plus casseroles and meat entrées (50-70NIS). Upstairs terrace; sleek indoors; lots of windows; stylish yet friendly. Sun-Wed 1000-2400, Thu-Sat 1000-0100.

$$ Mala Bar, Ein Karem, T02-6422120. Glowingly inviting indoor cave or intimate street-side tables, it's the place to be seen (in a good way), always buzzing. Wonderful salads/pasta, good drinks selection. No English sign, look for the chandelier and candles. Weekdays 1730-0200, or from morning at weekends.

Also **Trezoro** for Italian/gelato (daily 0830-2400), the Lebanese Restaurant for a more casual experience, and **Karem** for meaty kosher delights (1130-2330 except Shabbat).

Abu Ghosh p137

$$-$ Lebanese Food Restaurant, 88 Ha'shalom, Abu-Gosh, T02-5702397, www.abo-gosh.co.il. Exit off Road 1 at the Hemed Junction, or take Bus 185, and it's the first restaurant at the entrance to the village on

the left; you can't miss it. The labaneh with mint/garlic is possibly the best around; hummus and other salads also fantastic (11NIS). Meaty mains 30-70NIS. Eat under the ancient mulberry tree. Despite its rambling size and many tables, it's hard to get a seat on Shabbat. Daily 0900-2300. No alcohol.

🎵 Bars and clubs

Jerusalem's nightlife used to be a standing joke, particularly amongst Tel Avivians, though this is certainly no longer the case. There is now a selection of bars and nightclubs to suit most tastes and pockets, with many staying open until the early hours. With very few exceptions, most bars are located in the New City, while the fashionable nightclubs tend to be out in the suburbs, notably Talpiyyot to the south.

Bars

Artel Jazz Club, 9 Heleni Hamalka 9, Russian Compound, T077-9620165. Live jazz every night at 2200; good range of drinks (the food is great too). Wi-Fi.

Austrian Hospice, 37 Via Dolorosa. The tranquil gardens and cloisters are perfect for a late afternoon beer. Nip up to the roof for the call to prayer and sunset over the Dome of the Rock. Daily 1000-2200.

Baroud Bar-Restaurant, Feingold Yard, 31 Jaffa, 102-6259081. Friendly: good for hanging out at the bar and a place solo women feel comfortable. The food is OK (particularly the calamari) but it's better for a drink. Mon-Sat 1230-very late.

Borderline, 13 Sheikh Jarrah, East Jerusalem, T02-5825162. Very popular place for boozing; naturally weekends are particularly good.

Cellar Bar, American Colony Hotel, 1 Louis Vincent, off Nablus, T02-6279777. For those on expense accounts, notably journalists, aid workers and Palestinian officials. A stylish and beautifully lit arched grotto, from 1800.

Dublin, 4 Shammai/Darom, T02-6223612. A

mega-pub, plenty of Israeli rock music (yes!) or even karaoke, plus trance. Big, busy and social. You can't miss the Guinness signs outside signalling the way in. Open until very late.

Mirror Bar, Mamilla Hotel, 11 King Solomon, T02-5482222, www.MamillaHotel.com. Art-deco styling in this new venue popular with the 'in-crowd'. Black walls covered with sheets of mirrored glass, stretched bar of lit alabaster, adjacent cigar bar, retro furniture. Fusion food is reasonably priced (3 courses 58NIS). Daily 1900-the last customer (usually about 0230, or at weekends 0400); DJ every night.

Uganda, 4 Aristobulos, T026236087. You know it's cool coz they serve Taybeh.

Versavee Bistro Bar, Greek Catholic Patriarch, Old City, www.versavee.com. Courtyard is always busy due to their prime location, but it's attractive with a well-stocked bar, high ceilings and pleasant atmosphere. Happy hour 1600-1800; free Wi-Fi. Good place to hang out. The food's not that cheap. Daily 0830-late.

Zabotinski, 2 Ben Shattach, T054-4928878. Familiar pub-feel, if that's what you are after. Always a few hardened drinkers sitting outside. Cheap drinks offers all day. Not a bad place at all and very handy location right in the centre.

There are a number of bars and pubs on Yoel Salomon and Josef Rivlin, many of which have some sort of 'happy hour', including: **Doors**, **Gent** and **Zolli's Pub**.

Clubs

Haoman 17, 17 Haoman, Talpiyyot Industrial Area. Thu and Fri nights only 2400- after sunrise. DJs from around the world; house-techno music. Dress up. Cover is 80-120 NIS. Long-standing Jerusalem favourite; there's also a mega-huge bar.

The Lab, 28 Hebron, T02-6292001. Dance club/bar in the grounds of the old Jerusalem railway station, a restored old Ottoman building. It's pretty laid-back. Music is quite rocky, though there is a mix. Also good for just drinking as opposed to 'clubbing'.

Yellow Submarine, 13 HaRechavim, Talpiyyot, T02-6794040, www.yellowsubmarine.org.il. In Hebrew 'Tzolelet Tzehubah', this venue for underground alternative music is found among the industrial warehouses of Talpiyyot. It might be punk-rock or salsa or a night of jazz, every night of the week till the early hours. See the website for schedules.

⏯ Entertainment

For full details of cultural, cinematical and theatrical performances, check www.jerusalem.com, the 'entertainment' section of Friday's *Jerusalem Post*, *Hello Israel*, *Time Out* (http://digital.timeout.co.il/), *This Week in Palestine*, and other such freebies that can be picked up at tourist offices and hotel receptions.

Cinemas

Barbur Gallery, 6 Shirizli Street, Nachlaot, www.barbur.org. Seriously art-house movies in a shed-like gallery space, Tue at 2000. In English or with English subtitles. By donation.

Cinémathèque, 11 Hebron Rd, T02-5654333 www.jer-cin.org.il. Jerusalem's main art-house cinema; highly recommended for interesting yet approachable films; check website for complete listings. Also hosts the annual International Film Festival (Jul) and Jewish Film Festival (Dec). Adult 36NIS, student 28NIS.

Cultural centres

American Cultural Centre, 19 Keren Ha-Yesod, T02-6255755, www.usembassy-israel.org.il/ac.Sun-Thu 1000-1600, Fri 0900-1200. Free Wi-Fi.

Beit Avi Chai, 44 King George, T02-621-5900, http://www.bac.org.il. Hosts frequent music concerts/lectures/events. All relate to Jewish or Israeli culture, but are held in an open as well as artistic milieu.

British Council, 31 Nablus, East Jerusalem, T02-6267111, www.britishcouncil.org/ps.

Mon-Thu 0730-1530, Fri 0730-1330; or 3 Shimshon, New City, T6736733. Mon-Thu 1000-1300 and 1600-1900, Fri 1000-1300.

Centre Culturel Français Romain Gary, 9 Kikar Safra, T02-6243156, www.ccfgary-jerusalem.com. Library with good stock of DVDs/CDs as well as books/periodicals; free internet. Sun and Tue-Thu 1400-1800, Mon 1000-1200 and 1400-2000, Fri 1000-1300; membership adult/student 350/280NIS a year. Also run French language courses and cultural events (various venues, listed on website).

Centre Culturel Français, 21 Salah al-Din, East Jerusalem, T02-6282451, www.consulfrance-jerusalem.org. Mon-Thu 1000-1300 and 1400-1800, Fri and Sat 1400-1800. Housed in a beautiful old building, hosts films, exhibitions, concerts, plus a worthwhile Christmas fair.

Music

The world-renowned Israel Philharmonic Orchestra performs at the **Binyanei Ha'Uma** (International Convention Centre) opposite Central Bus Station, T02-6558558/6237000, www.ipo.co.il, box office Sun-Thu 0900-1900, Fri 0900-1300; whilst the Jerusalem Symphony Orchestra and Israel Chamber Ensemble often play the **Jerusalem Theatre/Jerusalem Centre for the Performing Arts**, 20 David Marcus, T5617167.

Classical music concerts and recitals are also held at **Beit Shmeul**; **Beit Ticho**, off Harav Kook.

Eden-Tamir Music Centre, 29 Hamaayam (by Mary's Spring), Ein Karem, T02-6414250, www.einKaremusicenter.org.il. A season of concerts (Fri and Sat) in enchanting surroundings.

Edward Said National Conservatory of Music, Regent Hotel, 20 Az-Zahra Street, East Jerusalem, T02-6271711, http://ncm.birzeit.edu. Concert series twice yearly (spring and autumn, check website for schedules) in Jerusalem and West Bank towns; a good opportunity to hear Arabic

music. Also has branches in Ramallah and Bethlehem.

YMCA (West), 26 King David, T02-5692692, www.jerusalemymca.org, 600-seat theatre, not just classical concerts.

Zionist Confederation House, 12 Emil Botta, Yemin Moshe, T02-6245206, www.confederationhouse.org. Organises the annual Oud Festival and is home to the Ethiopian Hullegeb Theatre; also Israel Museum, see 'Sights' on page 124, every Tue at 1800.

Live outdoor concerts (classical/folk/rock) are occasionally held at the **Sultan's Pool**, just to the southwest of Jaffa Gate.

Theatres

The Khan, 2 David Remez, T02-6718281. Theatre, music, stand-up comedy, restaurant, art gallery; but most performances in Hebrew.

Palestinian National Theatre, Nunza (near American Colony Hotel), T02-6280957, info@pnt-pal.org. Critically acclaimed (and highly politicized) theatre, usually in Arabic but sometimes English/Turkish/Greek.

O Shopping

It's difficult to exhaust Jerusalem's potential for shopping, though if you're looking for a trinket or souvenir you will have to wade through a sea of rubbish before you find anything tasteful in the Old City. As a general rule, shops in the New City tend to be fixed-price, with prices prominently displayed. In the Old City it's a free-for-all, with protracted bargaining required to make the most of your spending power. In the Old City, David Street/Street of the Chain and the Via Dolorosa are crammed with small shops staffed by multi-lingual merchants with a keen eye for the tourist dollar. Initially stunned by the bright colours, unusual objects and accumulated junk, closer inspection usually reveals that all the stalls are pretty much selling the same stuff. There's some choice rubbish aimed at the pilgrim market, most notably the 3-D picture of Jesus with the winking eyes, or your own personal crown of thorns. Shops listed below are just a tiny selection of what's on offer.

Arts, crafts and Judaica

Quality Judaica pieces can be very expensive; they are generally more tasteful in the New City rather than the shops along the Cardo in the Jewish Quarter.

Eight Ceramists, 6 Yoel Salomon, T02-6255155. Handmade ceramics from pottery cooperative, much in demand.

Frank Meisler Galleries, Annex of King David Hotel, 21 King David, T6242759. Beautiful Judaica.

Gallery Anadiel, 27 Salah al-Din, T02-6282811. Contemporary Palestinian art.

Gift Box, American Colony Hotel, T6734046. Daily 1000-1200 and 1730-2000, closed Sat morning. Nice range of classy gifts and beautiful antiques, but at a price.

House of Quality, 12 Hebron, near Mount Zion Hotel, T02-6717430. In a romantic building opposite Mount Zion Hotel, new and established Israeli artists and quality crafts, ceramics etc, well worth investigating. Sat-Thu 1000-1300, Sun, Mon, Tue and Thu 1700-1900, Fri 1100-1300. Not cheap. Selection of work by artists in their studios.

Palestinian Pottery/Armenian Ceramics, 14 Nablus, opposite US Consulate, T02-6282826, www.palestinianpottery.com. Hand-painted designs. Family business since 1922, fixed price.

Sunbula, 7 Nablus, opposite Mt Scopus Hotel, Sheikh Jarrah, T02-6721707, www.sunbula.org. Quality embroidery work, rugs, clothing, olive oil, soaps, jewellery, gifts etc, with profits going to 14 Palestinian cooperatives spread over the West Bank and Gaza. Mon-Sat 1000-1800. The original venue at St Andrew's Scottish Guest House, 1 David Remez, was closed for refurbishment at the time of writing but should soon reopen on Sun only 1000-1400 (or by appointment).

Trionfo, 9 Dorot Rishonim, T/F02-6232368, trionfo.webs.com. Sun-Thu 1000-1900, Fri 1000-1400. Tempting Aladdin's cave of Judaica and Israeliana, plus antique books (Hebrew and English), old photos, posters, prints, maps and heaps of LPs in the basement. Unique but expensive (save for the second-hand books).

Bookshops

Book Gallery, 6 Schatz, T02-6231087. Multi-levelled labyrinth packed with books in several languages, from first editions to second-hand basics.

Dani Books, 3 Even Israel, T2624-8293, Sun-Thu 0900-1900, Fri 0900-1400. Good selection of new and old fiction; will buy/swap; sells second-hand books for around 30NIS.

Educational Bookshop, Salah El-Din, East Jerusalem. A good information point, plus there's a café. You can pick up the Alternative Tourism Group (ATG) guide *Palestine and the Palestinians*, an excellent guide for travelling in the West Bank.

Elia Photo Service, 14 Al-Khanqah, Christian Quarter, T02-6282074, www.eliaphoto. com. Sells superb black-and-white photos of Jerusalem in the 1930s-60s; prices fixed (large beautiful silver-coated prints cost 250NIS). Owner Kevork Kahvedjian also signs copies of the book Through My Father's Eyes, a collection of many of his late father's famed photos. Mon-Sat 0900-1900.

Gur Arieh, 8 Yoel Salomon, T02-6257486. An eclectic collection of second-hand stuff, some (overpriced) travel books and new stock. Plenty in English. Sun-Thu 1000-2000, Fri 1000-1500, sometimes Sat evening.

Libraire Française, Jaffa, sells French-language books, newspapers and magazines.

Munther's, American Colony Hotel, Louis Vincent, East Jerusalem. T02-6279777. Wide selection of books on the region; also readings by authors. Daily 0900-2000.

Sefer ve-Sefel ('Book and Mug'), 2 Ya'Avetz/49 Jaffa, T/F02-6248237. New and second-hand odds and ends; good selection, largely in English. Sun-Thu 0900-1900, Fri 0900-1400.

Steimatsky, 7 Ben Yehuda, 33 Jaffa, and 9 Mamilla. The latter (in the historic house where Hertzl slept) is the biggest, with best choice of travel and fiction by Israeli/Arab authors in English. Café and toilets. Sun-Thu 1000-2200, Fri 1000-1400, Sat 1 hr after Shabbat-2300.

Trionfo, 9 Dorot Rishonim, T/F02-6232368, trionfo.webs.com. Great antique maps, posters, books, plus good old (but cheap, 5NIS) English titles in the basement. Sun-Thu 1000-1900, Fri 1000-1400.

Camping gear
Camping Jerusalem, Ben Hillel. Army surplus, lots of knives, etc. Less about tents and camping gear.

Orc'ha, 12 Yoel Moshe Salomon, T02-6240655. Here in Jerusalem for the last 32 years, it's where the locals go for all their equipment needs.

Steve's Packs, 11 Ben Hillel, T02-6248302. Outdoor and camping gear, also has a branch in Jerusalem Mall, Malkha T02-6482003.

Supermarkets
Supersol, Gershon Agron. Sun-Tue 0700-2400, Wed 0700-0100, Thu 24 hrs, Sat end of Shabbat-2400.

2000 Drugstore, Shamai. Booze, fags, groceries, but controversially open 24 hrs, 7 days per week.

On the corner of Lunz, there is a 24-hr supermarket which is useful (as they say, they "don't have a door").

▲▲ Activities and tours

Children
Time Elevator, Beit Agron, 37 Hillel, T02-6248381, time-elevator-jerusalem.co.il. An "interactive experience" (three giant screens, moving seats and stage) takes you through 3000 years of Jerusalem's history

(eight languages, frequent showings). Not recommended for pregnant women or children under five! Sun-Thu 1000-2000, Fri 1000-1400, Sat 1200-1800, adult 49NIS, student/internet booking 42NIS.

Hiking
Those intending to hike in the Jerusalem area (and elsewhere in Israel) are advised first to consult with the SPNI (see under 'Tour companies and travel agents' below).

Leisure centres
Cybex Fitness Centre, David Citadel Hotel, T02/6211111. One of the nicest in town.

Jerusalem Spa, Regency Hotel, French Hill, T02-5331234. Full facilities and fitness centre, fabulous setting.

YMCA West, 26 King David, T02-5692692. Aerobics classes, swimming, squash, tennis, etc.

Swimming
Jerusalem Pool, 43 Emek Refaim, T02-5632092. The city's only Olympic-sized pool (which is under threat of closure) has sauna, fitness room, lawns. Adult 500NIS, child 40NIS. Buses 04 and 018. Daily 0700-1900.

Mitzpeh Ramat Rahel Pool, Kibbutz Ramat Rahel, T6702920. Balloon-covered heated pool, weight and fitness room, tennis; coffee shop; year and half-year membership.

Tour operators
For tours that present a Palestinian perspective, in Jerusalem and the West Bank, also see box, page 201. **NB** Tours generally do not include entry fees to sites. Remember to take your passport with you.

Al Quds Tours, Centre for Jerusalem Studies, Khan Tankiz, Souq Al-Qattanin, T02-6287515, www.jerusalem-studies.alquds. edu. Jerusalem/Bethlehem tours from a Palestinian perspective, call for schedules.

Alternative Tours, c/o Jerusalem Hotel, off Nablus, T/F02-6283282, mobile 052-2864205, www.alternativetours.ps. Experienced and reliable Abu Hassan runs

'Masada Sunrise Tour'

For those visitors to Israel with limited time, the 'Masada Sunrise Tour' offers a cheap and convenient way of seeing some of Israel's most spectacular (but remote) sights. Packed into a non-stop 12 hours you will get to climb Masada for sunrise, float in the Dead Sea, hike in Ein Gedi , pass by Qumran and enjoy the panoramic view of Jerusalem from the Mount of Olives. And, unless you are on a tour led by an Israeli, you'll probably visit Jericho and see St George's Monastery in Wadi Qelt as well. All this for just $50 (excluding entrance fees). Too good to be true? Of course there are both advantages and disadvantages to seeing Israel in this way. For a start, the tour is extremely rushed. Mount of Olives, St George's Monastery, Jericho and Qumran are little more than 'photo stops' (with most people too knackered to even bother getting out the minibus at the latter), whilst the short time spent at Ein Gedi Nature Reserve does not allow you to get away from the hordes of visitors who just pop in for an hour or so. Further, the 0300 departure time is a real killer (and

very cold if the minibus is late), whilst some people feel the "sunrise over the Dead Sea" is not all it's cracked up to be! That said, there are enough advantages to make this tour worthwhile, particularly to those on a tight budget. For example, the cheapest accommodation at Masada and Ein Gedi is some $30 per night, so you're half-way to saving the tour price already. Also, you need not worry about the Dead Sea Region's irregular transport connections; to do the same tour by public transport would probably take three to four days. And finally, by travelling as a group you gain the advantage of reduced admission prices.

If you do take the tour, make sure that you bring some warm clothes for the Masada climb (and wait for the bus), drinking water and food (most the places you pass are expensive), swimming costume and towel for the Dead Sea, and money for admission fees. And backpackers, please, organise all these things the night before so you don't wake up the rest of the dorm with the rustling of those bloody bags!

a variety of Palestinian-orientated tours including Bethlehem (3 hrs, 120NIS), Hebron (5-6 hrs, 150NIS), Jericho (half-day, 140NIS), Nablus (1 day, 180NIS), plus refugee camps (3 hrs, 100NIS), and Qalqilya/the wall, (full day, 180NIS). Also organises transport to airport/Allenby Bridge etc. Recommended.
Archaeological Seminars, Jaffa Gate, T02-5862011, www.archesem.com. A variety of walking tours with a Jewish slant for up to 10 people, half ($200) or full ($350) day, plus dig-for-a-day at Beit Guvrin archaeological park ($30 plus 20NIS entrance fee, 3 hrs).
Ateret Cohanim, T02-6284101, www.ateret.org.il. This organization is involved with 'settling' Jews in the Christian and Muslim Quarters of the Old City. They

arrange short tours in the old city and will explain their viewpoint.
issta, 4 Herbert Samuel, T02-6211888. Good for student-priced flights, etc.
Green Olive Tours, T03-7219540/054-6934433, www.toursinenglish.com. Tours around East Jerusalem, West Bank and Israel, single or multi-day, some political and others focussed on sights. Comprehensive list on website, easily booked online. Fred runs his office out of the Gate Café, by Damascus Gate. Recommended.
Holycopter, T050-2411339/050-9313144, www.holycopter.co.il. Helicopter flights over the city for $150 per person.
Jerusalemp3 Tours, www.jerusalemp3. com. Take yourself around, with a free

downloadable audio tour. Lots of interesting (and less run-of-the-mill) destinations are covered, eg Ein Karen, Nachalot.

Mazada Tours, 9 Koresh, T02-6235777, www.mazada.co.il. Runs buses to Cairo on Sun and Thu, $90 single, $110 return, departs 0830, takes around 12 hrs; prices exclude border taxes of $55; buses also pick up in Tel Aviv. Their Cairo office is at the Cairo Sheraton (T00202-33488600); buses back to Israel Sun and Thu at 0800. Buses to Amman daily (min 3 persons required), each way $88, departs 0830, takes 6 hrs; prices exclude border taxes of $49; buses also pick up in Tel Aviv. Also run tours to Egypt and Jordan from Jerusalem/Tel Aviv, and from Eilat to Petra/Wadi Rum, plus choice of other tours.

Mike's Centre, nr Station IX (off Souq Khan al-Zeit), T02-6282486, www.mikescentre. com. 1-day tours to Galilee $65 (Wed and Sun) and Masada (Mon, Tue, Thu and Sat) $50; half-day (Tue and Fri) to Bethlehem $40.

Sandemans New Europe, c/o Steimatzsky's Bookshop, Mamilla Avenue, T02-6244726, www.neweuropetours.eu. You can't miss the guys in red t-shirts just inside Jaffa Gate offering free tours (on a tips basis) at 1100 and 1430 every day, lasting around 3 hrs. It's a jovial introduction to the old city with a fair sprinkling of history. Office Sun-Fri 1200-1900, Sat 1200-1330.

Society for the Protection of Nature in Israel (SPNI), 13 Heleni HaMalkha, T02-6244605, tourism@spni.org.il, www. teva.org.i/englishl. SPNI organize a series of excellent guided tours in Israel, all of which involve some hiking, with accommodation in field schools: 3-day Galilee and Golan ($395), 3-day Upper Galilee crossing ($395), 4-day Negev and Eilat ($485), 2-day Masada, Ein Gedi and Dead Sea ($295), 1-day Wadi Qelt ($125), and Jerusalem Old City, Mt of Olives ($95). Individuals can join but a minimum of 10 persons is required; email them for schedules.

Zion Tours, off 19 Hillel, T02-6254326, mark. feldman@ziontours.co.il. Cheap airfares, Sun-Thu 0830-1730.

Zion Walking Tours, near Jaffa Gate (opp entrance to Citadel), T/F02-6261561, 052-5305552, zionwt.dsites1.co.il. Long-established tour company; tours last 3 hrs: Old City $30, Mount of Olives $40, 'Underground' City $35 (good way to see the Western Wall Tunnels, book in advance), Bethlehem $40, Mount Zion and City of David, plus others.

Transport

Air

The vast majority of airlines only have offices in Tel Aviv. **Arkia**, T*5758, for reservations in Israel; www.arkia.co.il). No flights on Shabbat within Israel, and few charter flights abroad. Call for schedules, as they vary according to demand. **Israir**, T0516-5931785, www. israirairlines.com. Domestic flights. **El-Al**, 12 Hillel. T02-9771111, Sun-Thu 0830-1830, Fri 0830-1300. **SAS**, 14 Az-Zahara, T02-6283235.

For details of air tours around Jerusalem, see above. There are buses from Jerusalem's Central Bus Station to Ben-Gurion Airport (see page 19), as well as taxis (see page 26).

Bus

Jerusalem's Central Bus Station is located on Jaffa Rd, to the west of the New City centre. See Ins and outs, page 30. Information booths are relatively helpful. The multi-storey bus station has a plethora of shops, toilets and places to eat. **Central Egged bus information** www.egged.co.il, T03-6948888 or speedial T*2800, Sun-Thu 0700-2000, Fri 0800-1500, Sat 30 min after conclusion of Shabbat to 2300.

Akko: go to Haifa and charge. **Ashkelon**: 437, Sun-Thu half-hourly 0630-2200, Fri last at 1630, Sat first at 1800, 1½ hrs, 24NIS. **Be'er Sheva** direct: 470, Sun-Thu every 1-2 hrs 0600-2200, Fri last at 1600, 1½ hrs, 31.5NIS. **Be'er Sheva** via **Kiryat Gat**: 446, Sun-Thu 2 per hr, Fri last at 1545, Sat first at 2045. Bet Shean: 961, every hr Sun-Thu 0700-2030, Fri until 1530, Sat 2040 and 2245, 2 hrs, 44NIS. **Bet Shemesh**: 417, Sun-Thu 2 per hr 0550-2400, Fri last at 1630, Sat first at 2100,

1 hr, 15NIS. **Bnei Brak**: 400, Sun-Thu every 15 mins 0630-2330, Fri last at 1600, Sat first at 1915. **Eilat**: 444, Sun-Thu 0700, 1000, 1400 and 1700, Fri 0700, 1000 and 1400, Sat 0000, 5 hrs, 73NIS, book 2-3 days in advance. '**En Gedi**: 421 and 486, 7 per day 0800-2030, Fri 5 per day, Sat bus 487 2200, 1 ½ hrs, 36NIS, or bus 444 (see 'Eilat, above') 1 hr. **Haifa** direct: 940, Sun-Thu every hr 0600-2000, Fri last at 1630, Sat first at 2100, 3 hrs, 44NIS. **Haifa** via **Hadera** and **Netanya**: 947, every 30 mins Sun-Thu 0600-2100, Fri last at 1630, Sat first at 2040. **Kiryat Arba** (for Hebron): 160, Sun-Thu every 30 mins 0530-2200, Fri last at 1630, Sat first at 2125, 1¼ hrs. **Kiryat Shemona**: 963, Sun-Thu 5 per day 0630-2330, Fri 0715, 1130 and 1400, Sat 2130 and 2330, 4 hrs, 61NIS. **Latrun**: 404, 432, 433 and 434, frequent service, Sun-Thu 0630-2330, Fri until 1640, Sat from 2000, 30 mins, 17NIS. **Masada**: see "En Gedi' and 'Eilat' buses above. **Nahariya**: go to Haifa and change. Netanya: 947, see 'Haifa via Netanya' above. **Ramla**: 433, 435 and 404, frequent service, 1 hr. Safed: 982, Sun-Thu 7 per day 0920-2320, Fri 7 per day until 1320, Sat 21250 and 2320, 3½ hrs, 44NIS. **Tel Aviv** direct: 405, Sun-Thu every 15 mins 0550-2350, Fri last at 1700, Sat first at 2030, 1 hr, 20NIS. Tiberias 962 and 963, Sun-Thu hourly 0630-2330, Fri last at 1600, Sat first at 2040, 2 hrs, 40NIS. For buses to Cairo see Tour operators, above.

For the West Bank mini-buses are the main transport link to **Ramallah** (north) and **Bethlehem** (south) from Jerusalem. Bus 18 to Ramallah (30 mins, 6NIS) departs from Suleiman, just outside Damascus Gate (exit Damascus Gate, turn right). For **Nablus**, go to Ramallah and change. For **Bethlehem** (45 mins, 4-6.5NIS), take minibus 21 to **Beit Jala** from where it is a 15 min walk to the centre of town, or minibus 124 to the large checkpoint on the outskirts of Bethlehem from where you need to get a taxi or walk about 30 mins. For **Jericho** change in Ramallah or Azariya; for **Hebron** change in Bethlehem.

Car hire

Most of the car hire firms have their offices on King David, near the Hilton Jerusalem. Note that most will not cover damage or theft that occurs on the West Bank (including East Jerusalem). Offices are generally open Sun-Thu 0800-1800, Fri 0800-1400. Book online to get special deals. **Avis**, 22 King David, T02-6249001, www.avis.co.il.

Budget, 23 King David, T03-9350015, www.budget.co.il.

Eldan, Eldan Hotel, 24 King David, T02-6252151/2, www.eldan.co.il/en.

Goodluck, Nablus (next to American Colony), East Jerusalem, T02-6277033, reservation@goodluckcars.com. Cars are insured for travel in the West Bank.

Nesher Taxis, 21 King George, T02-6257227. The best way to get to Ben-Gurion Airport (45 mins); book ahead and they will pick you up. Allow plenty of time since the taxi may drive all over Jerusalem picking up other pre-booked passengers. In the Old City they will usually only arrange to pick you up from outside the tourist office at Jaffa Gate. The Ben-Gurion sherut operates on Shabbat, but reservations aren't taken: you'll need to book on Fri morning if travelling between Fri afternoon and Sun morning.

Another option is **Mike's Centre**, nr Station IX (off Souq Khan al-Zeit), T02-6282486, www.mikescentre.com. 24-hr service, leaving from Jaffa or New Gate, 4 hrs before departure, 65NIS per person.

Sheruts

Sheruts to and from Tel Aviv arrive and depart from the junction of HaRav Kook and Jaffa, close to Zion Square (50 mins).They also wait outside the Central Bus Station for departures to Tel Aviv. Sheruts run on Shabbat.

Train

Jerusalem's train station is inconveniently located in Malha to the southwest of the city. Route and fare information can be

found at www.rail.co.il; T03-6117000 or
speed dial T*5700, Sun–Thu 0600–2300,
Fri 0600–1500, Sat from half an hour after
Sabbath until 2300. On weekdays there are
10 services to Tel Aviv (1½ hrs, 20.5NIS one
way) and, though it's slower than the bus, it's
a very pleasant journey.

❶ Directory

Banks Banking hours are Sun, Tue and
Thu 0830-1230 and 1600-1700, Mon, Wed
and Fri 0830-1200. All banks have 24-hr
ATM machines offering shekel advances
on most cards. Hotels are bad places to
change money. Note that post offices offer
commission-free foreign exchange for
travellers' cheques. There are also a number
of legal money-changers inside Damascus
Gate who offer good deals on travellers'
cheques and cash. Those travelling on to
Egypt or Jordan are recommended to buy
a supply of Jordanian Dinars/Egyptian
Pounds in advance. **American Express**, 18
Shlomzion HaMalka, T02-6240830. Sun-Thu
0900-1700, Fri 0900-1300, member services
including clients' mail. **Embassies and
consulates** Many nations still refuse
to recognize Jerusalem as Israel's "eternal
undivided capital", and so retain their
embassies in Tel Aviv. Some, however,
maintain consulates in Jerusalem, though
you may be referred to Tel Aviv for certain
matters. **Belgium**, 5 Biber, Sheikh Jarrah,
East Jerusalem, T02-5828263; **Denmark**,
10 Bnei Brith, T02-6258083; **France**, 5 Emil
Botta, T02-6259481, and Sheikh Jarrah,
East Jerusalem, T6282387 626-2236,
www.consulfrance-jerusalem.org; **Italy**, 16
November, T02-5618966; **Spain**, 53 Rambam,
T02-5633473; **Sweden**, 58 Nablus, East
Jerusalem, T5828117 02 582-8212/13;
UK, 19 Nashashibi, Sheikh Jarrah, East
Jerusalem, T02- 6717724, and 5 David
Remez, West Jerusalem, T02 -6717724,
www.britishconsulate.org; **US**, 27 Nablus,
East Jerusalem, T02- 622-7221/6287137
(come here for visa services), or 18 Agron,

T02-6227230, http://jerusalem.usconsulate.
gov/. **Ministry of Foreign Affairs**, Press
Office, T5303343. Ministry of Information,
Beit Agron, 37 Hillel. The place to come
for your Israeli press card. Visa extensions
from the Ministry of Interior, 24 Hillel Street,
T02-6294726, *3450. **Hospitals** The world-
famous **Hadassah Hospital** in 'En Karem
(T02-6777333, www.hadassah.org.il), or its
sister on Mount Scopus (T02-5818111), are
capable of dealing with all emergencies,
though you should make sure that your
medical insurance is up to it. **Bikur Cholim
Hospital**, 74 HaNevi'im, T02-6461111,
www.bikurholim.org.il, may be a better bet
for the budget-minded. **Terem Immediate
Medical Care**, Magen David Adom Building,
7 HaMemGimel, T1-599-520520, www.
terem.com, offers what its name suggests.
Internet Café Net, 3rd Fl, Central Bus
Station, T02-5379192. Sun-Thu 0530-2400,
Fri 0530-hr before Shabbat, Sat hr after
Shabbat-2400. Cheap, fast, half-price happy
hour Sun-Thu 2300-2400. **CCS**, 17 Zahra,
East Jerusalem, T02-6261705. Computers for
use 10NIS 1hr, Sat-Thu 0700-1800. **Internet**,
31 Jaffa St (opp Holy Bagel), T02-6223377.
Good for night-owls, 15min 5NIS, 1 hr
14NIS, 10 hr member 110NIS. Sun-Thu
0900-0600, Fri 0900-1600, Sat 1930-0600.
Internet Café, 2 HaRav Kook (corner with
Jaffa), T052-4831038. Fast computers, new
and relatively quiet, but only 1030-2400,
closed Fri and Sat. 15 min 5NIS, 1 hr 14NIS,
2 hrs 25NIS. **Mike's Centre**, nr Station IX (off
Souq Khan al-Zeit), T02-6282486, www.
mikescentre.com. Cheapish: 5 mins 1NIS,
1 hr 10NIS. Daily 0900-2300. **Old City Net**,
Latin Patriarchate, Jaffa Gate. Nice setting.
Sandemans New Europe, c/c Steimatzsky's
Bookshop, Mamilla, T054-8831447/02-
6244726. Free internet in this friendly
independent travellers' centre where there's
also bike hire. **Sports Bar**, 10 Agrippas. Up-
to-date technology; alcohol available (happy
hour daily till 2000); smoking section; sports
on LCD screens, 1 hr 14NIS (8NIS with flyer).
Sun-Thu 0900-0300, Sat after Shabbat -0300.

YE Communications, 31 Emek Refa'im, T050-5242091, www.asim.co.il. Sun-Thu 0900-1900, Fri 0900-1300. 30 mins 10NIS.

Language Courses **Al-Quds University Centre for Jerusalem Studies**, Khan Tankaz, Suq Al-Qattanin, Old City, T02-6287517, www.jerusalem-studies.alquds.edu. Regular 2-month Arabic courses. **Gerard Behar Centre** (Beit Ha'am), 11 Bezalel, T02-6240034/6254156. Intensive courses only, 5 times per week. **Hebrew Union College**, 13 King David, T02- 6203333, hsaggie@hotmail.com. 3-month ulpan twice a week; tourists accepted. **Milah**, 4 Mevo HaMatmid, T02-623 3164/6249834. www.milah.org. Intensive course 4 days a week. **YMCA**, 26 King David, T5692673/05-2674770, www.simplehebrew.com. 3 days per week, 900NIS for 3 months; geared towards English speakers. **Laundry** **Mike's Place**, nr Station IX (off Souq Khan al-Zeit), T02-6282486, www.mikescentre.com. 2.5kg 17NIS, 4.5kg 30NIS, wash only (add 10NIS for drying). Daily 0900-2300. **Post office** Post offices are generally very busy and operate on a numbered ticket system. **GPO**, 23 Jaffa, T02-6244745. Sun-Thu 0700-1900, Fri 0700-1200. Poste restante, parcel mail. There are branch offices in the New City on Ezra M Mizrachi, in East Jerusalem on Salah al-Din (Sun-Thu 0800-1800, Fri 0800-1200), in the Old City opposite Citadel (open till 1400) and the Jewish Quarter.

Contents

Footnotes

Index